Faithful
As She Fades

Faithful As She Fades

A Memoir of Love and Dementia

Robert Fischbach
As Told to Vivien Cooper

Columbus, Ohio

Faithful As She Fades: A Memoir of Love and Dementia

Published by Gatekeeper Press
2167 Stringtown Rd, Suite 109
Columbus, OH 43123-2989
www.GatekeeperPress.com

ISBN (hardcover): 9781642376951
ISBN (paperback): 9781642376944
eISBN: 9781642376968

Printed in the United States of America

Foreword

When examining the life of a single family, one often discovers a microcosm of the world. In one family's history is found all the happiness and sadness, all the successes and failures, and all the triumphs and tragedies which human beings can experience.

In my ministry of almost fifty years, I have never seen a family who does not know, intimately, the vicissitudes of life. No family is spared. As my grandparents used to say, "If everyone placed their bag of troubles on the table, we would ultimately retrieve our own bag."

One of the privileges of a career in the congregational ministry is the opportunity to work with families at the heightened moments in their lives, both the happy and the sad. This is a rare privilege but, at the same time, a heavy responsibility. That intimacy with others is what I most appreciated in my life's work. What I learned and experienced sustains me to this day.

I met Bob Fischbach in 1964 while we were both college students in Cincinnati. At the time, Bob was studying community planning at the University of Cincinnati's School of Design, Art and Architecture. He was living in the Sisterhood Dormitory of the Hebrew

Union College-Jewish Institute of Religion, just across the street from the U. C. campus. I was then engaged in an intensive Hebrew program at the College-Jewish Institute, in preparation for my entrance into the first-year rabbinical class.

I recall so clearly Bob's warm, engaging personality, of which I have been a beneficiary ever since. At the very same time, I also met Janie Pressman who would later become Bob's wife. Janie's personality was outgoing and I especially liked the fact that she was forthright and pulled no punches.

During that very same time, I became seriously ill with a lung condition. Upon learning of my illness, Janie mentioned that her cousin was a pulmonologist at the University of Cincinnati and said that I might want to consult with him. In that respect, Janie saved my life.

After I had gone weeks without a diagnosis, Janie's pulmonologist cousin recognized my ailment as histoplasmosis, a fungal disease which is particularly prevalent in the Ohio and Mississippi River valleys. At the time, very few doctors were able to make the diagnosis. This chain of events tied me to Janie in a special way for the rest of her life.

In 1980, I moved to Atlanta to serve as Senior Rabbi at the congregation where, coincidentally, Janie and Bob were members. Sixteen years had gone by since our last encounter. Our reunion was *bashert*—a function of destiny. What made my encounter with the

Fischbachs even more significant was the fact that they now had two wonderful sons whom I would have the privilege of teaching. It is no understatement to say that those two boys were the light of Janie's eyes.

During my Atlanta years, I would encounter Janie and Bob often. It was not unusual for them to attend my classes and lectures. The warmth of Bob's personality was always cherished and Janie's humor always kept me smiling.

Then, during the late 1990s, Bob and Janie began to attend my Tuesday morning classes. It was not long before I noticed a change in Janie. She was as friendly with me as she had always been but I noticed that her vibrant spirit was no longer a defining feature of her personality. Months went by and it became evident that Janie's speech was also being affected. After a time, she was unable to communicate at all.

The Fischbach family was reticent to speak about Janie's worsening condition and I never dared to ask. But then one day, someone informed me that Janie had been diagnosed with frontotemporal dementia, a progressive degeneration of the temporal and frontal lobes of the brain. At one time referred to as Pick's disease, this prognosis for both patient and caregiver is devastating.

With grace, dignity and unstinting dedication, Bob retired in order to look after Janie. In this way, he enabled her to stay in their home and, for eight and a half years, to be cared for there. At the time, I could only imagine the toll this was taking on Bob as Janie's caretaker.

During the period when the disease had become well-advanced, I performed the wedding of their son Scott in the Fischbach home, in the presence of Janie. She was only a shadow of the young woman I had known in Cincinnati so many years earlier.

With pride in my friendship with Bob and in memory of Janie, I extend my best wishes to any person who chooses to read this book. May insight be gained into one of the most catastrophic diseases which can afflict a human being. May the reader, as well, be guided, strengthened, and encouraged by the example which Bob Fischbach has so lovingly and thoughtfully provided.

We all have stories to tell. Let us listen and let us learn.

—Phil Kranz, Rabbi Emeritus,
Temple Sinai (Atlanta)

One

My wife Janie was so full of life that her words tumbled out of her at the speed of light. I was always saying, "Would you slow down a little and repeat what you just said?"

Then in 2003, I noticed that she wasn't speaking at quite the same speed. She was also beginning to fumble for words here and there. Since she seemed like herself otherwise, I didn't think too much of it at first. She was managing fine around the house during the hours that I was at work. And in every other way, she was still the force of nature she had always been.

When her speech problems did not clear up on their own, I realized I was going to have to address it with her. One day I said, "Hey, bunny, you're not speaking clearly. Are you okay?"

"Really?" Janie said. "I'm not speaking correctly? I hadn't even noticed. But don't worry...I'm fine."

"You're probably right, but I'm thinking we should go see the doctor and have you checked out. Better safe than sorry."

We had used the same internist for years (Dr. Adam Leaderman) and were on a first-name basis with him. When we met with the doctor and I explained what I was hearing (and not hearing) from Janie, he gave her an examination.

Dr. Leaderman told us, "I'm not seeing anything here that gives me great cause for concern. But maybe you should go for some speech therapy, Janie."

We agreed that this was probably a wise course of action so I called Emory University. Janie went to speech therapy and returned home from her sessions with homework, comprised of writing exercises. Janie had to complete sentences and answer questions to simple problems. It became apparent right away that Janie could not complete the homework. I, on the other hand, was doing a bang-up job with the answers and the sentences. Of course, I wasn't supposed to be doing the homework for her.

When I observed that Janie was unable to complete this simple homework, I realized that I was going to have to take her back to see our internist. I decided that I wanted to speak with him privately before I took Janie back in for further testing.

"Adam," I said when I got him on the phone, "Janie's been going to speech therapy but it's not really helping. She's not even able to complete the simple homework. I've already made an appointment with your office for a follow-up but I wanted to talk to you privately before we get there."

"Given that speech therapy didn't really help, maybe we ought to have her go take a brain scan," he said.

"I think that's a good idea," I agreed.

Two

I was twenty years old and Janie was nineteen in the fall of 1963 when we first met at a fraternity party on campus. Joining the fraternity was beyond my financial means at the time, and I was there as the invited guest of friends of mine. As the party got underway, I looked across the room and noticed her—a gorgeous girl in a brown knit dress with an argyle print on the front. She stood about five-foot-five and was wearing brown high heels.

I was riveted, watching her from across the room. She had dark eyes, dark hair, an absolutely magnificent figure, and an outgoing personality.

I've got to meet that girl! I said to myself.

I started investigating the situation and found someone who knew her name. He said, "She's taken, though." And then he told me the name of the guy she was dating.

The guy happened to be an acquaintance of mine, so I went over to him. "I understand you're dating Janie Pressman," I said. "I'd love to meet her."

I really could have cared less whether she was already dating someone or not. I had to meet her. I happened to be dating someone myself.

My acquaintance introduced me to her. "This is a friend of mine, Bob Fischbach," he said to the beautiful girl. "And Bob, this is Janie Pressman."

We had a brief but pleasant exchange and I found out that she was from Cincinnati. Then a couple of weeks later, my acquaintance called me and said, "I'm going over to Lynn's apartment and Janie's going to be there. Would you come over and even up the odds?" Lynn was a mutual friend of both his and Janie's.

"Sure!" I said. I was already wowed by Janie and jumped at the chance to be around her again. I didn't accept the invitation with the intention of stealing her away but of course I had ideas.

During the evening at Lynn's apartment, Janie and I hit it off. We had some good, casual conversation and became fast friends. She was very charismatic with a wonderfully outgoing personality. And I found her to be absolutely gorgeous.

I thought, *If nothing else, hopefully we'll become friends.*

I believed, as I do to this day, that it's a good idea to become friends before becoming dating partners. I knew that Janie was a townie, a hometown girl from Cincinnati, so there might also be the possibility of a home-cooked meal for this New Yorker.

We saw each other on campus and talked about school. I wasn't that into the girl I was dating and I found out that Janie wasn't that into the guy she'd been dating (my acquaintance).

As we approached the Christmas vacation break from school, I said to Janie, "Why don't you drop me a line in New York while I'm home, or call me..."

"You call me," she said, "if you want to talk to me."

Once Janie and I returned to college on January 2nd or 3rd of 1964, I gave her a call. After we talked for a few minutes about how we had spent our Christmas break, I said, "How would you like to go out to a movie? My friend Bob's got a date and a car. I was thinking it might be fun to join them."

I was happy when she agreed to join me and wowed when she showed up at the door wearing a red faux-suede jumper with a bib and straps, and a patterned blouse underneath.

The four of us went into downtown Cincinnati to Fountain Square and, during the movie, I reached over and took Janie's hand. Afterwards, we all went to dinner, and then Bob drove us to Janie's house and I walked her to the door. I had been taught to be very respectful of women by my parents.

I leaned in and gave her a kiss goodnight, and then I walked to the car where Bob and his date were waiting to drive me home. As I got into the car, I thought to myself, *Maybe I'm imagining things but I think she kissed me back!*

Years later, Janie's mother would tell me, "I waited up for Janie that night. And, when she walked into the house after your goodnight kiss, she was swooning a bit!"

At the time of my first date with Janie, I was still seeing the girl I was dating before I met Janie. This went on for a week or two until I decided I'd better make up my mind. It was a no-brainer as to which girl I was going to pick. Meanwhile, Janie had already broken things off with the overconfident guy she had been dating.

I was pretty confident myself, and had a large outgoing personality I had inherited from my dad. Dad was named Harry. My mom, Elizabeth, was known as Betty. I would start out calling my parents Mom and Dad but later in life I would nickname my mother Liz and my father Stubby. I don't know how to account for the fact that I had given my parents these nicknames and insisted upon using them rather than the customary Mom and Dad. I do know that I was always a bit of a clown and a jokester. I may have inherited this trait from my father.

I was born in New York City on June 29th, 1943, a couple of years before the end of World War II. In 1921, my mother's family had emigrated to the U.S. from Russia (Minsk, actually) right after the Bolshevik Revolution.

Mom was gorgeous with pitch-black hair, and she stood about five-foot-eight-or-nine inches tall—in my mind's eye anyway. In reality, I would later find out that my tall, regal Russian mother only stood about five-foot-two-or-three inches tall. She was an honest, scrupulous, straight-laced, no-nonsense woman of great strength and character. She was also a very proper lady and never cursed. So, the one time in my life I heard her say a foul word, it came as a shock.

My mother was the youngest of nine children and had a very mothering, protective nature. She took good care of us. When we were very young, for example, she would polish our white shoes each night after first removing the laces so they wouldn't get covered in polish. Mom was also a great cook, thanks to lessons from Dad's mom, Grandma Sadie. We had a good relationship, even though our bond wasn't particularly warm and cozy.

Dad was my best friend and we were very close. He was stocky, strong, toned and barrel-chested. He had fair skin, red hair, freckles and blue eyes. So did his older brother, my uncle Ben, and their mother, my grandma Sadie. By the time I came into my father's life, he had only a rim of hair, so I couldn't tell you whether or not it had ever been full and thick.

Dad claimed to be five-foot-eleven-and-a-half in height. When I got to be six feet tall myself, I told him that he couldn't possibly be as tall as he thought.

He kiddingly hit me in the arm and said, "I'm five-eleven-and-a-half and don't ever forget it!"

Between my mother and my father, it was my dad who had the more gregarious, outgoing personality. He was fun to be around and a jokester but he was not a guy you wanted to cross. He would tolerate a lot before he lost his temper but once he reached his breaking point, you didn't want to be standing in front of him.

When I was eleven years old and my brother, Danny, was thirteen and getting bar mitzvahed, I witnessed an outburst from my dad that I wouldn't soon forget. The instigator of the incident was Mom's brother-in-law, my uncle Mac. He was married to Mom's sister, Sophie, whom we called Aunt Sonny. Uncle Mac was in the jewelry business and was very successful.

Here's what happened. Danny's bar mitzvah party was held in the evening at a reception hall. During the entire party, Danny was wearing the watch that Uncle Mac had given him as his bar mitzvah gift. Apparently, at some point in the evening, Uncle Mac made an insulting comment to my father, things got heated, and words were exchanged. I never did find out what was said.

The next thing I knew, Dad was standing in front of my brother, saying, "I need the watch on your wrist! Don't worry...I'll replace it tomorrow."

Then Dad marched over to where Uncle Mac was standing, took the watch, and cracked it on the table or a chair, busting the crystal. This was followed by these words: "If you don't leave, I'm going to shove what's left of that watch up your ass!" (The very next day, he bought Danny a similar watch.)

Uncle Mac may have made an insulting remark about the fact that Dad was a beautician. When Dad first started out in his profession in the post-Depression 1930s and '40s, it was considered a manly profession. The beauty industry was perfect for my naturally creative father because it provided an outlet for his creativity. Later in life, he would also take up painting. (Some of his paintings grace my walls to this day.)

Dad and Uncle Mac didn't speak again until just before my dad died. Dad's position was that he would only talk to Uncle Mac if he apologized.

Aunt Sonny called and said that Uncle Mac wanted to see my father.

Dad said, "Only if he apologizes before he gets here."

Uncle Mac did apologize and then he and Aunt Sonny came over.

Both my parents worked but family was always of the utmost importance to them. Work was never first priority. Mom was as protective as a mother hen and completely devoted to her family, but that devotion did not translate into a particularly affectionate nature.

My parents had both grown up in the Bronx and then moved to Great Neck, Long Island after their 1938 marriage. Every Sunday, our family would get in the car and go visit both sets of my grandparents.

I didn't have a maternal grandmother. Grandma Dina had passed away in 1929, only eight years after emigrating to America. Mom was only ten years old at the time she lost her mother. When Mom was fifteen, Grandpa Harry remarried. His second wife, whom we called Aunt Leahna, was the only maternal grandmother I ever knew. She was the quintessential Russian grandmother—a strong, somewhat stern woman. She was not warm and friendly like my paternal grandmother.

Interestingly enough, Aunt Leahna's daughter would go on to later marry a guy with the last name Fishkind. And Mom's maiden name was Fishkin. I later joked that my mother married my father to avoid changing the monograms on the bathroom towels.

Any time we were preparing to leave their house after a visit, Mom would say to me, "Give Grandpa a kiss goodbye...and go give Aunt Leahna a kiss too." My mother never referred to Aunt Leahna as Mom or Mother, and we didn't either. And, by the way, I never did kiss her goodbye.

My paternal grandmother, Grandma Sadie, was the prototypical Jewish grandmother and an amazing cook. On the weekends, she would bake fresh challah and handmake meat-and-veggie knishes, starting with the dough. Each and every visit to my paternal grandparents' house was filled with incredible food. It was like attending a food festival. She never served us anything she hadn't made by hand. She even handmade syrups from oranges, lemons and strawberries and mixed those with seltzer water instead of serving us bottled soda.

Grandma Sadie was from Austria. Around 1906 while she was still a teenager, she had an argument with her father and moved to the United States on a boat (steerage class). She settled in the Bronx, and there she met my grandfather-to-be, Grandpa Julius, also from Austria. The Bronx was mostly Jewish with a large immigrant population. So it wasn't that surprising, but it was still a bit of serendipity.

They got married and my grandmother got pregnant with my father's older brother, Uncle Ben, who was born in the Bronx in 1908. In 1909, Grandma Sadie received word that her father was sick and dying. While pregnant with my father, she took Uncle Ben, who was still a baby, and got back on a boat in steerage class. She traveled all the way back to Austria while Grandpa Julius stayed behind in the Bronx.

My father was subsequently given birth to in Austria, and Grandma stayed there with the two kids until her father died. Then she took a boat all the way back to the States in 1912. Dad arrived here as a two-year-old. Grandma was a tough cookie. No question about it.

Three

The appointment was arranged, and Janie was sent for a brain scan.

"See this little spot right here?" Dr. Leaderman said, showing us the results of the brain scan. "It could be an indication of a mini-stroke and it could be nothing. But I want you to go to Emory University to see Dr. Alan Leavey, the head of the Emory Alzheimer's Disease Research Center."

Then Dr. Leaderman wrote down the name of the doctor at Emory. This was 2003. Janie was fifty-nine at the time. I was a year older.

"I don't want to go," Janie told me when we got home. "I don't think there's any problem. I'm fine."

I wasn't going to let her sweep the problem under the rug. "Bunny," I said, "there's something going on and it's better to find out sooner than later. Adam thinks you ought to do it and I do too. You weren't able to complete much of the homework."

After being together for so many years, I knew my wife. And I knew that she didn't want to face the music. She sensed that there was something wrong with her and she didn't want to find out that it was something bad.

When Janie was in her late forties, she had said to me, "I think I'm going to get Alzheimer's one day..."

That was the last thing I wanted to hear so I downplayed it at the time. Now, I remembered that moment and it sent a cold chill up my spine. I said to myself, *She may have noticed something different about herself even ten years ago and felt it coming on.*

I finally convinced Janie to go to Emory University for the appointment, and then I called Dr. Leaderman.

"Adam, please send everything you have on Janie to Dr. Leavey," I said. "I've got an appointment set up for her."

We met with Dr. Alan Leavey, and he put my wife through a battery of tests. He had her answer questions, both oral and written. He also looked at the medical records Dr. Leaderman had sent over to him for review. And, he ordered an x-ray to see if perhaps a concussion or some other injury might be causing the problems.

While Dr. Leavey was examining Janie and administering the tests to her, I was relegated to the waiting area. I'm sure this is done as a precaution so that well-meaning spouses don't end up coaching their loved one. It felt like an entire week passed as I paced back and forth, anxious for the results.

Finally, Dr. Leavey called us into his office and, with his nurse present, had us sit down.

"I'm sorry to tell you this," he began, "but Janie has frontotemporal dementia. There are many forms of dementia, not just Alzheimer's. Frontotemporal dementia is a disease affecting the frontal and/or temporal lobe of the brain..."

The doctor might as well have taken a hammer and hit me in the gut. I felt all the air go out of me.

"...The cells deteriorate," he continued, "and the brain shrinks. You essentially lose that part of your brain."

Every sentence was another blow to Janie and me, and we were both sobbing by this point.

"...While Alzheimer's primarily affects the memory," Dr. Leavey explained, "frontotemporal dementia affects the memory somewhat but primarily behavior and personality."

We left the hospital in tears. Everything had happened so fast, and the dementia diagnosis was such a blow, we were both in shock. We drove home in stunned silence.

That night we sat together and cried some more.

"I need you to make me three promises," my wife said to me. "First, keep the family together."

"Of course," I agreed.

"And, secondly, I do not want anybody other than the boys to know about this. Promise?"

"Okay. If that's what you want me to do, I will promise you that. Absolutely."

Meanwhile, I was thinking, *My promise is not going to ensure that nobody knows about her condition! Eventually, it will become obvious to everyone.*

"And lastly, you have to promise me that you will not put me in a facility."

That was the word she used—facility. Not "home" or "nursing home."

As part of the diagnostic process, the doctor had asked me about correlating factors. "Does anyone in your wife's family have any type of dementia?"

"Not that I know of...or not anything that was diagnosed, anyway."

In retrospect, I think that Janie's father may have had some dementia later in life, but it was never diagnosed. He ended up in The Jewish Home, the best nursing home in Atlanta, before he passed four years prior to Janie's diagnosis. She visited her father regularly and hated seeing him there. This was no doubt a factor in her determination to avoid being put in a facility.

When her father died, Janie said, "I'm never setting foot in that building again!" She certainly didn't want to be seen as someone who was confined to a nursing home. As far as she was concerned, that was a place where people went to die.

"I will not put you in a facility," I said. "I promise."

I couldn't possibly have known what I was in for when I made these promises to my beloved wife.

Four

By the time of my brother's bar mitzvah in the mid-1950s, my dad had grown sensitive about his profession. It had begun to attract homosexual men and Dad didn't want it assumed that he was gay. He was not bigoted in any way against others; he was just a husband and family man and wanted to be known as such.

Dad didn't just work at the salon—he owned it. It was located at 107 Middleneck Road in Great Neck, Long Island. Great Neck was an extremely affluent town and we were a very working-class family. The only sign of affluence in our house was the baby-grand piano that sat in the living room and had a player-piano attachment. I can't imagine what kind of a deal Dad had gotten on the piano, but he must have pulled out all the stops in terms of his negotiating powers. Otherwise, we could never have afforded it. I suspect that he traded it for services rendered at the shop.

Mom worked alongside Dad at the salon. She mostly did the customers' manicures and pedicures, while Dad did their hair. A friend of Mom's named Marsha also worked at the salon for many, many years and was like an aunt to us kids. There was also a nice Italian woman named Terri who worked there for many years.

Marsha was married to an African American man named George and they had one son, George, Jr., from George's prior marriage. It was unusual to see a biracial couple in that era. For that matter, there were very few African Americans in our neighborhood, period. I did have one good friend in high school who happened to be African American, and we played sports together.

Dad had regular customers every week for thirty-two years straight, without missing a single week. In those days, most housewives with financial means had a weekly appointment at a hair salon. Dad's customers were so loyal, they wouldn't have even considered letting another stylist anywhere near their hair. One of Dad's wealthy customers, Mrs. Salmonson, used to travel abroad. Before her trips, she always had my father mix up some hair color for her to take with her.

Mrs. Salmonson would always say to me, "I don't think I've ever seen you without a cast or a bandage on, Bobby!"

She was right. I was very athletic and Dad's customers got used to seeing me banged up from one sports activity or another. I grew up at the salon because it was two blocks from home and two blocks from my elementary school.

When I was fifteen or sixteen, Dad suggested I come into the salon over the summer so he could teach me the trade. "That way, you'll always have something to fall back on."

"Sure, Dad." I would have done anything he asked.

When I got there on the first day, he handed me a pair of scissors and a comb. At the end of the day, I handed him back the scissors and the comb.

"Dad," I said, "I would rather pick seeds out of a pile of horse manure with boxing gloves on. I don't know how you put up with this every day. I've got to get out of here!"

I hated all the gossip between the clients, and between the clients and the stylists. It was like being a psychologist, having to listen to everyone's stories and troubles about husbands and boyfriends, wives and girlfriends, and kids who were acting up. It occurred to me that maybe that's why my father had a temper—because he couldn't release his frustrations at work.

In all the years Dad was in business, he never hired one man to work in his salon. He was concerned that by hiring a man, he was setting himself up. He envisioned a scenario where a guy would work for him for six months and then go take out a bank loan to start his own business.

"The more men in this industry, the more competition I will eventually have," he once explained to me when we were by ourselves in the salon, cleaning up, as we were on most weekends.

My mother left the salon ninety minutes before closing time, every day like clockwork. Since we lived only two blocks away, it didn't take Mom long to get home. On the way, she would stop and buy groceries for the evening meal. Then, when she got home, she would slip into a housecoat and prepare dinner.

My father never had his own key to the front door. Instead, he would arrive at the door like he was a suitor, arriving to take Mom on a date. When Mom heard the doorbell ring, she would go to the door, open it, and give Dad a warm hello and a kiss. They conducted themselves like they hadn't just spent the entire day together, working at the salon. Every night, we would eat dinner together as a family. This daily ritual epitomized my parents' long marriage.

Dad was twenty-eight years old and the president of the hairdresser's union when he met Mom, who had gone to the union to join. Dad fell in love with her at first sight. They married on April 10th and Mom turned twenty a couple of months later on June 10th. They went on to have a thirty-two-year-long happy marriage.

I can't say whether faithfulness and commitment are learned traits or genetically passed down from one generation to another. Either way, I seemed to inherit these things from my parents. I saw them take care of their parents, and I saw my mom take care of my dad before he died.

I believe that much of who you are is learned rather than inherited—how you think, how you react to people, your priorities. I am very easy to get along with but I also have my father's not-to-be-messed-with attitude.

Five

Once I had gotten my thoughts together, I called Dr. Leavey and said, "With all due respect, I need you to give me the names of six experts around the country that you respect. I need to get a second and third opinion on Janie's condition."

The first doctor recommended by Dr. Leavey was an expert in neurological diseases at the Mayo Clinic in Jacksonville, Florida. Within a couple of weeks of Janie's diagnosis, we drove down to Florida. It was a five-hour trip by car and a tense one, with barely a word spoken between us. We were both all too aware of the gravity of the situation.

When we arrived, the doctor told us that he had all of Dr. Leavey's notes in hand and had reviewed them before we arrived. "If you don't mind," he said, "I would like to do some of my own tests. Some of these tests are the same ones done by Dr. Leavey. I have made my own subtle changes on others. I'll be administering some of the tests myself and some will be administered by my staff."

Once again, the doctor relegated me to the waiting room while Janie underwent this second round of testing. When Janie was finished, we made our way to our hotel and passed a restless night. We returned to the doctor's office the following morning for the test results.

When we were seated in front of the doctor, we heard the news we had been dreading: "I'm sorry to deliver this news, but I concur with Dr. Leavey's diagnosis. I believe it is correct. And just to be sure, I also emailed the test results to the Mayo Clinic in Rochester, Minnesota for review. We are all on the same computer system. I'm sorry but my colleague there also concurs with the diagnosis."

As we left Jacksonville and made the long drive back home, we felt as if there was a dark cloud following us. We were struggling to find words to say to each other in the face of such grim news.

The doctor at the Mayo Clinic in Jacksonville had been unequivocal in stating his agreement with Dr. Leavey's assessment of Janie's condition, and so had his colleague in Rochester. So, we had now effectively been given professional opinions from two and a half doctors—Dr. Leavey, the doctor at the Mayo Clinic in Jacksonville, and his colleague in Rochester via long distance. (While we had seen Dr. Leaderman, he hadn't really given an opinion on Janie's condition.)

If even one of these doctors had waffled at all, or given me the slightest sense that they were uncertain about the diagnosis, I would have gone in search of one more opinion. As it was, I felt that we had our answer—even if it was the last answer we wanted to hear.

Six

Our family lived in a two-bedroom, one-bath apartment in a large building with a hundred units or so. The building was arranged in a u-shape, with one wing on each side and a lobby in the middle. My parents took one bedroom and we three kids slept in the other bedroom. Then when my sister got a little bit older, my parents relinquished their room to her and slept on a pull-out bed in the living room.

My brother, Daniel ("Danny"), and I slept in the same room until he went away to college but we never shared a close bond. He had my mother's personality and I had my father's. Danny was quiet and introspective, with few friends. As I've said, I was very outgoing and socially and athletically active. I was always out doing something, surrounded by a group of guys or girls.

The distance between us began when we were quite young. We had plenty of sibling rivalry in our relationship. As the oldest son, Danny was paraded around like a little king. His every move was announced and applauded. "Look at Danny walk! Look at Danny talk!"

I don't think Danny ever considered me his intellectual equal. He was always finding something to tease me about, and when provoked, I would go after him. He had very strong hands and would grab me by the wrists to hold me at bay. Then he laughed at me when I couldn't break his grip.

Only once did I ever break his grip on me, and that caused quite a scene. I was so angry, I beat him to a pulp. I had a lot of pent-up rage from all the times he had grabbed me, held me down and laughed at me. When I unleashed that rage, I went nuts. My dad had to pull me off of Danny. I am very easy to get along with, but don't cross me.

In later years, Danny would say to me, "I was always jealous of you!"

I was the maladjusted middle child. He was the golden firstborn child who blossomed in college and went to Georgetown Law. So, I said, "Jealous of me? What in the world for?"

"I used to ask to do things and was always told not to do them. But you could always do them!"

I learned early on that it was much easier to beg forgiveness than ask permission. My philosophy has always been to never ask a question you already know the answer to, especially when the answer is no.

By contrast, I always had a close relationship with my sister, Randee Sue, who was born in April of 1946. Randee would grow up to be five-eight-or-nine inches tall. She was thin with dark hair and dark eyes. Personality-wise, she was outgoing and social like Dad and me, and quite athletic. My sister and I had much more interaction than I ever had with Danny.

Danny and I were expected to keep an eye out for Randee. We were told, "Look after your sister! Don't let her get in trouble! Take her with you!"

When I was young and forced to take my sister someplace with me, I made her walk ten to twelve steps behind me because I thought it would make me look uncool if we walked together.

Both Randee and Danny played our grand piano. Being the family clown, I liked to agitate my sister while she was playing, sneaking up behind her and banging on the keys to mess up whatever piece she was playing. She took it good-naturedly, laughing as she told me to get the hell away from her. Of course, this just spurred me to bug her even more.

As the only daughter in the family, Randee became the apple of our father's eye. Dad was fond of saying to Mom, "It's a good thing Randee was born because we were going to keep having children until I got a daughter!"

I didn't feel threatened by my dad's close relationship with my sister. He and I always remained close, and he never objected when I wanted to go with him to clean and wax the salon. I jumped at any chance to spend time with him. I knew things about my dad's business that even my mother didn't know. It felt great to know that Dad trusted me. I will forever keep his confidences.

Belonging to a working-class family in the wealthy town of Great Neck was hardest on Randee. Women of all ages tend to have a harder time with peer pressure in that kind of situation. All the other women had the finest shoes in every color and skin available, but Randee couldn't afford such things. Feeling left out made Randee miserable in Great Neck. Danny shared her feelings.

Being involved in athletics was an easy way for me to fit in with the wealthy guys. When I was playing sports, I wasn't expected to show up in fancy clothes. All I really needed was a good pair of sneakers. That made it much easier to keep from standing out as different. I also had an attitude of, *I may not be rich but this is who I am. You can take me as I am or don't take me at all. I don't really care.*

At the time that my parents moved to Great Neck in 1938, it was a very non-Jewish area. Mom and Dad were Jewish and both sets of their parents were Jewish and religious to some extent. We were mostly culturally Jewish, observing Rosh Hashanah and Yom Kippur. Mom also lit candles for Shabbat but I don't recall us ever doing any praying around the house. Just like my brother, I was bar mitzvahed but Randee didn't have a bat mitzvah.

Although our parents were not religious, per sé, they still expected my brother and me to marry Jewish girls and Randee to marry a Jewish guy.

Danny came home from college one day and announced that he had gotten lavaliered (a preamble to being "pinned") to a girl. He referred to her as "my girlfriend, but not my only one."

"That's nice," said Dad. "What's her name?"

Danny told Dad the girl's first name and then said that her last name was O'Reilly or some other Irish name.

My father went off the rails. He may not have been a particularly observant Jew, but he was definitely Jewish. And, he was not about to see any of his children marry outside the religion. (Both Danny and I would end up married to Jewish girls. When Danny got divorced, he remarried a catholic girl. Randee never did get married.)

Dad's salon customers would never know he was Jewish—at least not by his name. Dad had sensed that Fischbach might be too conspicuously Jewish a name for his customers to accept. So, around the salon, he was known as Mr. Harris, taken from his first name, Harry. That was the only name his customers ever called him. It was sort of an informal version of the Ellis Island name-changing and name-shortening practice followed by so many Jews who arrived in America from other countries.

In the ten years between the time my parents moved in and I started school at the elementary school a block from our house, the community completely changed. It became predominantly Jewish, to the extent that schools closed for all the major Jewish holidays. There was one Reform, one Conservative, and one Orthodox synagogue in our neighborhood. (Today, Great Neck's population is predominantly Orthodox.)

In 1951 when Danny was ten, he started taking Hebrew lessons in preparation for his bar mitzvah which would take place three years later in 1954. I was eight at the time Danny started lessons, and my bar mitzvah would take place two years after his.

"Mom," I said, "if Danny's going to Hebrew school, I want to go too!"

My mother took me at my word and let me start Hebrew lessons. After two weeks, I went to her and said, "You know what, Mom? I think I'd rather wait until I'm ten."

"I'm sorry," she said, "but you started and now you're going to finish."

By starting my Hebrew lessons when I was eight, I had doomed myself to five years—rather than the usual three—between the time I began my studies and the time of my bar mitzvah.

Rabbi Wolfe, my Hebrew teacher, was the rabbi of a small Orthodox synagogue. The Conservative and Reform synagogues had too long a waiting list to get in, so we had to join the Orthodox synagogue for the purposes of Danny's and my bar mitzvah lessons.

Each week, I did my Hebrew studies and my readings and I made my way through the entire Torah. I could recite both my Haftorah and my Torah portion by rote, like a parrot, but I couldn't have told you what any of it meant. The rabbi wasn't much help in that regard. He was an old-school rabbi, with the long beard and the black hat. His one and only goal was to get me through my studies and prepare me for my bar mitzvah in a way that reflected well on him.

After five agonizing years of speaking Hebrew without understanding a word of it, the time had finally come. In 1956, I showed up at the Orthodox synagogue where I had spent so many Tuesdays and Thursdays in study. In an Orthodox synagogue, the lectern where the bar mitzvah boy and the rabbi speak is situated in the middle of the room and the men and women are seated on separate sides of the room.

Rabbi Wolfe pulled out a hatpin from under his jacket. "You see this?" he whispered to me in a low voice under his breath.

"Of course I see it," I whispered.

"Well, if you make a mistake, you'll *feel* it!"

With these words, the rabbi was letting me know that any mistakes I made would reflect poorly on him as my teacher. He wasn't concerned about me making a fool of myself but he was not about to let me embarrass him.

I did not get stuck with the hatpin that day. Everything went off without a hitch. But I hated Rabbi Wolfe and I didn't appreciate learning my Hebrew studies like a parrot. My horrible bar mitzvah experience drove me away from the synagogue and I stayed away for fourteen years. Even then, the only reason I returned was because my father passed away. (While

I was away from the synagogue for all those years, I retained the ability to say the prayers from memory. I can't claim that I ever understood all of the prayers, but at least I remembered how to say them.)

I suppose my experience was probably close to the norm in the Orthodox tradition where there is only Hebrew in the prayer book—no English. In Conservative synagogues, there is a little bit of English in the prayer book, and in the Reform synagogues, there is Hebrew on one page and English on the opposite page.

Today, I am more observant than my family ever was, thanks to Janie. She slowly brought me back into the religion. Janie was from an ultra-Reform, German Jewish background. Cincinnati is the home of Reform Judaism, and Hebrew Union College is the rabbinic school for Reform rabbis. Eventually, Reform Judaism made its way across the country.

Currently, I belong to a Conservative synagogue. Along with five other guys, I study once a week with an Orthodox rabbi named Rabbi New. He happens to be the head Chabad rabbi for all of Georgia. Rabbi New refers to us six as his street people because we are so unknowing. I think he likes teaching us because we absorb everything he says without questioning. I think the world of Rabbi New. We study the Torah, the history of the Jews, and whatever else crosses his mind. On some days, he'll email us and say, "When we meet next time, just bring me questions."

One year when Danny and I were about nine and seven respectively, Marsha (who worked in Dad's salon) and her husband George wanted to get a Christmas tree for us kids. They were very fond of my siblings and me. They knew we were Jewish but that didn't stop them from promoting the Christmas tree idea.

Every time Marsha mentioned to my Jewish parents the idea of getting us a Christmas tree, the answer was always, "No, no, no..."

That Christmas season, Marsha said to Mom and Dad, "This year, I am not taking no for an answer!"

So, one Saturday night after the shop had closed, Marsha and George appeared at our apartment building with a Christmas tree in tow.

My parents felt like they couldn't say no, and they allowed Marsha and George to come in and set up the tree. Marsha and George then joined us for dinner and drinks and left later in the evening.

I looked at the Christmas tree more like a toy than a religious symbol. It was something we had never had before and I enjoyed the novelty of it. But we certainly didn't put presents under the tree or celebrate Christmas.

The morning after Marsha and George brought over the tree, my mom's sister and her husband, Aunt Rene and Uncle Willy, went by and picked up Grandpa Harry for a drive.

"I want to see the kinder," announced Grandpa Harry, an Orthodox Jew. (Kinder is a Yiddish word for children.)

Suddenly, all three of them arrived at the apartment. Mom was flustered. She knew she couldn't very well refuse the visit from her father or her sister and brother-in-law. So, she opened the door and invited them in.

Once inside our apartment, Grandpa's eyes naturally went straight to the Christmas tree.

My dad (also named Harry, if you will recall) took Grandpa Harry aside and said, "A woman who has worked for me for a long time brought over the tree. We felt we couldn't refuse the gift. It doesn't mean anything..."

Dad later told me that Grandpa Harry had stopped him midsentence and said in Yiddish, "Look, you don't have to prove anything to me. You live your life the way you want to and I do too. No harm done."

Grandpa Harry was a very proper man and every bit the Russian immigrant. I never saw him in anything other than a three-piece suit and tie, with a pocket hanky. He was not particularly warm or cuddly. (Mom's personality and demeanor followed his.) He was not the type of man you casually went up to and hugged. He was an old-school Russian Jew—the type of man who would take a seat and allow you to present yourself to him. Once you were properly presented to him, you would get a slight hug from him.

My grandfather's journey to America had been arduous. He and my grandmother had started out with nine children but the oldest had died in the Russian army. The remaining eight came to the U.S. with them. I still have Aunt Rene's passport showing the many countries they had to pass through to get here, starting in Russia and going through Amsterdam to get the boat.

Grandpa had been a dressmaker for the royal family in Russia. He became a furrier in the fur district until his children made him retire at ninety-one. I told them they were making a big mistake by forcing his retirement. He died at ninety-three. (As you may recall, my maternal grandmother Dina had passed in 1929, only eight years after emigrating to America, when my mother was only ten.)

Grandpa's handling of the Christmas tree incident left a lasting impression on me. Here was my Orthodox Jewish grandfather, someone completely devoted to Judaism, and yet he was not about to press his beliefs on anyone else.

I had always admired Grandpa Harry and thought very highly of him. This incident endeared him to me even more. On the Saturday of Danny's bar mitzvah, I was awarded the honor of walking Grandpa Harry three miles to the synagogue.

Seven

It was time to break the news to our boys so I called them and had them meet me for lunch. I had used my better judgment when I decided not to have Janie meet with the boys and me. I felt that, with her present, the lunch would have had the potential to become an emotional nightmare. I worried that it might have been more than any of us could take. There were too many unknowns in terms of what Janie might say or do, and how the boys would react.

Drew was thirty-four by then, Scott was thirty-one, and they were both working in real estate. They had gone through some of the ups and downs in the real estate business with me, and already knew the pitfalls. But they both liked the business so they formed their own company.

I came up with the name: M&M2S. It was an abbreviation for "Me and My Two Sons," although my role in the company was limited to that of advisor and banker. I put up some seed money and gave my input when needed.

The boys bought a couple of houses at the courthouse steps, remodeled and flipped them. They eventually split up their partnership but both remained in real estate.

"I need to break up with Scott if I want to continue to love him as a brother," was the way Drew put it to me.

"It's not working out well with you two working together?" I asked. "Does Scott feel the same way?"

"I think so," said Drew.

Drew found himself a new real estate partner. Meanwhile, Scott went to work for a real estate syndicator. I totally understood and supported their decision to break up their business partnership.

On this fateful day, my sons met me for lunch at Goldberg's Deli in Atlanta. It broke my heart when I thought of the terrible blow I was about to deliver. I knew how much the boys loved their mother and me. There was no question that they would have done anything for either of us. Unfortunately, I was about to tell them that the worst had happened to their mother and there was nothing any of us could do about it. If only I could have written a check to solve the problem.

My oldest son, Drew, walked into the deli first. When I saw him, I was taken back in time to a doctor's appointment that took place when he was still a little tyke.

I asked the doctor, "How big do you think he will get?" I was worried because Drew was on the small side.

"Six feet and about two hundred pounds!" the doctor had said, putting my mind at ease.

I needn't have worried. The doctor was right. The young man who walked into the Atlanta deli that day looked cut and ripped, thanks to his intense workouts.

When the three of us were seated, I took a deep breath and came right out with the news about Janie's diagnosis.

Drew immediately became very emotional. He hung his head and sobbed. He usually deflects emotion and strives to give the impression that he is a tough guy. But behind his gruff exterior lies a marshmallow heart.

With Scott, what you see is what you get. He is outwardly and inwardly the sweetest, most caring human being you would ever want to meet. Even though he is the one who wears his heart on his sleeve, he didn't shed a tear in front of me or his brother. He just bowed his head and cried inwardly.

(Years later, when Janie's mother was dying in the hospital, Scott—whose emotions are usually so close to the surface—was the one who was able to go into her hospital room and hold her hand. Drew, whose deepest feelings are usually hidden under a ridge of muscles, couldn't bear to face it.)

The boys had a lot of questions, like, "I thought Mom was just going for speech class! When did you take her to see Dr. Leavey? And when did you take her to the Mayo Clinic?"

I had thought it best to refrain from distressing them unnecessarily. I also knew that if the news was as bad as it seemed, there would be time enough to fill them in once I'd gotten the diagnosis confirmed.

Eight

When I was in high school, I was very much into social activities and athletics and played on several school sports teams. Even though Dad and I were very close and I considered him my best friend, he wasn't the kind of dad who went out and played ball with me. He was, however, quite happy to have me with him in the salon ("the shop") or at the dock, repairing the boat. I helped him clean up the salon and we enjoyed spending time together.

I looked up to my father, admired him, and thought of him as a very smart man. So, I was always surprised when I saw him bypass opportunities that came his way throughout his career. For example, he had the chance to open additional salons in other communities on Long Island. This would have been a great opportunity for him.

Unfortunately, any time Dad would run one of these opportunities by my mother, her response was always the same: "No, we can't afford to take a chance on something like that. We have the kids' expenses and college coming up..." The message was always the same—that they needed to plan carefully and be conservative.

One day when I was fifteen years old, I heard one of these conversations where Dad told Mom about a great opportunity and she shot it down. Listening to this, I felt a resolve lock into place inside me.

I vowed to myself, *I am not going to die a working stiff because I am afraid of taking a chance in life!* The vow I made to myself that day would guide the course of my life.

My mother came by her cautious, conservative nature honestly. As I said, Mom was only ten years old when her mother died. Mom's father didn't remarry until she was fifteen. So, Mom grew up in a household without the stability of a mother present. Her older siblings took care of her while their father worked, and no doubt had to be very conservative, especially with money.

When my nineteen-year-old mother married my father, she lived by the credo, "We'd better not take any chances! It's better to play it safe."

Even as a teenager, I already sensed inside myself an entrepreneurial spirit. I knew that I was unsuited to have someone telling me what to do and I didn't envision going to work for anyone else. I needed to be out on my own.

I can't say whether I was born with that entrepreneurial spirit or developed it. I do know that my brother, Danny, was much more traditional than I. He went to Northeastern for his undergraduate work—a co-op school in Boston. He then went on to Georgetown Law School. Upon graduation, Danny walked the nine-to-five corporate path as a CPA and tax lawyer. He lived the very life that would have made me want to jump out a window. I was not cut out for the status quo.

In all the years my brother and I shared a room, I knew how he saw me—as a clown, and as someone who was not his equal. It wasn't until I went away to college that my brother finally began to treat me as an equal. His attitude (and Mom's) was representative of a value system that prioritized great job security, ensured by a person going to college and earning a degree.

When it came time for me to go to college, I was told that my parents could not afford to send me away to school. I was going to have to go to the local commuter college and live at home. I hated that idea in the worst way. The last thing I wanted during my college years was to find myself in a position where I would be getting social invitations, having to ask my parents if I could go, and explaining what time I would be home.

I had my heart set on the *true* college experience—living on or near a campus far from home. I wanted to be on my own and experience independence for the first time. Nevertheless, I did as I was told and applied to local schools like Pratt Institute in Brooklyn and Cooper Union in Manhattan. Both schools would have been an easy commute and, as it happened, both schools accepted me.

I also applied to Rhode Island School of Design, which offered me a small scholarship, more for basketball than academics. (Speaking of basketball, I was jealous of my brother only in regard to his six-foot-two height. He had two inches on me, and it was wasted on him. He didn't even play basketball.)

Along with my applications to those three schools, I applied to the Design, Architecture and Art School at the University of Cincinnati, with an eye toward becoming an architect. I had discovered that they offered a work-study co-op program which enabled students to help pay their way through college. (I knew about co-op colleges thanks to Danny having attended one.)

The program was set up in such a way that students attended school for the entire first year and, in each following year, they would alternate one quarter of work with one quarter of school. This arrangement was not without its downside. For one thing, it would take me five years to complete college instead of four. Secondly, I would still need to apply for student loans to supplement the money I would earn in the co-op program because the co-op job would not pay well enough to cover the cost of school.

The upside was irresistible. I would have the chance to go away to college, and to graduate with nearly two years of work experience under my belt. I was very happy to get to have a true away-from-home college experience. Meanwhile, my parents were happy because I would be covering most of my own college costs. My decision was made.

I would end up living in a dorm for the first year and then living in a series of apartments with school buddies. Interestingly enough, I even spent two years (my third and fourth years) living in a dorm at the original branch of Hebrew Union College-Jewish Institute of Religion, the school where people went to become a Reform rabbi. This situation arose because Hebrew Union College had more dorm space than students, and was able to open its dorms to Jewish students from the University of Cincinnati.

Getting to live at Hebrew Union College was a great blessing for me. They had a fabulous library, an indoor swimming pool and a wonderful gymnasium where I could play basketball. I had my own room which was cleaned daily by a maid who also picked up my dirty laundry on Tuesdays and delivered it clean on Thursdays. I had three meals a day served to me by waiters. On Friday, Saturday and Sunday afternoons, we were allowed to invite female visitors to our rooms. It was like a high-end fraternity house and I loved living there.

Janie, meanwhile, never lived on campus at University of Cincinnati School of Education. She would visit her friends in the dorms and sleep over when she needed a break from home.

Nine

The boys asked, "What's going to happen to Mom? How long will it take?"

I let out a big sigh and said, "It's a terminal illness."

"How long does she have?"

"Nobody knows. The progression of frontotemporal dementia averages between eight and fifteen years."

I tried my best to soft-peddle the news, but any way I framed Janie's diagnosis, it carried with it a dire outlook for the future.

All three of us had tears running down our faces by this point. Drew and I were openly crying and dabbing our eyes with napkins from the table. Scott had his head in his hands, crying quietly to himself.

Nobody could have loved her children more than Janie. No two kids could have loved their mother more. And no two people could have loved each other more than Janie and me. We were a very tight family. That's not to say there weren't bumps in the road, of course. Nothing is ever perfect.

After our lunch, Drew and Scott went to see their mother. I was glad I had decided to give the boys time to digest the news before seeing Janie. I wanted to soften the blow for them—something I wished someone had been able to do for me.

It was 2004, Janie was fifty-nine, and I was sixty years old. The eight and a half years that followed were far and away the worst of my life. I would not wish that pain and devastation on anyone.

To this day, I ask myself how I got through it. All I can say is that I just kept putting one foot in front of the other and staying laser focused on my priorities: caring for my wife, keeping the vows I made to her on our wedding day and on the day of her diagnosis, and cherishing every last minute we were given.

Ten

At the end of my first year at University of Cincinnati, I had to temporarily drop out so I could return home to earn the money I needed to re-enroll for my second year. I returned to my hometown and went to work at a haberdashery called Gramatan Men's Shop where both Danny and I had worked during summers and holidays while we were in high school. My brother had the haberdashery job first and I inherited it from him.

I worked in the store's tuxedo-rental department. I also filled in from time to time as a hat model, thanks to my sample-size head. The store decided whether or not to buy certain hats based upon how they looked on me.

Whenever I had to measure a guy for a tuxedo rental, I measured the outseam of their pants. After all, I was a nineteen-year-old self-respecting male and I wasn't about to go near another guy's inseam. So, I measured the outseam from the top of the pants at the belt loop all the way down. The problem was, the difference between the inseam and the outseam (the "rise" of the pants) varied between ten and twelve inches, depending upon cut and style.

I would do my outseam measurement and jot a note to the tailor stating, for example, that the measurement was forty-two inches, "give or take an inch." (Arthur was from Bermuda and the other tailor was island born as well.)

Arthur would see my note, come out onto the floor from the back room where he was doing his alterations, and start yelling, "Bob! What the hell are you doing? What is this supposed to mean?"

"Arthur," I would say, "don't worry about it! He's not buying the suit...he's just renting it. I'll adjust it with the suspenders."

He would shake his head in exasperation and go back to his alterations room.

While I worked, I took night classes at Pratt Institute in Brooklyn, an architectural, art and design school which had a very fine architectural program. In that way, I was able to make up some of the classes I was missing while not attending University of Cincinnati.

Between student-loan money and my earnings from the store, I had enough money to return to The School of Design, Art and Architecture in Cincinnati after one year away. As I mentioned, working every other quarter *helped* pay for college, but the co-op system didn't pay students enough to be able to afford college without student loans.

When I graduated, I would do so with a couple of cases of payment-coupon books for repayment of my student loans to Chemical Bank of New York. I owed over two thousand dollars in student loans and repaid it over ten to twelve years, at the rate of $18.10 per month. That amount is forever branded in my brain.

Despite the fact that the co-op system didn't completely cover the cost of college, I found it to be a very worthwhile program. I had no regrets. I would highly recommend it to any prospective college student without the funds to go away to school, and anyone who wants to get some work experience while learning.

For my first co-op job after returning to school following my yearlong absence, I worked at the Planning Commission of Cleveland. After two quarters there, I was assigned to work at the Planning Commission of Cincinnati. The way it worked out, I was in school the first and third quarters of the calendar year, and I worked the second and fourth. So, the end of my fourth-quarter of work always coincided with the Christmas-New Year's break from school, and I was able to return to New York to spend the holidays with my family.

When I was in Cleveland on the weekends, I took a bus to the outskirts of town and then hitchhiked to Janie's house and spent the weekend with her. Hitchhiking wasn't considered as dangerous as it is today but it was definitely a race against the sun. Once it was dark outside, no one in their right mind would pick up a hitchhiker, and no hitchhiker would want to get into a stranger's car.

When Janie and I had plans to go out and I wasn't meeting her at her parents' house, she would come pick me up at my apartment in her mother's car—a 1957 Chevrolet convertible. Being in Ohio to attend school, I was without a car of my own.

Janie and I were now seeing each other exclusively. So, when my close friend Ricky told me that he was getting married in Brooklyn and wanted me to be his best man, I naturally invited Janie to be my date for the wedding. Going to this wedding together would mark the first time Janie would be meeting my parents. It would also burst her illusions that I was as wealthy as the other residents of Great Neck and just being modest when I had tried to convince her otherwise.

Janie wasn't the only one who had envisioned me as a well-to-do suitor. Apparently, so did her mother. When Janie's mom found out that I really did come from a working-class family, despite living in tony Great Neck, she tried to talk her daughter out of dating me. Her logic went like this: "But, Janie, you like nice things! You should marry someone older and established." It wasn't that Mrs. Pressman disliked me; she just knew her daughter.

The moment of truth about my financial status came when Janie and I traveled together to New York to go to Ricky's wedding. We pulled up in front of the apartment building where I lived with my family when I wasn't away at school. I could see the realization dawning on her that I really *was* from a working-class family. Janie covered her surprise very well but not before I saw the expression on her face.

When my parents met Janie, my father loved her right away. He recognized in her a kindred spirit. Their outgoing personalities and gregarious natures drew them to each other, and my dad enjoyed her very much. My mother was always the picture of politeness and class, to the point that she never set foot in anyone's house without bringing them a gift. Mom welcomed Janie and made her feel at home, but her reserved personality was not a natural match for Janie's outgoing one. Mom and Janie may not have been two peas in a pod like Dad and Janie, but my mother liked Janie very much.

The banquet hall where the wedding was held was lovely and I was honored and happy to be Ricky's best man. All the way around, it was a wonderful function and Janie and I had a great time together. We couldn't have known at the time that this wedding was the first of many we would attend together throughout the years, including our own.

Eleven

Janie was getting worse by the month.

Friends started saying to me, "Do you realize you're finishing Janie's sentences for her? What's wrong with her?"

Trust me, nobody ever finished Janie's sentences for her—not before she got sick, anyway.

"No, nothing's wrong," I said, lying through my teeth. I had promised my wife I would keep her secret and I intended to do exactly that for as long as I could pull it off.

As Janie's illness became more and more obvious and I continued to deny its existence to our friends, many of them became more and more upset with me.

My first loyalties were to my wife and kids. I felt that Janie's desire to keep her illness a private matter within the family trumped anyone else's desire to know. It was my job to preserve her dignity.

I also felt that Janie's condition was none of anyone's damned business, and I wasn't afraid to let people know my feelings if they pushed the issue.

At one point when Janie's illness became quite advanced and I had retired to look after her, I had to call one particular woman and let her know what was what. She kept insisting that something was wrong with Janie and that everyone, including her, had a right to know.

"Look," I said, "there's nothing wrong with Janie and it's none of your business. And until you've walked in my shoes, you have nothing to say!"

By the time I was done telling off this woman, she was in tears.

At this point, Janie's illness was manifesting itself only in her speech, not in her physical being. Neither Janie nor I were aware of the toll her dementia was taking, the direction it was heading, or how fast it was accelerating.

Dr. Leaderman had given me generalities because that was the best he could do. He had told me at one of Janie's doctor's appointments, "Remember, not everyone with frontotemporal dementia reacts the same way. So, I can't tell you exactly what to expect."

I knew that Janie would eventually experience personality problems. And she was already experiencing obvious speech problems.

In the meantime, Janie did her best to avoid drawing attention to herself. She was known as a force of nature with a huge personality and she intended to maintain that persona for as long as possible. The last thing she wanted was for anyone to think she wasn't herself. She didn't want anyone to see her in a different light until it became impossible to get around it.

Twelve

When I got to be sixteen or seventeen years old, all the guys in my circle became interested in cars. Every one of them got a car—a Chevy or Ford hardtop or convertible. (That was the pre-foreign-carmaker era.) I didn't get a car at that age but my longstanding attitude was, "This is who I am. If you don't like me, it's fine with me."

My father taught me how to drive. He believed that the only way I would learn to drive a stick-shift was by having me drive to the top of a steep hill, put the car in neutral, and try to get going again without rolling backwards. He made sure I learned the delicate, precarious dance between the clutch and gas pedal that all new drivers have to master if they are to drive a stick-shift without causing an accident or killing themselves or someone else. While I was learning, I went through a few episodes of the car jerking up and down.

That was my dad. He didn't believe in the easy way out and always made me work for everything. I laugh every time I go to the beach and see the kids in the water, crying that they don't know how to swim. My dad dragged me into the water at Jones Beach when I was eight or nine years old and made me learn to swim.

I was sixteen when Dad bought a bright yellow Bonneville automatic convertible with black bucket seats. My eyes bugged out when I saw it. I had no idea what had possessed my father to buy such a car. Such a purchase was completely out of character for him and not something I could imagine someone his age driving.

We were a one-car family so I knew I would eventually get to drive that great machine. I couldn't wait to get behind the wheel. At the first opportunity that presented itself, I said to my father, "Let me have the keys to the car!"

"Okay, here," Dad said, cautiously handing me the keys, "but be careful."

I hopped into the car and immediately put the top down. I had only gone three or four miles when I heard a siren behind me. *Oh, my G-d!* I said to myself. *What did I do?*

The policeman pulled me over. When he walked over to the car, I recognized him as a sergeant who was friendly with my dad. My father knew every cop in Nassau County, Long Island where we lived. This firsthand acquaintanceship with the police was a side benefit of the pistol-shooting competitions Dad liked to enter.

"I just want you to know," said the sergeant, "that every cop in the county knows this car and license plate. So, do not be caught someplace you shouldn't be!"

The police officer was keeping me on the straight and narrow. I was known as being a little on the risk-taking side of life so the warning was not completely unwarranted.

I took a very deep breath and went on about my business. That night at the dinner table, out of the blue and without looking up, my father mentioned that he knew I had seen the sergeant earlier that day. That was his way of letting me know, "I know where you are at all times. Don't be anywhere you're not supposed to be!"

This wasn't the first or last time during my youth that I was picked up by one of dad's police-officer buddies and deposited back home.

Another incident that drew the attention of law enforcement officers occurred on foot. A fellow ruffian friend of mine and I were walking down the street with a handful of guys when a group of guys in motorcycle jackets (we called their type "rocks") came up on us and started taunting us. One of the rocks threw out an insult and my friend retaliated.

I figured our odds of prevailing were pretty good or at least even because we had an equal number of guys on each side. Or, so I thought. When I glanced behind me, I saw that the remainder of our friends had hightailed it out of there when the skirmish started.

One thing led to another and my friend and I ended up in a tousle with two or three of the rocks. Since this was happening on Middleneck Road, the main drag through town, we caught the attention of police. A couple of police officers came over and broke up the fight and then one of them escorted me home.

"I'm not going to arrest him," the cop said to my dad. "Just let him cool off for a while."

There was no question that I came by my bravado honestly. As my Dad's high-school friend Murray (known as Uncle Murray to me, despite the fact that he was not a blood relation) said many years later at my father's funeral: "As sad as I am to see him pass away, when I think about it, I realize it's amazing he lived as long as he did. He was just so unfiltered and bigger than life. Everyone knew not to mess with Harry. No one insulted him and got away with it!"

I knew this to be true. I had witnessed this trait of my father's on more than one occasion. I've already told you about the incident at Danny's bar mitzvah where Dad crushed the watch. Then there was the fall day when we were headed to the dock where we stowed our boat.

We were driving down a very narrow road. Parking was allowed on only one side of the street so as to allow room for two cars to pass. We reached a point in the road where either our car or the car facing us had to back up. The other car was a fancy car, a Cadillac maybe. The driver began exerting his perceived luxury-car authority by honking at my father and motioning for him to back up and let him pass.

Dad and I stuck our heads out the window and surveyed the situation. It was clear that the other driver had only one car behind him and empty spaces at the curb. Behind us was an entire block filled with cars that would have had to back up.

Finally, the other driver got fed up. He opened his car door, got out, slammed it shut and stormed over to our car.

Dad rolled down his window in time to hear the other driver say, "Can't you hear well? I said to back up this piece of garbage so I can get through!"

Dad never said a word. He simply got out of the car and, in a single motion, removed his glasses and tossed them through the driver's-side window and onto the seat. Then he cold-cocked the guy across his jaw. After flattening the man, my father walked over to the other car and motioned for the guy's wife to roll down her window.

"Come get your husband and put him in the car!" Dad said. "And back up this car...we're coming through!"

My father had grown up on the streets in the Bronx. To some extent, he still lived by the rules of the street. There was no way on earth that he was going to let anyone look down upon him or talk to him in a disrespectful manner just because he wasn't driving a fancy car. Once the other car had backed up to let us through, we drove on.

Another interesting car story involving my father and me took place in 1961, during my freshman year in college, before I had met Janie. I was heading home, along with four female friends and a male friend who owned a 1951 Studebaker. My friend was driving us from

Cincinnati to the East Coast to spend Thanksgiving with our families. I was going to be surprising my parents, who weren't expecting me home for the holiday.

The five of them were headed to New Jersey. They dropped me off at the New Jersey tubes so I could take the subway to Penn Station, and the Long Island Railroad to Great Neck. I waited for the first train headed to my hometown. It was around four or five o'clock in the morning when I boarded the Long Island Railroad train and promptly fell asleep. After the seventeen-hour car ride, I was exhausted.

When I woke up, I was at the Manhasset stop—one stop past Great Neck. I was so anxious to get home by then, I didn't give two thoughts to the fact that I didn't really have a lot of money in my pocket. I hailed a taxi anyway and arrived at my parents' apartment building around 6:30 a.m. Thankfully, I ended up with just enough money to pay the cab fare.

My mother, may she rest in peace, never let herself fall into solid sleep until she knew all the kids were home safe and sound. At that point in time, my brother was away at school in Boston, and my sister was still living at home. Since I was surprising my parents for Thanksgiving, I knew my mother wouldn't be expecting me and would be fast asleep.

I planned to tiptoe inside and fall asleep on the couch until everyone woke up. I very slowly turned the key in the lock, trying unsuccessfully to avoid the loud click. Figuring I might have awakened someone, I listened for a minute to see if I could hear anyone moving around inside. When I heard nothing, I opened the door and the lights came on.

There was my father, standing in the corner with a gun pointed at me. "Oh, it's just you," he said and went back to bed.

I suspect that my mother heard the click, elbowed my father and said, "Someone is breaking into the apartment!" At that point, my father went and got the gun.

I spent the Thanksgiving weekend with my family. On Sunday, it was time to head back to New Jersey so I could meet up with my friends and ride with them back to school. Both my mom and dad were going to drive me to New Jersey, and then stop off in the Bronx afterwards to see their parents.

"Don't let Mom go!" I whispered to my father.

Dad made up an excuse about needing to run an errand along the way and got Mom to agree to stay behind. When Dad saw my friend's Studebaker with its doors tied shut because they wouldn't lock, he said to me, "Good decision! She never would have let you in the car. Be careful and call me when you get there."

Thirteen

A few years later, I was in town for my brother's wedding. During that trip home, I bought a car from Uncle Murray for one hundred dollars. It was a 1958 army-green Hilman-Minx convertible. I had been asking for a car for ages before this windfall finally came my way. It felt great to have my own wheels.

"Now, listen," Dad said to me, "if you're buying this car, that's fine. But make sure you also have enough money for gas, insurance and repairs. Don't call me if the thing breaks down!" The car was not exactly a practical purchase and my father knew that there was an excellent chance that it would break down at some point.

After my brother's 1964 wedding, it was time for Janie and me to return to Cincinnati for school. We had flown to New York and Janie's parents insisted that she fly back. They may have been afraid that we would stop over at a motel if we were permitted to drive back. I'm sure they suspected that our relationship had already progressed to the physical stage but they certainly had no intentions of aiding and abetting any sexual encounters.

Hungover from the wedding, I drove my car back to Cincinnati very slowly, barely able to focus on the road. The highway kept getting wavy on me, moving back and forth. I had to pull over two or three times. Finally, I decided to take a nap and then follow it with a stiff cup of coffee to clear my head.

When I got back to Cincinnati, my father's warning about making sure I could cover the repairs on the car was still ringing in my ears. So, I checked the junkyards, looking for a spare engine for a Hilman-Minx.

Miraculously, I found one. I bought it and put it in the backseat of the car. Any time I needed a part, I would take the part off the spare engine. Thankfully, I inherited mechanical aptitude from my father, who always worked on the family car himself, and even singlehandedly fixed our T.V.

I was passably good with mechanical repairs but an amateur compared to my dad. I was reminded of this fact when I changed my own spark plugs and failed to get the gapping correct. It took me two days to get the car started.

Fourteen

Between the middle and the end of 2005, I started to notice Janie's disease progressing at a faster rate of speed. By the end of 2005, her speech had vanished completely. She knew the words she wanted to say, and was able to form words with her mouth; she just couldn't make the sound to go with the shapes.

The last conversation we ever had occurred sometime in the last few months of that year. For the next several years, it was very lonely around the house. My wife was there with me and yet she was completely unable to speak to me.

I got nervous about Janie driving a car by herself. I envisioned her getting lost and stopping to ask for directions—and then being unable to express herself properly due to her speech issues. I had panic attacks over that.

She was still able to walk at this point. So, during those moments when I was not next to her, she was able to come over to me and hand me a note she had written. She could also indicate with a gesture of her index finger that she wanted me to follow her. Then she would point at something she needed me to do for her, and I would catch on.

I would think, as she pointed at the coffeemaker, *Oh, she wants me to make a cup of coffee for her. She knows she wants a cup of coffee but she's forgotten how to make it.*

We had been married for so long, I could practically read her thoughts. I knew what she was thinking and wanted to say.

I had not planned on retiring quite so early, but I had a compelling reason: it was obvious that I needed to stay home and take care of Janie. She needed care twenty-four hours a day, every day of the year.

Fifteen

Her beauty, attractiveness and great personality made Janie quite desirable. There were plenty of guys who would have loved to steal her away from me. One of these guys was an attorney local to Cincinnati who was three or four years older than I. He fit the profile of the older, established guy who could give Janie the type of lifestyle to which she supposedly wanted to become accustomed.

Janie's mother thought that this attorney might be a good match for her daughter. The potential matching of Janie and the attorney didn't sit well with me. As I mentioned earlier, my relationship with Janie's parents was a good, close one and they liked me very much. I even occasionally worked part-time at Janie's father's auto-parts-and-repair store. Thankfully, the pairing of Janie and the attorney would remain nothing more than an idea in the mind of Janie's mother.

Years later, Janie and I would laugh about the attorney. "I knew you would end up being successful," she said. "I just didn't think it would take you this long!"

We had been dating for two years and I was ready to close the deal and take Janie off the market. So, I started thinking about asking her to marry me. I was barely twenty-two years old, but it was customary in those days to marry young.

(It is interesting to note that Janie's mother, Helen, had not gotten married until age thirty-five. That's when she met her Philadelphia-born husband, who was eight or nine years her junior, on a beach trip to Atlantic City. For a bride to be over twenty-five, much less over thirty, was almost unheard of in those days. It was also highly unusual in those days for a wife to be older than her husband. Helen was forty-three when she gave birth to Janie. She'd been thirty-seven when she had Janie's sister, Gail. Helen was a very attractive woman in her day, and I have no idea why she didn't get married earlier.)

I was ready to propose to Janie but I didn't have two nickels to rub together for the engagement ring. Luckily, my dad collected loose diamonds, which he may have acquired in exchange for hairstyling services. I knew that there were times when Dad's customers would take thousands of dollars of their husband's off-the-record earnings and put it towards their weekly visits to the salon. They would say, "Here you go, Harry! Just let me know when the money's used up."

So, it wasn't much of a stretch to envision Dad's customers giving him diamonds in exchange for services.

Dad had taken three of the loose diamonds from his collection and made a ring for himself. He removed the center diamond from his ring and gave it to me so I could make it into a ring for Janie. It was a magnificent carat-and-a-half stone. Then Dad sent me to a jeweler he knew to buy a setting for the ring and a couple of side diamond baguettes.

Many years later, I was in a novelty store somewhere and I would see a kid's toy ring with three little plastic carrots. I bought it, took it home, gift-wrapped it, and gave it to Janie as a gag gift.

When Janie opened the box containing the three-carrot ring, we both had a good laugh.

"I'll replace this with three *carats* sometime soon," I promised.

Two years after Janie's diagnosis, on our fortieth wedding anniversary, I bought Janie a very beautiful ring with a setting I designed myself. Then I waited until she left the house for some reason, and went and found the little toy ring with the three carrots on it. I tied the three-and-a-half-carat ring to the three-carrot ring.

One night shortly thereafter, as Janie and I were heading out to dinner with Drew and his wife, I hid the ring in my jacket pocket. At some point during the evening, I pulled out the ring box and handed it to my wife. "This is what I promised you I would do many years ago," I said.

When Janie opened the box, she immediately recognized the three-carrot ring and started laughing. Then her laughter turned to bittersweet tears and she cried all the way home from the restaurant. The ring was absolutely gorgeous and it reminded us both of our long, happy marriage.

Anyway, around the same time I was having Janie's engagement ring made, Dad and I took our usual evening walk. This was our routine: every night around nine o'clock, we left our apartment building together and took a walk around the block. Usually it was just the two of us but occasionally Dad's friend from the building joined us. Our destination was Frederick's, an establishment which sold sandwiches as well as newspapers and other sundries. Dad always bought the next morning's paper.

This had been our evening ritual dating all the way back to my elementary school or junior-high-school days and continuing through high school. Once I got into my college years, we took our evening walks together only when I was home during breaks from school.

On that particular walk, we were talking about the fact that I wanted to marry Janie.

"Let me ask you a question," said Dad. "Do you know how to satisfy a woman?"

Needless to say, the question took me by surprise. I looked at my dad and said, "Yeah, Dad, that's not a problem."

"Okay, good. I'm glad."

I'm not sure why my father thought to ask me such a question. He must have felt that he should have that father-son talk with me before I got in too deep with my soon-to-be wife. I have no idea what he would have said or done if I had said no. Maybe he was planning to send me a hooker to teach me the basics.

I returned to Cincinnati. When I came home from college on my next break from school, Janie's engagement ring was ready and waiting for me.

One evening in December of 1965, Janie and I were back in Cincinnati and out for the evening. We had seen a movie or had dinner, and afterwards we took a drive. I pulled the car into the parking lot of a bowling alley.

I fumbled around with my words for a minute and finally said something to the effect of, "I'm starting to run out of funds and I need an income, and well, you have one, so..."

She earned only a hundred dollars a week ($5,200.00 per year) as an elementary-school teacher. (Yes, she was already in the work force. During her college years, she always went to summer school instead of taking a summer job. So, she graduated two quarters early in December instead of May.)

"...maybe we should get married," I said.

Janie started laughing, which was good because I was kidding around—not about the proposal but about wanting to marry her for her fifty-two-hundred-dollar-a-year salary.

Sixteen

Our wedding took place two years and nine months after we started dating. Janie's birthday was August 17th, four days before our wedding. So, every year thereafter, she would remind me that she missed out on one gift by having the two occasions fall so close together.

The wedding was held on August 21st, 1966 in the sixth-floor ballroom of the Terrace Hilton Hotel in Cincinnati. It was a black-tie affair with all the bells and whistles. We had about a hundred and thirty guests. As was standard operating procedure during that era, the bride's parents picked up the tab for the wedding.

My brother was my best man, as dictated by tradition and protocol. I could feel the unspoken pressure and expectations from my parents. So, I did as I was expected to do and asked Danny to do the honors. (He had already been married for two years by then, and I had been the best man at his wedding.) If I'd had the freedom to *choose* my best man, I would not have chosen my brother. As I've said, we had completely opposite personalities and weren't close at all.

The bridesmaids included my sister, Randee, Janie's sister, Gail, and a few other friends of Janie's. I adored my sister but neither Janie nor I liked Gail. She rubbed me the wrong way. Janie was six years younger than Gail, and the two were as different as Danny and me.

Grandma Sadie had chosen a beautiful gown for the wedding but it failed to make its way into her suitcase. She had no choice but to wear the same dress for the ceremony that she had worn to the rehearsal dinner.

Sadly, Grandma Sadie and Grandpa Julius were attending the wedding separately. After fifty years of marriage, they had separated. Interestingly, they stayed apart for the rest of their lives, but never divorced. The wedding photo of the two of them shows them standing shoulder to shoulder—but turning away from each other. I never knew what had caused them to separate after such a long marriage. Grandpa Julius was a wonderful, easygoing guy and I had always adored Grandma Sadie.

As I mentioned earlier, Cincinnati was the home of Reform Judaism, thanks in no small part to the fact that Hebrew Union College was located there. So, not surprisingly, Janie's parents belonged to a Reform synagogue. The rabbi from their temple officiated at our wedding.

I was completely at peace and free of any wedding-day jitters or cold feet. As you've no doubt gathered by now, I am a very secure person by nature and not the nervous type. And even if I had been prone to anxiety, there was nothing about marrying Janie that gave me pause. I was completely in love with her and certain that I wanted to share my life with her.

Janie's parents and I got along well. And I knew that my mother liked my wife very much, and my father adored her. Janie and Dad were compatible on many levels and loved to joke around together. That signified that my father accepted Janie completely. I was in heaven, having Dad approve of the girl I was marrying. Any time he said no about something, it was hard for me to feel as good about it.

As I stood at the altar and watched my bride walk down the aisle toward me, I was completely starstruck. Janie was such a beauty, she looked good in everything and anything, and she looked especially exquisite in her wedding dress and veil. The gown was white with sleeves slightly fuller than cap sleeves. It was tightly fitted from her shoulders to her hips and then flared out.

I was wearing a black tuxedo and a yarmulke—and the rabbi was wearing a white dinner jacket.

"Is that the waiter or the rabbi?" my mother asked when she spotted him in his white dinner jacket. Unfortunately, there was nothing we could do at that point but accept the rabbi's attire. Needless to say, my mother wasn't too thrilled with the rabbi and neither was I.

We were married under the chuppah and took the traditional step of smashing the glass beneath our feet. We said our vows, which were in keeping with tradition and not out of the ordinary in any way.

At the reception, as everyone danced the hora, Janie and I were both lifted up in the air in chairs. I also danced with my mom, and Janie danced with my dad.

At one point during the reception, I was standing in the corner, having a drink with a couple of friends when I decided to light a cigarette. The minute the flame lit up the tip of my cigarette, my father came striding across the floor in my direction.

Dad had always been a heavy smoker. He considered smoking to be a terrible habit and one he was stuck with, after several attempts at quitting.

"If I ever catch you with a cigarette again..." Dad said, snatching the cigarette out of my mouth and crushing it beneath his shoe. The issue was not up for discussion.

I may have been a twenty-three-year-old married man but I was still my father's son. And, no son of his was going to follow in his footsteps and become a smoker. Not if he could help it.

(Unfortunately, I did become addicted to cigarettes, just like my father, and continued to smoke until 1979 when I was thirty-six. I smoked a pack a day. When I was out on the weekends, enjoying a few drinks, I could easily find myself opening a second pack. I smoked Lark Cigarettes and told myself that they were healthier than other brands, thanks to their charcoal filter.

There's an interesting story behind me finally quitting smoking. It happened when Drew was nine years old. We were out to dinner as a family the night before the first day of school, as was our tradition. I felt like Drew hadn't been living up to his potential during the previous semester at school. So, over dinner, I told him,

"If you will promise you'll do your best in school this semester, I will quit smoking."

My son agreed, we shook hands, and I threw a pack of Larks in the trash. I had tried to quit a hundred times before that night, but always picked cigarettes up again. But that time, I was motivated by my love for my son. That's what finally did the trick. I haven't touched a cigarette since.)

Anyway, other than Dad's reaction to me lighting a cigarette, there were no real surprises at the wedding or reception. Everything went pretty smoothly.

After the festivities, Janie and I went back to our room at the Hilton and changed into our traveling outfits. Then we spent our wedding night at a hotel at the Cincinnati airport. We had an early flight the following morning. As Janie and I slipped into bed for some wedding night intimacy, we discovered that some of my jokester friends had short-sheeted the bed. We had a good laugh over that.

The following day, we flew to the Caribbean island of Nassau and checked into the Nassau Beach Hotel. I joked that we were a long way from Nassau County, New York, where I was born. Many years later, we returned to Paradise Island, a small island off the main island of Nassau. During our honeymoon, the bridge from Nassau to Paradise Island had not yet even been built.

We had a wonderful honeymoon, including an outing to a European-style casino located in a house.

Thankfully, I am not a big gambler. So, there was no danger of me gambling away my nest egg before our life together had even begun—not that I had much of a nest egg yet. We also visited the straw market in downtown Nassau where natives sold their handwoven straw hats and purses. And we spent a lot of time enjoying the water. We returned home with a sexy photo of Janie standing on a rock, her bathing suit half on, half off.

The day before we were due to leave and head back to the States, the baggage handlers in Nassau all went on strike. This made it impossible to leave the island by plane. Somehow, I managed to wrangle a room for us on a cruise ship headed to Miami. Once in Miami, we caught a flight back to Cincinnati.

Getting ourselves off the island and onto that ship was no easy feat. It entailed a lot of aggravation we didn't need after our peaceful honeymoon in paradise. But it made for a great story later and enriched our memory of the trip.

All in all, our honeymoon was terrific, and our future looked rosy. I was on cloud nine and felt like I had died and gone to heaven. I was madly in love with my wife, and she with me, and that's how we would stay for all the years G-d gave us together. Of course, no marriage is without its bumps in the road. Ours was no exception but we always managed to work through them.

Seventeen

After returning from our honeymoon, we walked right into the apartment we had located, rented and furnished before we got married. It was on Newbedford Avenue in Roselawn, a suburb of Cincinnati. It was a very nice two-bedroom, one-bath place in a four-family apartment building with two units per floor. Each unit had its own garage, which meant that I had to park my car outside. I didn't mind. I was married to the woman of my dreams and happy as could be.

Janie and I decided that we wanted carpeting instead of the hardwood floors that came with the place. I said to myself, *I'm sure I'm at least as smart as whoever the carpet store will send out to do the installation.*

So, when we went to buy the carpeting, I asked a bunch of questions about installation and got all the information I needed to install it myself.

Meanwhile, thanks to the extended duration of the work-study program at college, I was finishing up my schooling during our newlywed period. And, Janie was loving her job as a teacher, her chosen vocation. Her passion for her work was rewarded when she was nominated for Beginning Teacher of the Year.

We had gotten engaged in late 1965 and married in August of 1966. In the interim, I had received a letter from Uncle Sam, officially inviting me to come in for my draft-board physical. The Vietnam War was underway and I was an able-bodied man of the proper age for the armed services.

I went to my college and collected letters from the dean, one of my professors, and a school counselor. The letters proved that, thanks to the work-study college model, I was shy of graduation by a year. Uncle Sam took pity on me and granted me one year to finish my studies before reporting to the draft board for my physical.

In April of 1967, not even a year after our wedding, I received a letter stating, "Your year is up!"

I responded to the letter with a statement that it would be a financial hardship for me to return to New York for the physical. I requested that I be allowed to take the physical in Cincinnati instead. Six months later the papers arrived and, in January or February of 1968, I went to the draft board in Cincinnati for my physical.

I had a bad varicose vein in my calf as a result of resuming playing football too soon after an injury. And, in anticipation of the physical, I already had an appointment set up for surgery. I also had a shoulder injury from my football days. And around the time we were married, Janie had noticed a small rash on the bottom of my left foot.

"What's that?" she asked.

"I don't know," I said. "I've had it for a long time. It doesn't itch or bother me or anything."

"I think you should go see Uncle Leon about it."

Janie's uncle was a dermatologist of national renown. I made an appointment with him, and during the examination, he diagnosed me with psoriasis. (Four or five months later, I would read an article in the paper stating that there was no known cure for the condition.)

"You should call Uncle Leon," Janie suggested, "and get him to write you a letter about your psoriasis to give to Uncle Sam!"

I went and saw Uncle Leon and was armed with a letter from him when I went in for my draft-board physical. I stood naked in a line, awaiting my inspection by the physician. I got tapped on the shoulder, indicating that it was my turn to lift up my right foot and then my left.

I lifted my left foot and my psoriasis became visible. I whipped out my three letters—one relating to my upcoming varicose vein surgery, one relating to my shoulder, and the final letter from Uncle Leon stating that he was treating me for psoriasis.

"Okay, go down the hall right now and see the doctor," he said, sending me to another room for further examination.

I did as I was told and went into the exam room where I took a seat. Then I showed the doctor my left foot.

The doctor took one look at the psoriasis on my foot and gave me a permanent 1-Y deferment. As I said, there is no known cure for psoriasis so that put a premature end to my physical. The U.S. Army may have been concerned that by accepting enlisted men with conditions for which there was no known cure, they were setting themselves up for claims for permanent disability compensation.

While I was there, I happened to run into an acquaintance from college. Prior to our physical exams, he sprinted into the draft board, all smiles, thinking he would get a deferment for testicular cancer. At the end of the physical, we ran into each other again, and he was no longer smiling. He was accepted into the Army, due to the five years that had passed since he had cancer. Sadly, he was considered cured.

Meanwhile, I had my deferment and I was smiling—but I had mixed feelings. I was relieved that I wasn't being sent overseas, but disheartened over the prospect of facing a permanent disability.

In retrospect, I wonder why I was excused from serving my country. I never understood why they didn't simply have me do a desk job where I would be wearing shoes. Ironically, by 1971, the last year I could have been drafted, my psoriasis rash was gone. It completely vanished. It was almost as if God had lent it to me.

Unfortunately, psoriasis remains dormant and can manifest as psoriatic arthritis. I discovered this a handful of years ago when I got arthritis in my wrists so severe that I could not turn a doorknob.

I went to see my doctor, who sent me to a rheumatologist who happened to be my neighbor and friend. X-rays were taken and I was asked to wait in the waiting room while they were read.

"Bob," said the doctor, who was looking at the X-rays. "Have you ever been a professional boxer?"

"No," I said laughing, "why do you ask?"

"Because the X-ray films show that every single one of your fingers has been fractured at one time or another!" said the doctor.

"Wow!" I said. "Well, I did play a lot of sports when I was young."

Occasionally, the pain and stiffness get so bad that I have to take prednisone for a short period of time. It completely erases the pain, which is wonderful. Of course, it is not the sort of medication you can take on an ongoing basis.

Eighteen

Janie and I had taken a year to enjoy each other before trying to start a family. Around the time that I reported for my draft-board physical, we had been actively trying to start our family. Once we did start trying to make a baby, we kept trying and trying for two years, to no avail.

We realized it was time to get a professional opinion on the matter so we went to see a fertility specialist. Janie and I both underwent some testing and then sat down with the doctor to discuss the results.

The doctor was uncertain about the origins of the problem we were having conceiving a child. He said that there seemed to be no obvious issue with either Janie's eggs or my sperm.

He explained, "I can't find any medical reason that you aren't getting pregnant, Janie, but this does happen sometimes. It might just be stress. If you decide to keep trying, you may or may not end up conceiving. We have no way of giving you a definitive answer."

In those days, there weren't all the fertility options that exist today. All we knew was that we had been trying for a couple of years and we were tired of waiting. We figured that we might as well move on and start the adoption process. We had heard stories of couples starting the adoption process and then getting pregnant because the stress was off.

We made a fairly quick and easy transition from wanting children of our own to discussing adoption. We weren't about to abandon our dream of having a family just because we hadn't conceived a child of our own.

Meanwhile, my parents kept asking us, "When are you going to have children?" I didn't want to tell them anything until I had something definitive to report.

By Ohio law, we were prohibited from starting the adoption process until we had been married for three years. While we passed the time waiting for our third anniversary, we spoke to adoption counselors at Jewish Family Services located in Cincinnati, Ohio.

Janie and I knew that there were no guarantees—no guarantee that we would be accepted as adoptive parents, and no guarantee that, if we were accepted, we would get a baby in the foreseeable future. There wasn't anything in particular in my background or Janie's that I saw as a potential impediment to adoption but I knew that any time bureaucracies and red tape are involved, it's possible to hit a brick wall.

One thing we did have going for us on the adoption front was timing. In those days, birth control was not yet prevalent so there were more women having children, and more children put up for adoption. Within a few years' time, the pill would become popular and abortions would become more commonplace, as well as single women keeping their children.

While Janie and I were going through the process of being approved as adoptive parents, disaster struck my family.

On Memorial Day of 1969, the building in which my dad's salon was located burned to the ground. Very early in the morning, Dad got the call about the fire, and raced down to the salon, which was only two blocks from home. He found out that the fire had started in the basement and may have been sparked by paper goods being stored there by the restaurant adjacent to Dad's salon. No one knew for sure. The fire was so intense, the origins of it were never determined.

What was certain was that natural gas had been the fuel for the fire. The fire had started as a small fire and, had it been caught it in time, it could have been quickly contained and the building salvaged. Unfortunately, for some unknown reason, the gas company failed to turn off the gas. Fueled by gas, the small fire turned into a roaring, destructive blaze.

The gas company was held liable for the fire and lawsuits were filed against them. My father settled with the gas company but this was cold comfort. Dad was fifty-nine years old at the time of the fire and didn't feel that it made financial sense to invest in rebuilding and relocating his business at that late stage of his life.

One factor in Dad's decision not to reinvest in his salon and relocate had to do with the six to ten months of time that it would have taken to get the new salon up and running. In that length of time, Dad would have lost all or most of his regular customers as they naturally went in search of a new hair stylist for their weekly salon appointments. So, Dad had to live with the anger and disappointment that came with knowing that he had lost his thriving salon business through no fault of his own.

Dad had always hoped that he might find a way to retire at sixty-two. After the fire, he made the decision to retire a few years early. Apparently, he was able to retire on a combination of several sources of revenue—savings from the salon, salary he received from administering the practical exam needed to get one's state license to work as a beautician, and his settlement from the gas company.

My parents were now free to travel and they decided that they wanted to see the country. In August of 1969, they set off on a cross-country road trip. Their first stop was Cincinnati to see Janie and me. They would end up seeing forty of the lower forty-eight states on their trip and coming back through Cincinnati on their way home.

"When are you going to have children?" my father asked me while they were visiting.

"I'll let you know," I said. I didn't reveal the fact that we were looking into adoption because I wasn't sure whether or not we would qualify. I was planning to wait to tell my parents until Janie and I found out that there was an actual child waiting for us.

Nineteen

In September or October of 1969, Janie and I finally got approved and accepted into the adoption program through Jewish Family Services in Cincinnati. A month or two later, we went to the first orientation meeting for adoptive parents. As we pulled up to the building, there were our good friends, Alan and Margie, pulling up right behind us. We were amazed to see each other. Realizing that we were all in the same predicament, we shared an emotional moment together.

For the adoption process through Jewish Family Services, we were put into groups of couples who went through the process together. In our case, there were eight couples in our group: Janie and I, Alan and Margie, and two couples from the previous group who were still awaiting children. It was great having Alan and Margie in our group.

"We do our best to match parents and children, and we take many factors into consideration," we were told. "We take into consideration the biological parents' family background, education, and physical attributes, among other things..."

Being the Doubting Thomas I am, I balked. I have always been the guy who operates less from guesswork and more from factual investigation. It seemed incredibly farfetched.

Who's kidding who? I said to myself. *They can't possibly match very accurately. If a child becomes available, they're going to give them to one of the couples in the group, regardless of whether they match or not.*

"Would you prefer a boy or a girl?" they asked us.

"We would be happy with either," Janie and I agreed.

Obviously, if one of the couples specified a preference for a boy or a girl and a baby of the opposite gender became available, the couple with the preference would lose out. We wanted to leave our options wide open.

"When a baby becomes available for one of you couples," they explained, "we will invite you down to view the baby. You will have the chance to read the information and background on the child before you say yes or no." The background usually pertained to the mother's side of the family, although sometimes they had information related to the father's side, as well.

I said to Janie, "I can't imagine a couple saying, 'No, I don't think this baby looks right. Show us who else you've got.'" We agreed that the idea was ludicrous. If we were lucky enough to be given the opportunity to adopt a child, we would thank our lucky stars.

From the time we started the program, it would end up taking about nine months before we got the call we had been hoping for—the same length of time it would have taken if Janie had been pregnant with our child.

In late January of 1970, as my parents returned from their trip around the country, disaster struck again. Grandpa Julius (my father's father) took ill and had to be hospitalized.

While Mom and Dad were at the hospital visiting my grandfather, my mother dragged my father to see their internist who happened to have offices in the same building as the hospital. Dad had been complaining of severe pain in his lower back and had refused to see a doctor. He was never one to voluntarily go to the doctor. Sadly, a simple blood test ordered by the internist revealed that my father had late-stage multiple myeloma (a type of cancer where calcium from the bones ends up in the bloodstream).

I immediately hopped a flight from Cincinnati to New York to see my dad and meet with his doctor. My mother and sister were at the meeting with Dad's doctor too, and my brother may have been there, as well. (There were many visits between our family and Dad's doctors over the ensuing months and they all blend together in my mind.)

"I'm sorry," explained the doctor, "but unfortunately, all we have right now is research drugs. We don't have a proven cure."

My family and I all agreed that we had no choice but to give Dad the research drugs.

I spoke on behalf of the family, saying, "We will authorize putting my father on research drugs. Just tell me where to sign. But, doctor, you must promise me that if you ever get to the point where you are sure the medication isn't working, you will tell me. That way, I can take him off the medication and let nature run its course. I don't want him suffering needlessly and I know he wouldn't want that for himself."

For the next six months, my father was in and out of hospitals. (Just to give you an idea of how often I was flying back and forth between Cincinnati and New York, I ran up over three thousand dollars' worth of one-way tickets.) Janie would quite often come with me.

I wasn't suffering under any delusions. I understood that Dad's disease was terminal. As for Dad, I'm not sure he ever knew he had a terminal illness. He never brought up his mortality or said anything that gave me the impression that he knew he was going to die. We had told him only that he had a bloodborne disease, that research drugs were the treatment for it, and that the doctors were hopeful.

Ironically, Grandpa Julius, who was in his mid-eighties by then, recovered from his illness. Dad, meanwhile, reacted well to the medication initially. Then he declined. Then he rallied back, but not as strong as before.

In April or May, I got a call from my father's doctor. "The medication is not working. I know I made a promise to let you know. Do you want me to stop the medication?"

I couldn't get a yes out of my mouth. I knew that the doctor was doing exactly as I had asked him to do but I couldn't go through with it. Stopping my father's medication and letting nature take its course was one thing in theory. It was something else entirely when I thought about putting it into practice.

Even while I was telling the doctor to continue Dad's medication for the time being, I was kicking myself. I felt like I was letting my father down by extending his suffering. Yet, I couldn't *imagine* a world without my dad in it. Ever since I was a small boy, Dad had been my best friend and confidante, just as I was his.

Knowing that Dad was sick and might not have long to live prompted me to tell my parents that Janie and I were starting our family. By now, Janie and I had been definitively accepted into the adoption program, so I knew I could safely spill the beans.

I chose April 10th, my parents' anniversary, as the date I would tell them that they were going to become grandparents. Thankfully, at the time I told them, my dad was still lucid enough to understand what I was telling him and engage in conversation about it. I told them the bad news first.

"Janie and I had been having trouble getting pregnant so we saw a doctor," I explained. "The doctor didn't know why we weren't getting pregnant. They checked us both and found out that Janie's eggs are fine and so are my swimmers. They can't tell us the cause. We have decided not to wait to see if things will change. We're going to adopt. We've already been accepted into the adoption program through Jewish Family Services."

My mother took it hard when she heard that we wouldn't be having biological children. She went into a slight depression. She couldn't shake the feeling that it was her fault somehow. My attempts to explain that it had nothing to do with her fell on deaf ears.

Mom's sadness over the fact that we wouldn't be giving her biological grandchildren soon gave way to excitement over knowing there would be children coming, even if they weren't coming from Janie and me biologically. After all, we now knew that at some point down the line, we would be getting a baby.

Given how close Dad and I had always been, he felt he needed to dig a little deeper before giving us his blessing for adoption. "Are you absolutely sure you and Janie want to stop trying to have your own children?" Dad asked. "Is adopting really what you want to do?"

"Yes, Dad, we're sure about adoption."

"Well, in that case, I'm excited for you both...and for your mother and me!"

About nine months after we started the adoption program, we got the call from Jewish Family Services with the good news—they had a baby boy for us! They invited us down to view the baby and read the background information on the child. When we arrived at their offices and started listening to the history, I was flabbergasted.

The baby's grandfather was an architect. I had gotten a degree to become an architect. The baby had red hair, just like my father. Those similarities were just the tip of the iceberg. There were other aspects of the baby's family background that were such a match, I couldn't believe it. All my thoughts about the matching process being nothing but a bunch of hot air and false promises went right out the window.

To be preparing to bring our son into our lives at the same time I was watching my father slip away was bittersweet—and incredibly exhausting. I continued to fly back and forth between Cincinnati and New York to see my dad, hoping and praying that he would live long enough to meet his new grandson, who had been born on June 9th.

During the month of June of 1970, my father went in and out of a coma. My mom would call me and say, "He's in a coma! Get here fast!"

I would quickly make flight arrangements and rush to the airport so I could be by Dad's side, just in case. By the time I got to him, my father would be out of the coma. The emotional whiplash was a nightmare.

On July Fourth weekend, we were called back to the Jewish Family Services offices to view the baby and take him home. We couldn't wait to meet the little guy. When we got there, we took a seat.

A social worker came in and handed the baby to Janie, along with a bottle of milk.

Janie was shaking so badly from excitement, she decided to pass the baby to me. "I promised Bob that he could give the baby his first bottle," she said, improvising an explanation as she placed our little bundle in my arms. He was as cute as a button.

Looking at him, I was struck by the symmetry of him arriving in our world just as my father was preparing to exit. I said to myself, *G-d is taking one redhead away from me and giving me another.*

I fed our son for the first time and then we took him home. We named the baby Andrew and gave him Harrison as his middle name. In keeping with Jewish tradition, our son's middle name was taken from the first letter of a relative who had recently passed—in this case, his maternal grandfather, Harry. That was the official story, anyway. In my heart, I knew the truth. We were really naming our son after my father, also named Harry, who was still alive at the time, but barely.

It pained me to know that I couldn't take the baby on a plane until he was a couple of months old. That meant that I had to content myself with telling my father about the baby and showing him photos.

Sadly, Dad's health had declined so much by then, he was often comatose, asleep or drugged. So, I wasn't sure how much he understood. That didn't stop me. I kept telling Dad about the baby, anyway, and showing him photos. I was beginning to get the feeling the two might never meet. I wanted to do everything I could to give my father the gift of knowing his grandson. The summer of 1970 was one for the history books, between watching my father decline and bringing home my baby.

As the end drew near, Dad decided he wanted to spend his final days at home rather than in the hospital. I went to visit him and, as I walked into the house, I saw him sitting straight ahead of me in the living room. Looking at him, I gasped and my stomach lurched.

Before his diagnosis, my father weighed about one hundred and ninety pounds. By the end, he weighed about one hundred and twenty pounds. And, according to his doctor's estimate, eighty percent of his bones were fractured. This was due to the fact that multiple myeloma results in bone deterioration.

(Tragically, it would be many years before drugs were developed to keep the disease at a manageable level. A cure does not yet exist but the medications now available make it possible to live with the disease. In fact, a good friend of mine is a physician who has continued to practice medicine since being diagnosed with the disease fifteen years ago. And a friend of mine who was recently diagnosed with the disease will be receiving stem-cell transplants and will likely have an even higher chance of recovery than my physician friend with the disease.)

Sadly, during the period of Dad's illness when he was lucid enough that I could have said a meaningful goodbye to him, we were keeping his condition a secret from him. By the time the cat was finally out of the bag, and he was aware that he was close to death, it was too late to say goodbye because he was in and out of a coma. I have always regretted not being able to say goodbye and tell my father how much I loved and admired him and that I considered him my best friend. I think he knew, but I wish I had said it.

Twenty

Sadly, on July 18th, 1970, two weeks after we brought home our son, my father died. I was only twenty-seven years old. And I was only two weeks into being a father myself. I was devastated. Right after Dad died, Mom came to stay with Janie and me for a month. Like me, she was horribly depressed over the loss of my father. They had shared such a long and happy marriage.

Dad never did get to meet his little grandson. As the years went by, it would become obvious to me that my father and my son would have been great friends. They were both hellions and wonderful fathers and husbands. I had those hellion tendencies as well, but in the days when I was growing up, the world was a much less dangerous place.

Grandpa Julius was in his early nineties and still alive when Dad died, having just survived his own medical ordeal. I was selected to be the one to go to Grandpa's home in the South Bronx to break the terrible news to him and bring him to the funeral. It had become a terrible neighborhood over the years, but one he wouldn't leave because all of his old cronies lived there.

When I got there, Grandpa Julius was out grocery shopping or running errands. So, I waited for him on the stoop, remembering how Dad used to tuck a gun into his belt whenever he visited his father. I was scared to death being in that rough neighborhood that was filled with drugs, gangs and all sorts of thugs.

My grandfather had known that Dad was ill but he didn't realize that he was near death. It is a terrible thing to have to bury your child, and it goes against the natural order of things. I knew how much Grandpa would suffer over the news of Dad's death.

"Why am I still alive and my son is dead?" he asked me, breaking down in tears.

Dad's memorial service was held at a funeral parlor in Great Neck. I was flabbergasted by the sheer number of people who showed up to honor my father. I had expected only family and close friends to come. Instead, it seemed like the entire town closed up shop that day so that all the Great Neck business owners could attend Dad's services.

For as much of a hellion as Dad was, and for as much trouble as he got himself into when he was young and confrontational, he was truly beloved. It wasn't hard to understand why. Dad was fun loving, fair and honest, and he would help anyone who sincerely needed an outstretched hand.

I got up to speak, with tears flowing down my cheeks. I talked about my relationship with my father, how close we were, and how much I thought of Dad as a man. I was so upside-down emotionally, I hardly knew what I was saying. I barely remember it to this day.

Uncle Murray, my dad's best friend and the man who sold me the hundred-dollar car years earlier, also spoke. This was the moment when he made that remark I referenced earlier about it being a miracle that Dad lived as long as he did, considering how fearless he was about getting into the face of anyone who crossed him.

Meanwhile, Grandma Sadie was still separated from Grandpa Julius after over fifty years of marriage and living in California. (They never divorced but remained separated.) She had moved for better weather, following her son, my uncle Ben and his family out west. Uncle Ben decided to shield Grandma from the truth of my father's death. So, as the funeral took place, she was completely unaware.

When I got back to Cincinnati after the funeral and shiva, I got a call from Uncle Ben. "You've got to do me a favor," he said. "Grandma and your dad and mom always had a weekly phone call and now I don't know what I'm going to do. I can't tell her about his death! It'll kill her. Can you call her every week and pretend to be your father? You've always sounded just like him over the phone."

"I'm not doing that!" I said. "First of all, she and Dad always spoke Yiddish. I can understand most of what's being said but I can't really speak it fluently. I could never pull it off. And even if I could, I'm not doing it.

It's not right. Grandma needs to know and you've got to tell her!"

Uncle Ben refused to tell Grandma that Dad had died. Instead, he called and pretended to be my dad, and my mom would also call, but separately. This might have worked seamlessly had Grandma not been accustomed to hearing both my mom and dad on the phone with her at the same time.

Every single time, Grandma would ask, "Where's Harry?"

And every single time, Mom would say, "Oh, he's out running an errand."

I don't know why—or whether!—my grandmother accepted the notion that my mother always called her when my father was out. It remains a mystery as to whether or not Grandma really bought the story or just chose to go along with the charade. If she ever knew, she didn't let on.

In 1972, after two years of my uncle and my mother carrying on this charade, Grandma Sadie died. Mom was desperately afraid of flying so she refused to attend the funeral, which was being held in California. My brother couldn't have cared less about going, for reasons unbeknownst to me. Randee didn't go either. She may have been unable to afford the airfare.

Grandma Sadie was my favorite grandmother and we had always been close. I wasn't going to miss her funeral. I booked a last-minute flight from Cincinnati to Chicago with a connection to a flight in Los Angeles.

The flight was scheduled to arrive at one or two o'clock in the morning. The plan was that I would then take a cab to the home of one of my father's cousins, and get some sleep there before the funeral the following day.

I was groggy due to the late hour and walking towards the airport exit to look for a cab. I was completely surprised to be met at the gate by Uncle Ben's oldest son, Ronnie, who was one year my junior. (Ronnie's younger brother, Gil, also lives in Los Angeles. He is more conservative than Ronnie politically, and we have had some interesting conversations over the years.)

We went back to Ronnie's house and stayed up all night, talking about the family and all the mishegas that went on. One of the topics of discussion that night was the breakup of the family. My father and Ronnie's father (Uncle Ben) hadn't spoken to each other for ten to fifteen years before my dad's passing.

The day of Grandma Sadie's funeral was very difficult and rather strange. There were relatives from my father's side of the family that I had never met before.

"Oh, my favorite nephew!" Uncle Ben said, coming my way just as I was about to go looking for him.

He had tears in his eyes as he came toward me. He was very emotional over the death of his mother and the estrangement between him and my dad. He knew that he was partially responsible for it. Now that my father had passed, any possibility of reconciliation died with him.

As far as I was concerned, the difficulties between Uncle Ben and my dad were actually Grandma Sadie's fault. She was a wonderful grandmother but she was not a good wife and not a good mother. She pitted one son against the other until they ended up at each other's throats.

She would say to one of her sons, "Well, *he* did this for me, so now *you* have to do that for me!" I never understood why Grandma did that but it didn't change the way I felt about her. I loved her dearly.

Back at Uncle Ben's house later, as everyone was sitting shiva, I told Uncle Ben that I believed that the broken relationship between him and my dad was really Grandma's fault, not his or my father's. I am not sure whether he took any comfort in my words or not.

It was a whirlwind trip, with me flying home right after the shiva. Years later, Janie and I were in California with the kids. We were on the freeway, driving from San Diego to San Francisco.

"Hey," I said to Janie, "This exit sure looks familiar! I think Grandma Sadie is buried around here."

I pulled off the exit and without much effort, found the Jewish cemetery where she was buried. "Wow!" I said. "I can't believe I was able to find the cemetery after so many years!"

I had now buried my father and my favorite grandmother in the short space of a couple of years. Meanwhile, on the home front, Andrew—whom we nicknamed Andy—was growing and changing by the day. He was a sweet, lovable, adorable redheaded kid. Unfortunately, he was on the small size, and this would make him the target of bullies when he got into his school years.

We had adopted Andy in a closed adoption, meaning that we didn't get to meet the biological parents. All we knew about them was what we were told by the agency. Janie and I had heard horror stories about closed-adoption families, where the kids end up in serious trouble with drugs, drinking or crime, and sometimes end up in jail.

We were blessed and lucky. Our son was a wonderful boy and we had absolutely no problems with him. He would briefly walk the ragged edge in his teen years but we didn't have to contend with anything particularly serious.

There were all sorts of rules and regulations that governed the adoption of our son through Jewish Family Services. The red tape included the requirement that the adopted child be given his own room. So, the organization had a representative making regular visits to our home to check out our living conditions. At any point during that first year, they had the legal right to remove our baby from our home.

Thankfully, there were no issues. At the end of that first year, we went to court to finalize the adoption.

When Andy was a little more than a year old, Janie and I decided to take a trip. It was the first time we had gone on vacation together since we started the adoption process, and it was like a second honeymoon. We had a wonderful nanny who agreed to stay with Andy while Janie and I were gone. We started our three-week road trip with a drive through New England.

I couldn't very well be in New England and not stop off in Boston to see my brother and his family. After visiting with them, Janie and I headed for Canada and spent time in Quebec, Montreal and Toronto. When we returned to the States, we headed back to Ohio by way of Detroit.

Twenty-One

Janie and I wanted to apply for a second child but we couldn't do so right away. We had to wait twelve months from the point of finalizing the adoption. By the summer of 1972 when we were permitted to apply for a second child, the number of children available for adoption had dwindled substantially. The prevalence of birth control, abortion and single parenthood had changed the landscape entirely.

Janie and I knew that we had to be completely flexible if we had any hope of bringing home a sibling for Andy. That meant that our desire to adopt a little girl had to take a backseat to our desire to bring home a second child of either sex.

We were told, "Don't call us. We'll call you. There are still families waiting for their first child!"

Interestingly, many Christian parents who put up their children for adoption preferred to have them adopted by Jewish parents. The feeling seemed to be that the child would receive a better education and better quality of life overall. (We welcomed Gentile children into our family without any questions or qualms—twice.)

In December of 1973, just a year and six months after we had applied for a second child, we got the surprise of a lifetime when Jewish Family Services called.

Janie called me at work, saying, "Honey, they called! They called! They have a baby boy for us!" She was hardly able to contain her excitement.

I ran home like a bandit, picked up Janie, and drove to the agency to hear the baby's history. We were over the moon.

Listening to the baby's history, I was again amazed by how closely they had matched the child with us. The child's mother was a teacher—like Janie. Usually the biological father has given up a child prior to it being put up for adoption, so it is somewhat unusual to find out anything about the paternal side of the family. But we had learned in Andy's case that his paternal grandfather was an architect—the field in which I had gotten my degree. In the case of our second son, we learned that his paternal grandfather was in the real estate business—like me.

The day we went into the agency to view the baby and bring him home, we were as dumbfounded as we had been with Andy. Just like the first time, the second time felt surreal. It was almost inconceivable that we were able to walk into the agency, simply take a seat on a couch, and have a social worker hand us a child.

The baby was utterly adorable. He had tow-head-white hair and was on the large size in contrast to his older brother. (This disparity would change dramatically as they got older.) He looked like he would remain big and grow up to be tall. Later, when we took him to the pediatrician, we would discover that he was literally off the size charts in terms of height and weight.

We named our younger son Scott Jason, taking the "S" and the "J" from the names of Grandma Sadie and Grandpa Julius, who were both deceased by then. While we had initially thought we wanted a little sister for Andy, we were absolutely thrilled to have our second son. We couldn't and wouldn't have loved him more if he had been a she.

Grandpa Julius had died at ninety-four after recovering from a mugging that took place in his rough Bronx neighborhood. It occurred a couple of years after his hospitalization that led to Dad seeing the doctor and getting diagnosed with multiple myeloma.

I have a memory of Janie, my mom and me going to visit Grandpa at the rehab place in the Long Beach area of Long Island, where he was recovering from the mugging. We had Andy in a stroller and Grandpa in a wheelchair, as we all took a stroll down the boardwalk.

I stopped and lit a cigarette, catching my grandfather's eye and noticing his look of longing. I offered him a cigarette.

"Grandpa, are you sure you want this? It's going to stunt your growth and your health." I was joking. He was already ninety-three at the time.

Grandpa took the cigarette, immediately tore off the filter and threw it on the ground. He had always smoked Camel unfiltered cigarettes. He wasn't about to smoke a filtered cigarette.

Another memory involving Grandpa Julius occurred one day when I was at Dad's salon, helping him repaint. Grandpa, who used to be a commercial painter, arrived at the shop unannounced, carrying a huge, heavy canvas bag. He proceeded to open it up and pull out a brush that must have been six to eight inches wide and five or six pounds in weight.

"What's that for, Grandpa?" I asked.

"I'm going to help paint!" he said proudly. Grandpa had come prepared for the job, and was ready to use his old-school method. He must have been seventy years old by then.

"Oh, Grandpa...you won't need the brush! We use rollers now. It's a lot easier."

I was sad to lose Grandpa Julius. He was a very sweet man. And now our second son carried the "J" in his name. Scott was a confident, outgoing little boy who was very mature for his age. And for many years, he remained considerably larger than his big brother. So, he protected Andy despite being three and a half years younger.

In sports, Scott had an advantage simply by virtue of being so much bigger than all the other kids. In youth football, for example, he excelled without ever getting his uniform dirty. All he had to do was push the other kids out of the way and they would fall down.

Right from the start, we let both boys know they were adopted. I even went so far as to tell them, "If you ever want to find your biological family, I will gladly help you! It won't hurt my feelings."

Janie wasn't so sure about me helping the boys find their biological families—but she absolutely agreed that it was important to use the word "adopted" ourselves before some wayward kid decided to tease or mock the boys for being adopted. We didn't want our sons blindsided by strangers who were using the word as a weapon. It can be a cruel world. Later when the kids got older, we explained in greater detail the process we went through when adopting them. While they were young, we kept it simple.

The boys were always very comfortable with us as their parents. I never really considered keeping the fact that they were adopted a secret from them. But if I had been inclined to keep it secret, I believe the boys would have been unhappy with us when they got older and found out.

Later in life, Andy—who was known as Drew by then—would end up saying to Janie, "Why would I want to find my birth mother? She only gave birth to me. You and Dad are my parents!"

Scott, meanwhile, is a techie and managed to find his biological family on the internet. One day a few years ago, he came to me and said, "Dad, I think I found my birth family!"

"Really?" I said, shocked. "How did you do that?"

"Well, I knew what day I was born and the town and the hospital. So, I went to the hospital records online, looked up the records of boys born that day, and found a family I think is my bio family."

"What is their last name?" I asked.

He ran the name by me and I confirmed that he was right.

Shocked, Scott asked me, "How in the world do you know their last name?" He knew that both he and his brother had been adopted in closed adoptions.

"Well, years ago, some guy in a law office in Cincinnati inadvertently sent me a document I should not have had. I have that document in a safety deposit box. I've been holding it for you in case you ever asked me for it. Now, you've gone and ruined it. You don't even need me."

The document was part of the final adoption papers and contained the last name of Scott's biological parents, as well as the first name they gave him at birth.

Ultimately, after thinking it over, Scott decided that he didn't care to pursue it any further.

Janie and I never looked back. We had two wonderful children, and we could never have been happier with our own biological children. In fact, we never thought of them as anything other than our own kids. I thank my lucky stars that we ended up with two great kids.

The funny thing is, a lot of people have said that Drew looks like me. I laugh when I hear this because I've always believed that we pick up the attributes of those in our family, simply by living under the same roof with them.

Janie and I were concerned that the difference in size between Andy and his brother might affect his self-esteem. So, we took him to a specialist at Emory University Hospital in Atlanta. After doing some tests that involved measuring a bone in Andy's wrist and looking at his family jewels, the doctor had his conclusion. He said that the test results were ninety-to-ninety-five percent accurate in forecasting how big a child might grow to be.

"Well," said the doctor, "I have good news and not-so-good news."

"What's the good news?" I asked.

"Your son will be six feet tall," said the doctor.

"Great! So, what's the not-so-good news?"

"He's a slow grower. Most kids stop growing by the time they're sixteen or seventeen. Don't be surprised if it takes Andy a bit longer to reach his full height."

Sure enough, Andy kept growing until he was twenty. In the meantime, he had the doctor's assurance that he was going to be six feet tall. This made him feel good and enabled him to relax, knowing he was not going to end up considerably smaller than his younger brother. By age twenty, Andy was six feet tall.

Ironically, Scott was six feet tall by his bar mitzvah at age thirteen and starting to show the beginnings of whiskers. He would grow one more inch to become six-foot-one.

Twenty-Two

In January of 1966, Janie had begun teaching first grade and, as I mentioned earlier, she was nominated for Beginning Teacher of the Year. She was a natural-born mother and this trait served her beautifully in her teaching career.

Janie was so outgoing, twenty-four/seven, her personality was like a flower in full bloom. The students loved her and she loved them, especially the outgoing, rambunctious boys who no doubt reminded her of herself. The kids' high energy was a match for her own.

When I think of this aspect of Janie's personality, I always recall the "first lady" nickname given to her by our housekeeper, Annie. She came to us in 1975 and, after forty-four years, she's still with me.

I have a fairly big personality myself so Janie and I were a good fit and a natural match. Our children were everything to us, the apples of our eyes, and that's where we put most of our attention. Janie took the boys with her in the car almost everywhere she went. She was a very safe driver, but she always had the pedal to the floor and went through forty-thousand-mile tires in twenty thousand miles.

With a wife and two young kids at home, I had more to lose than I ever had in my life. I am not a big worrier but the one thing that could put me into a panic was the thought that my wife or one of our kids was in trouble.

One day, for example, when Andy was two-and-a-half years old and Scott was barely one, the tornado sirens went off while I was at work. As I raced home to protect my family, I was scared of what I might find when I got there. Thankfully, I found the three of them safe and sound, huddled under a built-in desk on the lower level of our house.

In December of 1974, I moved from Cincinnati to Atlanta for work. Janie and the kids were supposed to follow shortly afterward.

I had always experienced Cincinnati as a very conservative town with an overall attitude of, "What was good for your great-grandparents will be good for your great-grandchildren." A perfect example of this is the fact that my wife was not known by her married name of Janie Fischbach at social gatherings, or even by her maiden name of Janie Pressman. She was known by her mother's maiden name, Janie Friedman.

I, on the other hand, did not have parents and grandparents who had grown up in Cincinnati. I knew that, no matter how long I lived there, I would never be considered anything other than an outsider. Both Janie and I were ready for a change when change came looking for me.

Here's what happened. By the time I left school with my degree in architecture, I knew I didn't want to be an architect or a city planner. I wasn't sure I was a natural-born architect, and I didn't want to spend the rest of my life bent over a drafting board. (Of course, these days such work is done on a computer, not on a drafting board.)

This self-awareness was one of the biggest gifts I received from the co-op program through school. By graduating with two years of experience in the field in which I had gotten my degree, I was able to get a sense of which direction I wanted to take *prior* to leaving school. Most college grads have to learn those lessons the hard way.

During my last co-op job at college, and then full-time after graduation, I worked for Bob Kanter in the real estate property management business. In that position, I was able to make good use of my education.

After getting my feet wet in the real estate business with Bob Kanter, I had the opportunity to work for The Marvin Warner Company, a real estate developer from Birmingham. My immediate boss was a guy named Burt Bongard. He and I had a huge argument, which wasn't surprising, considering the tremendous stress I was under at the time. (I worked there while I was dealing with my father's illness.) This led to Bongard firing me.

That experience reinforced my feeling that I should be in business for myself. That was not a new feeling; I had always felt that I was inherently better suited for being the boss than being an employee.

(Many years later, Bongard would get caught up in the nationwide savings-and-loan scandal and end up in prison. A good friend of mine from Cincinnati cut a photo out of the newspaper and sent it to me. It showed Bongard still wearing his Rolex watch while he was in shackles. I thought to myself, *That will teach him to argue with a Fischbach!*)

When I left The Marvin Warner Company, I spent three years working for The Mayer Company, another real estate company in Cincinnati. They gave me autonomy and allowed me to work independently for the most part. That's where I was working when serendipity happened along. My name was mentioned to a headhunter looking to fill a position in Atlanta. It turned out that my background and expertise were a perfect match for the position.

The headhunter's client was a construction lender to commercial real estate developers. The lender had gotten into trouble when the borrowers had failed to pay back what the company was owed. So, I was brought to Atlanta as part of what is called "a workout team," a group of new people that come in to help take a company through Chapter 11 bankruptcy reorganization. My position would entail foreclosing on developers, getting the properties back, finishing, renovating and operating them. The goal was to slowly take the company from a lending institution to an owning-and-operating company.

Even though Janie and I had been talking for a long time about leaving Cincinnati if an opportunity came my way, she remained resistant. Her feeling was, "No, I don't want to leave my hometown. I've got my entire family here—my mother and father, my sister, and my aunts and uncles. Not to mention lifelong friends. And this is also where we adopted our kids! How can I leave my hometown?"

"Babe," I said, "I don't think I have much of a future here if I really want to get into my own business."

Janie already knew that I wanted to be an entrepreneur. She agreed that it suited me so much better than working for someone else. We went back and forth for a while, with her saying, "I don't think I want to," and me saying, "Come on, take a chance in life!"

Then the company from Atlanta contacted me with the job opportunity. Before I even agreed to talk to them, I talked to Janie again. "I just got a call from this company in Atlanta and they have an opening they think might be a fit for me. I want your blessing before I go down there and talk to them. I don't want to even go if moving there is not a possibility for us."

Over the next week or two, Janie gave it a lot of thought and I did too. We would talk about it on a daily basis. I explained to her, "Cincinnati is a very closed town. I don't foresee opportunities for myself here. I've done some research on Atlanta. It's a very young, growing city, with people moving there from all over the country. It would probably be a good move for us." Slowly, I convinced her and she agreed to the move.

In a strange coincidence, four months prior to this, Janie's sister, Gail, had moved to Atlanta with her husband, Bernd, and their two daughters. Bernd had retired from working for the CDC in Cincinnati and accepted a professorship at Georgia Tech. I had never liked Gail and Janie wasn't overly fond of her either. Then again, Janie now knew that she would have some family members in Atlanta, and that changed the way she looked at the move.

I went down to Atlanta to meet with the company. During the interview, it became clear that the position would entail me taking on a project where I would slowly work myself out of a job. I knew that my role of converting the company, Great American Mortgage Investors (GAMI), from a lending institution to an owning-and-operating company was a two-to-three-year gig.

There was always a chance, of course, that I would end up staying on with the new iteration of the company. After giving it some consideration and talking it over with Janie, I decided to take the job.

Twenty-Three

Janie and I flew to Atlanta to look for housing. We saw a few houses we liked but ultimately decided to rent an apartment and get settled before looking for a house to buy.

I found an apartment in an area I liked called the Buford Highway neighborhood, which had a lot of apartments with young couples just starting out. The complex was reasonably new and featured swimming pools and tennis courts. We liked the property, the amenities, the area and the tenants we met and decided to take the apartment. I even found someone to fill the role of onsite manager of the complex—a good friend of mine who worked for me in Cincinnati and was also looking to move.

One weekend over the holidays, we had a terrible scare. I had already quickly made the move to Atlanta so I could start my new job, but Janie and the kids had not yet followed. I happened to be home in Cincinnati for the weekend with the family when I woke up in the middle of the night to the sound of Scott's cries. He was about a year old at the time.

I went in to check on him and discovered that he had a high fever. Just by looking at him, I could tell that he was really sick. I initially tried getting his fever down with cold washcloths and the usual home remedies. When that failed, I went in and woke up Janie.

"Scott's sick and running a high fever! I'm driving him to the E.R. It'll be faster than an ambulance. Call your uncle Eddie right now and have him meet me there." Janie's uncle was Scott's pediatrician.

I secured Scott into the baby carrier, tied him down with the seatbelt and started the drive to the hospital. As I drove, I kept glancing at him in the rearview mirror to see how he was holding up. I could see that he was turning blue!

I was in a panic, trying to get my son to the hospital as fast as I could while still remaining safe. I blew through every stoplight between our house and the hospital and finally pulled up in front of the E.R. I ran inside holding my son and went up to the desk.

The woman at the desk put a form in her typewriter and began very calmly asking me questions in a monotone voice.

"Put the forms away, lady!" I demanded. "Can't you see my son is blue? He needs to see a doctor, now, dammit!"

A nurse came and put Scott and me in a room. Before too long, a doctor walked in. After a quick examination, she said, "He's got the croup!" and opened the windows." It was wintertime in Cincinnati and the doctor seemed to believe that cold, damp air would be good for my son.

I got the feeling that the doctor had no idea what she was dealing with, so I had little confidence in her diagnosis. It did not ring true to me.

"I want another doctor," I said. "I want the head person on staff to see him now! Get whoever is on call in here right now." The doctor did not argue with me.

While I waited to get a more senior doctor to come in, I watched Scott turn bluer and bluer.

At last, a five-foot-four Hispanic doctor wearing a stethoscope, khaki pants and a plaid shirt, walked in and extended his hand. "Dr. Martinez," he said, by way of introduction. He was the most unlikely looking doctor I had ever seen.

He took one look at Scott and started shouting orders to everyone, including, "I want an anesthesiologist in here...stat!"

Then, Dr. Martinez turned to me and said, "Hold his head still for me. I need to put a tube through his nose and down his throat. His epiglottis is inflamed and infected. It swells so much in small children, it can cut off the air passage and the child can start suffocating."

When the doctor started the procedure of threading the tube down Scott's nose, Scott started screaming.

"Would you step out of the room for a minute, please?" said Dr. Martinez.

I went into the hallway and called Janie. She was home with Andy, who was asleep. It was four or four-thirty in the morning by then. I asked her if she had managed to reach her uncle.

"He told me to take Scott to the E.R. and I told him you had already taken him."

"Wait a minute," I said, remembering something. "You know that ENT doctor you see sometimes? Dr. Peerless? Why don't you try giving him a call?"

"Oh, that's a great idea!" said Janie. "I'll also call Mom and Dad and have them come stay with Andy so I can come to the hospital. See you in a little while."

A little while later, Dr. Peerless arrived. He was dressed in a formal jacket and tie and looked like he had just come from a fancy ball. He took off his jacket and went into the exam room where Dr. Martinez was working on Scott.

Dr. Peerless came out a minute later and said, "I'm taking Scott to surgery! I'll be back..."

Then he took Scott into surgery and performed a tracheotomy on him. About half an hour later, he came out and announced that Scott was going to be just fine. Janie had arrived by then and was standing beside me when we got the good news.

"By opening up his airway a little bit with a tube, Dr. Martinez saved your son's life!" explained the doctor. "Then, I was able to perform a tracheotomy, which allowed me to remove the tube and replace it with a tracheostomy."

Hearing this from Dr. Peerless, I was finally able to breathe again. I was scared to death.

Scott had to spend several days in the hospital before they would release him to come home. It was unbelievably distressing to see our young son in that condition and both Janie and I were total wrecks.

One day while we were at the hospital, we met another young couple whose child had climbed into a chest of toys and inadvertently locked himself inside. The chest had no air holes, and the child nearly suffocated. The parents got him to the hospital but it was too late. The little guy didn't make it. We were so sad for this couple over the loss of their young son, and only too aware that it could have been us.

During the week that Scott spent in the hospital, Janie went home at night. Meanwhile, I was flying back and forth between Atlanta and Cincinnati.

Several days later, the doctor removed the tracheostomy from Scott's throat. On the day that Scott was due to be released from the hospital, he started coughing and choking while Janie was holding him.

"Nurse!" screamed Janie, "get over here! Something's not right! Get a doctor."

"No, he's fine," the nurse said, implying that Janie was being an overreactive, nervous mother.

Janie could curse like a sailor and she used a few choice, sharp words with the nurse. They did the trick.

A doctor was called over and he examined Scott. "Well, it looks like the trach caused some scar tissue to form and it's blocking his air passage! We're going to have to take him back into surgery."

Scott was taken back into surgery to remove the scar tissue. Afterwards, he had to stay in the hospital again for two days. The entire ordeal was extremely trying and exhausting for both Janie and me, not to mention our poor little son. It was a scary couple of weeks for all of us.

In February, Scott was finally out of the woods. We felt it was now safe for Janie and the kids to join me in Atlanta. We settled into our new apartment and lived there for seven or eight months before we started looking around for something to buy.

One day when I got home from work, Janie told me, "I found the house we're going to live in!"

"Really?" I said, laughing at her signature bravado. "Do you mind if I take a look at it first?"

"You can most certainly look at it," she said, smiling, "but that's the house we're moving into. It's a really nice house on a cul-de-sac. It's on a little hill, slightly above street level. And it has a nice backyard and a creek in the side yard."

The house had three bedrooms, a dining room, living room and kitchen. There was also a playroom for the kids behind the garage. From the kitchen, we could keep an eye on the kids when they were in the playroom.

When Janie took me to see the house, I liked it but felt it needed some fixing up. "There are some things I'd like to do," I said, "but we don't have to do it all at once." (It was my intention to hire out most of the renovation work to contractors.) We bought our house and moved into it in December of 1975.

I initially found the people of Atlanta to be rather southern, but as time went on, I noticed it less and less. So many carpetbaggers were moving to Atlanta—a migration which has not really slowed in all these years!—and there were a lot of things happening in town. Compared to Cincinnati, I found Atlanta to be a place filled with opportunities for someone who was ready to take a chance. I certainly fit that description.

On the work front, GAMI had mortgage loans on properties from Texas to Georgia and mostly in the southeast. So, I was doing quite a bit of traveling during this time. We were taking back properties from borrowers who owed the firm a lot of money and should never have been granted construction loans in the first place. These loans were made during the good times but then when the economy hit a downturn, everyone took a second look at those mortgage loans that were in default and lending came to a screeching halt. Most of the properties were multi-family apartment buildings as opposed to office buildings or shopping centers.

I would generally catch an early-bird flight around six o'clock in the morning and fly home around ten or eleven o'clock that same night. Once I landed at my destination, I would go and talk to the borrowers-owners. I explained that we were going to foreclose on them. Usually, I was able to talk them into giving me the keys so we didn't have to foreclose.

At the old Atlanta airport, there was a very small parking lot right in front of the building with a ramp that led into the airport. One morning, I was racing to get to the airport in time to catch my flight. I whipped the car into a parking space, and ran up the ramp and to my gate. I made my flight on time, spent the day doing company business, and caught a late flight that got in around ten o'clock that night.

When I got back, I walked down the ramp and toward the parking lot. Reaching into my pocket, I came up empty—no car keys. When I couldn't find them, I panicked. I found my car, thankfully, and walked towards it. When I got to my car, I found this note on my windshield: *We found your car running at ten o'clock this morning. Please see the parking attendant for your keys.*

I felt like such an idiot. As I approached the attendant to ask for my keys, I was searching my mind for a way to save face. Suddenly, I had an idea.

"My battery was a little low when I got here this morning," I said, "so I decided to leave the car running for a while so it could recharge."

This story perfectly illustrates how exhausted I was during those days. Between being a husband to Janie, a father to two young boys, and an employee who was constantly flying all over the country, I was so drained, I could hardly think straight.

I'm sure all the traveling I was doing was also hard on my family. Janie had quit teaching to stay home with the kids. Scott was home with Janie a couple days a week and in daycare three days a week. Andy was four or five at the time and in preschool. Having the kids in daycare and preschool gave Janie a little break so she could meet up with friends and pursue some of her favorite activities. She had a huge circle of friends, most of whom had kids who were close in age to ours.

We went on this way for a year and a half or two, with Janie staying home with the kids and me traveling extensively for work. Since my job entailed going out and taking back properties from the borrowers-owners and trying to re-sell them to recoup our money, real estate developers who knew we had these properties for sale were always waltzing into our offices. They were there to try to buy the properties from us for peanuts. Often, these developers had trumped-up personal financial statements.

It started to dawn on me that I knew as much about the business as these real estate developers. So, I decided that this might be the right place and time to start my own business. I decided to go to the Board of GAMI. I would tell them that I knew I was working my way out of a job there, and wanted permission to go out and buy properties with a business partner for pennies on the dollar. I planned to explain that I would not be buying these properties from the company. Nevertheless, I was aware that they might see this proposal of mine as a conflict of interest.

Both my business partner (who shall remain nameless) and I went to the managing trustee and told him that we knew we were working our way out of a job. "So, here's what we want to do," I said, explaining our plans. "We would like the Board's approval to seek our own avenue going forward. We'd only do it on the weekends, so it wouldn't interfere with our full-time work for you."

The trustee took our request to the Board and, to my great surprise, they approved it. Perhaps they were swayed by a combination of two factors: they were liquidating the business anyway, and they knew we wouldn't be buying the properties from GAMI.

The approval was the good news—but there was also bad news. I had just created a situation where I was going to have to work seven days a week in order to go into business for myself. I knew that it would be a temporary hardship and that in the end, it would be worth it.

I never forgot the vow I had made to myself, that I would always seize opportunities and never shy away from risk. I was doing it for me—but also for my dad, who never had the chance due to my mother's fears and concerns.

Twenty-Four

Monday through Friday, I worked my full-time job. On the weekends, my business partner and I ran around looking at properties. Thankfully, timing was on our side, as the real estate market, currently in a valley, was about to make an upward turn. We were buying properties for what would turn out to be pennies on the dollar when the upswing was factored into the value.

I subscribed to the tenet so popular among real estate professionals: "Location, location, location!" The truth is, you can't move real estate. So, if a place is not desirably situated, there are no features or assets about the property itself that can make up for it. Luckily, we found a 214-unit English-Tudor-style apartment complex in the Atlanta suburb of Marietta. It was ideally located and the building's occupancy at the time was only fifty percent. That meant that we had plenty of units we could start renovating.

When we sat down and tallied up the numbers, we concluded that we would need $314,000 for the cash down payment to buy the building. The rest we would finance. We put down a deposit of $20,000 ($10,000 each), and said to each other, "You know, that's not all that much money to raise, between family and friends.

Let's give ourselves until February 1st to come up with the money. If we can't come up with fifty percent by then, we can cancel the contract and get our deposit back."

On December 14th, 1976, we put the property under contract and then set out to raise the money we needed. I had no savings, so I started by hawking my life insurance policy.

I had told Janie about my new venture with my partner, and she knew that we were spending our weekends looking at properties. I did *not* tell her that we had found this property and were trying to raise the money to buy it. And I certainly did not tell her that I had cashed out my life insurance policy.

I was terrified that if I told my wife everything, I would find myself reliving what my father went through with my mother. I never wanted to find myself in that position. I was driven by the promise I had made to myself: I would not die a working-class stiff because I was afraid to take chances.

As we faced our looming February 1st deadline, my partner and I looked at each other and said, "Now, what? We haven't raised the first dollar!"

We both wanted to continue in our pursuit of the money. We had already let the deadline lapse for getting our deposit back, so we felt we had nothing to lose by pressing forward.

I pitched to everyone who would stand still long enough to listen. It just so happened that Birmingham

Trust National Bank was a co-lender with GAMI so I already had a relationship with the senior vice president.

I was there on business one day and approached him. "Hey, Jim," I said, "let me tell you a story." I then proceeded to give him my pitch.

He listened intently and said, "Interesting...but not up my alley. However, the bank owns a company that does fee-only financial planning for high-income clients. I think I can get you a date to meet with the company and offer it as a potential investment. We'll see if they might be interested in putting investors in the deal."

"Great!" I said. "How soon do you think I could get an appointment?"

"How about next week?" he said, smiling.

The following Saturday, my business partner and I drove to Birmingham for a board meeting and took our seats beside each other at a long table. I started giving my spiel about how the building was run down and the occupancy low, and what great opportunities that presented for all concerned.

In the middle of my speech, my business partner piped up and said, "Yeah, and not only that, but there's some guy named Underwood wandering around the property in cowboy boots and he has no idea what he's doing!"

I wanted to elbow my business partner in the ribs to get him to shut up but it was too late.

Suddenly, a man sitting opposite me at the far end of the table slowly pushed back his chair. He put one very large foot—wearing what looked like a size-thirteen cowboy boot!—up on the table. "Well, my name is *Bob* Underwood. Did his boots look anything like these?"

This move let me and my business partner know that *we* were the ones who sounded like we didn't know what we were doing.

After my business partner shut up, I took over speaking to the board. When I finished, there was a long pregnant pause at the table, followed by nervous laughter. They gave us assurances that they would get back to us. It couldn't have been more awkward.

Then the meeting ended and goodbyes were said. As luck would have it, Bob Underwood ended up being absolutely no relation to the other guy. Funny enough, over the years, Bob became one of our dearest friends and ended up raising millions of dollars for us. (Unfortunately, he died at an early age due to Type 1 diabetes complications.)

Miraculously, the firm agreed to put the entire $314,000 we needed into our deal as a lump sum from their investors.

When we got the promise of the money, I was excited. I knew the time had come to tell Janie everything.

"Bunny, we put this deal under contract and raised the money for it," I explained. "We're going to close in

April and that will be the start of my new business. But, don't worry...I'm not quitting my job yet."

Janie was shocked, excited for me and also a little bit reticent.

"I don't understand," she said. "Where did you get the money?"

"This group in Birmingham invested the money we needed," I said, skirting her underlying question.

"I mean the *deposit* money. Where did you get that?" She knew that there was more to the story.

"Well," I said, taking a deep breath. "I took the equity from my life insurance policy..."

"Are you out of your f***ing mind?" She could use colorful language when the occasion called for it.

"Wait, I'm not finished. Once we got the money from the investors, I put the deposit money back. Don't worry, if I croak, you and the kids are covered."

She looked unconvinced.

"Bunny," I explained, "I was just fearful. Remember when I told you that my mom always kept my dad from taking a chance in life? I was fearful that you would do that to me. And I made myself a promise a long time ago that I would not be afraid to take a chance."

She wasn't overly sympathetic. "You moron," she said lovingly.

I was a husband, the father of two children, and a homeowner at that point in my life so the chance I had taken was a big one. I had risked throwing myself under the bus on a venture that could have gone bust. I had gotten very lucky.

We closed on the property—our first acquisition!—in April of 1977. The deal entailed giving investors a preferential return on their investment of seven-to-eight percent per year and after that, they got seventy cents on the dollar and my business partner and I got thirty. We also got a five percent property-management fee, as well as a small upfront fee for supervising the renovations.

The $314,000 was the equity requirement in order to buy the apartment complex for $11,700 per unit. We owned the building for twenty-seven months and then sold the property for $30,000 per unit. The return on investment was fantastic for us and almost incalculable for investors. It was the equivalent of hitting a home run in the bottom of the ninth inning of the seventh game of the World Series.

Your first deal is always the toughest. You don't yet have a track record and yet you're saying to investors, "Believe in us! Believe in us! We can do it."

My partner and I now had a win. Having something to show for ourselves put us in a much better position. A year after we bought the first building, we found another multi-family apartment building across the street from the first one, and went back to the same group of investors. This building was a 208-unit property and we bought it for $15,000 per unit. About three years later, we sold the property for $30,000 per unit.

The investors now thought highly of me and my business partner, thanks to the excellent return on investments for both buildings.

I attribute our good fortune to a few different factors. First, I was absolutely sure of what it would take to renovate. Secondly, we bought at the bottom of the market, based on a sense that the market was about to go on the upswing. We lucked out when the market did indeed go up quickly. We also had a good sense of what similar units rented for in that area, and whether or not there was a market for the units. The city was growing at a rapid pace and that also helped our cause.

We ended up selling both the first and second building to investors—big firms looking for steady income from rental property. By our third deal, the investment group from Alabama was tapped out. So, Bob Underwood introduced us to a fee-only financial planner in Texas. Once again, we got lucky and the financial planners' investors put money into our deal.

In our years together, my business partner and I would end up having investors in forty-five different properties. We developed a real solid track record, with properties from North Carolina to Florida and as far west as San Antonio, Texas.

As I mentioned, when I first got to Atlanta to work for GAMI, I was part of a workout team converting them from a lending institution to an owning-and-operating company. And I knew that I was there to work myself out of a job. After being there for two and a half years, my job was just about done.

I started looking for another job. I was out on my own already to some extent but hadn't yet had enough acquisitions to justify totally going out on my own. In the summer of 1977, I went to work with the Robert A. McNeil Corporation, a very large real estate syndication firm with headquarters in San Mateo in northern California. In my role as a regional vice president with the company, I was located in Atlanta.

For the most part, my work relationships in my new position were harmonious. I was given plenty of autonomy and the leeway to do my work as I saw fit. No one really got in my way—until one particular incident.

I was tasked with looking into the real estate taxes on a particular property. The number I came away with was contingent upon the county taxing authority assuring me that the property would be reassessed. Unfortunately, the reassessment was put off, which caused the net operating income to be much larger than I had budgeted for.

One of the big bosses paid me a visit and was demanding that I account for the discrepancy.

"Listen," I said, "if you look at the numbers and see that I am not performing well in my job, you're welcome to scream and holler at me. Or fire me if you see fit. Otherwise, just stay out of my way. It's not my fault they decided not to reassess the property."

Unfortunately, year-end bonuses were awarded commensurate with an employee staying within certain financial margins. Now, they were using this discrepancy as a basis for withholding my bonus. I was doing a great job in my role and this seemed patently unfair.

I ended up giving the boss a piece of my mind and then saying to him, "You're so sure your way is right? Fine. Let's take it to the president and see what he says!"

"Nah, it's okay. I'll let you have your bonus."

He preferred to avoid conflict. So, I got my bonus after all. I worked there for about three years in total and eventually left of my own volition. Even though I stayed for years following that run-in with my superior, I was now more convinced than ever that I was meant to be in business for myself. I was resolved to make it happen but it would be a little while longer before I put the wheels in motion.

Twenty-Five

When Janie and I bought our house in Cincinnati in 1970, it was my first detached house, after a lifetime of apartment living. When we moved to Atlanta, we bought our house and were perfectly happy there. But I had always had the desire to build my dream home. I had the architectural background and had been waiting for the right time to present itself.

Now that my financial situation had improved, I wanted a bigger house—one with a swimming pool and a backyard, for starters. I was ready to build my dream home.

"I'll tell you what," I said to Janie, "let's go look for a lot. Once we find one, I'll build the house and be responsible for the exterior and room sizes. And you can be responsible for decorating the interior. In the meantime, let's also take a look at some existing houses."

"I've already hired the interior decorator," said Janie. That was my wife!

Scott was seven years old and Andy was eleven as we began to look for a lot to build our dream house. I found one on a cul-de-sac street, but not on the cul-de-sac itself. The lot was just north of the Atlanta city limits in Sandy Springs. I wasn't in love with the lot.

There was a lot I loved, however, on the actual cul-de-sac. With a little bit of digging, I found out that the lot was owned by a Delta Airlines pilot. He lived in San Francisco and had bought it with the intention of eventually settling in Atlanta and building a house there.

I found his contact information and called him. I explained that by selling his lot to me, he could make money on the deal now, and then buy another lot later when he was ready to settle in Atlanta. Thankfully, I was convincing and he sold the lot to me.

I knew that I would never be able to get self-respecting subcontractors to come work for me, knowing that my dream house was the only house I planned to build. A good, busy subcontractor will always be contracted to a builder who is involved in building several houses. I had an idea of how I could get around this obstacle.

Once I got the permit for my dream house, I got in touch with a builder I had come across while Janie and I were looking at existing houses. I knew that this builder was an engineer by education and that his houses were built really well. I have the mentality that I am going to do things correctly or not at all, so he and I were perfectly matched. I offered to pay him a fee to use his subcontractors in the building of my house and he agreed. We set up our arrangement in such a way that the builder did the accounting and paid the bills and then I reimbursed him.

As we began building and digging, we hit a creek. We had to pipe it out from under the house and the long winding driveway and into what would become a nice coy pond in the front yard.

"What do we need *that* for?" Janie asked.

"Well, I've always wanted to live on water!" I joked.

The pond was beautiful when it was finished, with ivy growing all the way down into the water. The boys would spend many enjoyable hours fishing in the pond. While we whiled away the months waiting for the ivy to do its thing, however, it was a real eyesore, covered in screens. Janie affectionately referred to it as Fischbach's Folly but changed her tune when she saw how time turned it into something beautiful.

With the builder's help, I ended up creating what I considered to be the best-built house in Atlanta. We used solid brick and a partial copper roof with copper gutters and downspouts. It was a four-bedroom house, with three bedrooms upstairs. It had a huge den-playroom where the kids could play and watch T.V. There were also two full bathrooms upstairs. The boys had a Jack-'n-Jill (or, this case, Jack-'n-Jack) bathroom connecting their rooms.

Downstairs was an entry foyer, a large dining room, a den which doubled as a library, a huge living room, a good-sized eat-in kitchen, and a huge laundry room. Between the dining room and kitchen, I put a nice, open stairway against the side exterior wall with a brass handrail and a floor-to-ceiling window. I had never been a fan of grand semi-circle staircases right in the middle of an entry foyer.

The master suite had a separate door which opened onto the back patio and pool, along with two enormous walk-in closets, one a little bigger than the other, with built-in dressers and a dressing area. (Guess which one I got.) The bathroom was unique, outfitted with two sinks with drawers, set back to back and perpendicular to the wall. Between the two sinks were two mirrors, back to back. The bathroom also featured a sauna, a steam room and a big jacuzzi tub. And the toilet area had not only a toilet but a bidet.

One day while the house was being completed, I had a visit from two redneck friends in the building industry.

Walking out of the bathroom, one of them said, "Something's wrong in the master bath, Bob. When I flushed the toilet, the thing spit back at me!"

After I stopped laughing, I explained, "No...you hit the bidet handle!"

"The what?" he said.

There was a full basement downstairs. I put fireplaces in the den off the center hall, in the living room, and in the master bedroom—but there was only one chimney on the house. This posed quite a challenge for the builder and me, and it took thirty thousand bricks before it was done. My workaround on this had me doing daily tests where I lit fires in each of the fireplaces to prove that the chimney was drawing as it should.

The setting was very picturesque with a view of the woods. Outside next to the garage, I had a swinging gate that led into the backyard. Next to that was a little outdoor kitchen with a split door leading into it, the lower half of which doubled as a serving shelf. I even put a bathroom out there. The patio was all brick and, for the retaining walls, I had hand-picked fieldstone trucked in from Tennessee. The pool was right in front of the patio.

I spared no expense—and yet, I managed to do everything at my cost. So, the expenditure was considerably less than if I'd had to contract directly with a builder to build the house for me. I had hoped to have the house finished inside of a year. It would end up taking eighteen months but such delays are to be expected.

Having sold our old house at the one-year mark, we had to find somewhere to live while our dream house was being finished. We moved into a townhouse close by and then, when the house was nearly done, we would move in.

Twenty-Six

Our dream house was about six months from being finished and was still very much under construction. The outside was done but we were still working on the interior. We didn't even have the hardwood floors laid yet. Yet, I decided to throw a surprise birthday party for Janie's fortieth birthday.

Since the house still wasn't wired for electricity, I had to connive a way to use the temporary electrical hookup for construction to power the house for the party.

When I told the boys that I was planning to surprise their mom with a party at the unfinished dream house, they said, "But, Dad, how can you do that?"

"Just watch me," I said, smiling. "*Your* job is to not let Mom in before I'm ready for her!"

Then I told my wife, "I thought it would be nice to have dinner with friends for your birthday. They're going to come by the house to see how it's coming along after dinner. Sound good?"

So, Janie and I and another couple went out to dinner. I'm sure that Janie figured that the dinner was her birthday celebration. Little did she know that our house was filled with thirty to forty friends and loved ones, all waiting to surprise her.

As we pulled up in front of the house after dinner, I was relieved to see that there was no sign of a party. I had told the guests I'd invited to park down the street in the neighbors' driveways, and they had followed my instructions perfectly.

As casually as possible, I opened the front door. When the guests heard me turn the key in the lock, everyone jumped out from behind the partial walls and yelled "Surprise!"

Janie was taken totally by surprise and very excited.

I had one more surprise up my sleeve. He was already there, dressed in the red vestment robes of a Catholic cardinal.

"Bunny, you told me you had always dreamed of having an affair with a priest or a cardinal," I said, introducing him to Janie. "Well, here's your chance. It's my birthday gift to you."

I had already instructed the cardinal imposter to take my wife into the bedroom and talk with her a little bit. I was by no means giving him carte blanche to do anything more than that. He played along, escorting her into the bedroom. After a few minutes of kidding around, they emerged.

"So, how was it?" I joked.

"Not as good as you!" Janie said.

We all had a laugh over it and I invited the "cardinal" to stay and join us for a few drinks.

Right as I started building my dream house, I had turned forty and Janie had thrown me a surprise party.

She arranged to have my attorney take me out for early drinks after work. She told me, "When you get home, we'll go out to dinner."

After we'd gone out for a few drinks and gotten a bit tipsy, my attorney Eric drove me home. When we walked inside, the guests jumped out of hiding and yelled surprise and the party got underway.

I noticed among the guests an unfamiliar woman dressed in army fatigues, and a guy who seemed to be her date. I asked my wife about her.

"Oh, she's just someone I met one day at the Merchandise Mart. I thought she had a great personality and wanted to invite her to the party."

Janie worked part-time at the Atlanta Merchandise Mart, a collection of showrooms in a big building located downtown. (I earned enough money that she didn't have to work, but she enjoyed it.)

I didn't question Janie's explanation. I already knew that my wife had a habit of bringing home strays.

Everyone was on the back patio, laughing, drinking and having a good time. All of a sudden, music started blaring. I turned around to see what was going on and saw that all the outside chairs were now in a big circle. In the middle of the circle was a chair.

The girl in the army fatigues led me to the center chair, sat me down, and proceeded to strip all the way down to her birthday suit. Then she took a seat on my lap and wrapped her arms around me. Meanwhile, a friend of mine was running around with a camera, trying to catch the naked stripper's best angles.

While the naked girl and I were hugging, we managed to offend Janie's sister, Gail. She was so horrified, she got up and walked out. It was fine with me. I didn't particularly want her at my birthday party anyway.

It turned out that the woman was a professional stripper named Precious and the guy with her was her security guy. As the party wound down, Precious confessed that she had been sent as a gift to me from my business partner. He was out of the country at the time and arranged it with her, sight unseen. He had enlisted my wife's help in pulling off the surprise, and that's how Janie came up with the story about meeting the woman at the Merchandise Mart.

Six months after my birthday party, it was my business partner's fortieth birthday. His wife arranged a (non-surprise) party for him. Knowing that he had hired Precious for my party sight unseen, I had an idea.

The party was held in a party room at one of the local hotels. Cocktail waitresses were milling about, offering the guests drinks and hors d'oeuvres. At one point in the evening, the music began blaring and a chair was placed in the middle of the room.

My business partner swung around and looked at me, as I was standing with one of the cocktail waitresses. She started beckoning him into the middle of the room.

"Oh, my God, you must be Precious!" he said, allowing himself to be led to the center chair for his lap dance.

"Turnabout is fair play!" I said, laughing.

Six months after Janie's fortieth birthday party, we had our dream home. It was finally finished. One day right before we moved in, while we were still living in the townhouse, there was a knock at the door. I opened it to find Uncle Murray's oldest son, Benny, standing there with his wife.

"Benny!" I said. "What a great surprise! What are you two doing here?"

He was in town for his daughter's graduation from Emory University Law School and decided to pay me a surprise visit. (My mother had given him my address.) Our two families were very, very close but Benny and I hadn't seen each other in a long time.

He looked like he had seen a ghost. "Wow, Red," he said, calling me by my father's nickname, "you look just like your father! It's scary!"

Dad's red hair and blue eyes had earned him the nickname Red. (Dad had died in 1970 and this was twelve years later.)

I had always heard that Dad and I shared certain characteristics. Funny enough, people now tell me that I look just like my mom. Janie and I had a wonderful visit with Benny and his wife and the next day, they flew home.

Now that the house was completely finished, it was time for Bo, the interior decorator Janie had hired, to work his magic. Janie and Bo were thick as thieves and everything was going very well on the interior decorating front. They had a beautiful bedroom set made for the boys. It featured interlocking beds, with one a bit higher than the other. The set also came with a Formica desk. (It held up so well that today, the bedroom set is in an upstairs bedroom we use as our grandson's room.)

Twenty-Seven

Our boys were growing by the day, as kids tend to do. They were every bit as adorable as when I first laid eyes on them, Scott with his towhead blonde hair and Andy with his red hair.

(Speaking of the boys' hair color, I am reminded of a 1980 trip Janie and I took with the boys to Israel. It was right after Israel made peace with Egypt. In fact, we were on the very first flight from Tel Aviv to Cairo. When we got off the plane, all the Egyptians started to crowd around the kids. Everyone wanted to see—and touch!—both my redheaded son and my towheaded son, known as Gingies in that part of the world. Gingies are a rarity over there and the local people couldn't get over Andy and Scott.)

By the time sixth grade rolled around, Andy suddenly started having issues at school. We hired tutors, had him tested and discovered that he had A.D.D.

Then one day when Andy was thirteen or fourteen and in eighth grade, Janie called me at the office and said, "Hurry up and get home!"

I hopped in the car and drove home to find a police car parked out in front of the house. "Oh, no..." I thought to myself, fearing the worst. It turned out that Andy had been caught smoking a marijuana cigarette in the woods.

Janie and I decided to take Andy out of Riverwood High School and enroll him in Woodward Academy, a very popular private school with an independent-study program and smaller classes. At Woodward, he was able to get one-on-one instruction on the subjects where he was struggling and matriculate with the class on the other subjects.

Then, when Andy was fifteen or sixteen, we took him out of Woodward Academy because it was clear to all concerned that Woodward had already given all it had to offer. We put him in a school called The New School for tenth grade and his first semester of eleventh. This school was strictly for kids with learning challenges.

The headmistress, a little old lady with a steel backbone, welcomed Andy to the school with these words: "I just want to let you know something. I've had everybody work me over and I've been around the block a time or two. Don't even try!" She was letting him know that he wasn't going to get away with anything—not on her watch.

"Look," I kept telling Andy, "you have a high I.Q.! It's not like you're stupid so don't get that into your head. It's just that some people have to learn differently than others."

It took Andy about six months to buy into that concept—that he was one of those people who had to go about learning in a different way—and then he started to excel.

One day during his first semester of his junior year of high school, Andy came to me. "I want to go to high school in Israel, Dad." It was a one-semester program, so if Andy went, it would only be for his second semester of his junior year.

"Israel!" I said. "Really? That's out of the blue."

"And I've decided that when I get back from school in Israel, I don't want to return to The New School," said Andy. "I don't want that to be the school I graduate from."

Everyone felt that Andy should stay at the New School, including Janie, the headmaster and some of the teachers there.

I thought about it for a minute and then said, "Okay, I'll send you to school in Israel...but while you're there, you'll have to earn the right to leave The New School. You prove with your grades that you don't need to be there. You did well with your grades at The New School. Now show me that you can keep them up."

Sometime that fall, I happened to be on a mission trip to Israel with The Jewish Federation, leading a group of people through the homeland. (I was pretty heavily involved with the organization and one year was chairman of the real estate division.) While I was there, I went to see the headmaster of the Israeli high school Andy wanted to attend.

I explained my son's situation to the headmaster.

"Don't worry," said the headmaster. "We'll take good care of him."

I convinced Janie that Andy would be in good hands at the high school in Israel and we began to make plans to send him there. Two or three weeks before he was due to leave for Israel, Andy came down with mononucleosis. He was over the worst of it and getting better but it was still lingering.

My mother got wind of the situation and announced, "You cannot send my grandson to Israel with mono!"

"Mom," I said, "he'll be fine. I'll convince him that he shouldn't drink until he gets better."

I was sending my son to Israel against my mother's wishes, and to some extent against my wife's. Janie wasn't too excited about Andy making the journey before he was completely well.

I kept telling them, "He'll be fine...he'll be fine." As it turned out, he recovered and was just fine. He didn't come home with any tattoos or pierced ears, thank G-d.

I felt confident that the headmaster at the high school in Israel understood Andy's learning issues. I was also confident that he had said "Go ahead and send Andy to us" because he thought my son would do well there.

As it turned out, the school's tactile teaching methods turned out to be a perfect match for Andy's tactile learning style. The school taught the kids about Israel's history, for example, by actually taking them to Masada and having them spend the day learning on the actual mountain. It was a dual-language program so Andy was taking classes in Hebrew as well as English.

Motivated by his desire to steer clear of The New School for his senior year, and at ease with the teaching style of the Israeli high school, Andy returned to the States with straight A's.

"Okay, Dad," said Andy, showing me his report card from the Israeli high school. "I did as you asked. I got good grades. Now, where am I going to school for my senior year?"

Janie and I considered which school might be a good fit for Andy. Then it hit me—Yeshiva High School, an Orthodox Jewish school where I happened to be a member of the board. Janie agreed that it would be a good choice.

I went to Rabbi Cohen, the headmaster there, and told him the situation. Then I asked him, "Would you take Andy just for his senior year?"

I knew what I was asking. Being a religious school, they preferred not to take on students just for one year. But the fact that Andy had already spent the second half of his junior year in Israel helped our cause.

Andy liked the idea of attending Yeshiva High. So, I enrolled him and he began to attend.

Around the same time, a fellow board member at Yeshiva High had donated some money for the building of a new gymnasium he wanted to name in memory of his late wife. This guy was quite a character.

"Would you be willing to build the gym for us?" the headmaster asked.

"I would," I said, "but only under certain circumstances. I don't work well by committee. In order for me to agree to do it, you'd have to give me a budget and then get out of my way. I'll give you the keys to the front door when I'm done."

He readily agreed.

In October at the parent-teacher conference, Rabbi Cohen saw me and said, "I need to speak with you in private right away. It's about your son, Drew." He ushered me and Janie into a room. Then he locked the door and handed me a piece of paper.

It was an essay written by Andy. It said, in essence: *I am not Jewish according to Orthodox belief because my biological mother is not Jewish...*

(As I mentioned, Janie and I had told the boys that they were adopted when they were very young. When they were old enough to grasp it, we also gave them some basic information about their families of origin. So, both of our sons knew that they came from non-Jewish families.)

Andy's note continued with these words: *...and so I would like to go through the Orthodox conversion process to become Jewish.*

During school happenings at Yeshiva High, Andy was prohibited from reading from the Torah because he was not Jewish—despite having been circumcised, bar mitzvahed and confirmed.

I looked at Janie and she nodded in agreement. So, I told the rabbi, "Well, if that's what he wants, we support his decision one hundred percent!"

"It's a big step," explained Rabbi Cohen, "so I just wanted to make sure."

"I'm sure. And I think we need to have it before Passover," I said. "He'll be involved with school finals and graduation if we wait until May."

"Great. I'll make the arrangements."

When we got home, I talked to my son. "I understand you are now known as Drew. When did this happen?"

"This year, Dad. I think Andy is too young a name for me."

"Why not use Andrew, your full name?"

"I like Drew better."

It would not be easy for me to call my son Drew all of a sudden, after so many years of calling him Andy. For quite a while, he had to constantly remind me, "Dad, I'm Drew now!"

Practically anyone is welcome to convert to Reform Judaism. Orthodox Judaism is pretty strict. A person seeking an Orthodox conversion cannot simply want or request it; they must be deemed to be *learned.* By the end of his senior year, Drew would be considered learned in the eyes of Rabbi Cohen. By then, he would have studied under Rabbi Cohen for a year and attended the high school in Israel for a semester.

When a man is going through an Orthodox conversion, he must undergo a mickva, which entails going into a ritual bath and having blood drawn. It's similar to what would occur during a circumcision. The convert must also go before a rabbinic court in a synagogue, comprised of three rabbis. Drew would have to submit to a series of questions and provide answers satisfactory enough to get all three rabbis to sign off on his conversion. It has to be unanimous among all three rabbis, who vote yay or nay.

Drew was learning more and more about his upcoming conversion. One day, he came home and said, "I've changed my mind, Dad."

"Really? Why?"

"Because they want me to keep kosher and observe Shabbat. Since I'm going away to college in August, I know I'm not going to keep kosher or observe Shabbat. Not while I'm away at school."

Drew was planning to study architecture at the University of Colorado. He had always been an outdoorsy guy. By going to school in Colorado, Drew would have the opportunity to pursue both of his loves—attending a great architecture school and spending a lot of time outdoors. He had gone away for a couple of summers with a group that climbed Mount Rainier in Washington, spending an entire month on a glacier, living off the land. At the end of the month, he had to find his way back to camp with just a few essentials.

"Drew," I said, trying to talk him into keeping his commitment to the conversion, "there are certain things in life you really regret if you don't follow through. Later, you might look back and wish you had done it. This may be one of those things."

Twenty-Eight

In order for Drew to go through with his conversion, he needed to feel that he could answer honestly when the rabbi posed the question, "Will you keep a kosher household and observe Shabbat?"

Janie came up with an idea. "We'll kosher our house so at least you can have a kosher house to come home to. Then you can tell the rabbi that your home is kosher."

This made Drew feel like his integrity was intact, and he moved forward with the conversion.

Now it was time to have some Orthodox rabbis come to our house and make it kosher. This was a complex and fascinating spectacle and one I wish I had videotaped.

The rabbis arrived toting two enormous rectangular pots that each covered two burners on the stove. Into them they placed our pots and pans for boiling, first removing any plastic handles that might melt. Then they took all ceramic dishes and placed them in the basement for a year so they could purify and become kosher.

The thinking behind this is that, in older times, the clay in ceramic dishes was more porous due to the absence of glaze, and absorbed food. This meant that there was the possibility that meat and dairy might have combined on those plates at some point in time, rendering them impure and therefore non-kosher. In kosher homes, they always have four sets of dishes: two sets for the basic part of the year, one for meat and one for dairy; and two sets for Passover, one set for meat and one for dairy.

Then the rabbi went through our pantry and looked at each separate food item, saying, "This is okay," or "This is no good!" Primarily, he approved items which bore the kosher hechsher—the insignia.

I was confused when I saw one of the items the rabbi put in the approved pile. "Rabbi, why is this one in the okay pile?" I asked. "It doesn't have the hechsher on it!"

"I know the mashgiach that goes to that factory," he explained. (A mashgiach is a kosher inspector who goes to a factory to make sure it's clean, pork-free, and not engaging in the practice of mixing dairy with meat products. They are basically the health inspectors for Orthodox Judaism.)

After the rabbi left, I called my mother. "Mom, you're never going to believe this. We just koshered the house!"

She nearly fell off her chair.

Last fall, I happened to be in New York visiting friends. I went to see a couple of plays and visited the cemetery where my parents are buried. While I was in Great Neck where I grew up, I decided to stop at a Dunkin' Donuts for a cup of coffee. On the window display was a sign that read *Strictly Kosher.*

I was stupefied. I looked at the two guys behind the counter—both clearly non-Jewish men from remote parts of the world. It turned out that one was from Malaysia and the other from Bombay.

"Is that really true? This place is strictly kosher? If that's true, you can't even serve half the usual Dunkin' Donuts menu!"

"That's right," said one of the two men, with a perfectly serious expression. "We don't."

Then, as if it had been scripted to prove their point, the door to the donut shop swung open and in strode a man with a long black coat and black hat—the mashgiach! He walked right into the kitchen, spent a few minutes inspecting everything to make sure it was kosher, and then walked back out the door.

Drew's conversion weekend began on the evening of Shabbat, a Friday night in June. Rabbi Cohen invited Drew, Janie and me to stay the weekend at his house. It was, as they say in gangster movies, an offer we couldn't refuse. That Saturday happened to be the longest day of the year. Shabbat didn't end until sundown finally arrived around ten o'clock at night.

On Saturday afternoon, Rabbi Estricher, a rabbi from the same school, taught a Torah class at Rabbi Cohen's house. Rabbi Cohen asked if I was interested in sitting in. Again, an offer I couldn't very well refuse.

We went to Saturday night services, and then we went back home to spend the night in our own beds before joining back up with the rabbis on Sunday for the conversion. About five minutes after we got home from the rabbi's house, the phone started ringing.

The call was from Rabbi Estricher, one of the three rabbis on the rabbinic court. He was the same rabbi who had given the class that Drew and I attended that afternoon. While we were there, it became clear that he was beloved by all his students.

He wanted to talk to Drew. "Drew, I need to see you right now."

So, Drew drove to Rabbi Estricher's house and was gone about half an hour.

When he got back home, he told me, "The rabbi was not feeling comfortable with granting me the conversion. He wasn't sure I was serious about it."

"Why not?" I asked.

"A few different reasons. For one thing, I've only been at Yeshiva High School for one year. And he wasn't sure I was serious about keeping a kosher kitchen, observing Shabbat, and laying tefillin." (Laying tefillin in Orthodox Judaism involves saying morning prayers while wearing two leather pieces, one on the forehead and the other wrapped around the hand.)

"How did you leave things with him?" I asked.

"I finally convinced him that I was serious about keeping shabbat, keeping kosher, and laying tefillin. There wasn't much I could say about being at Yeshiva High for just a year."

When Drew first started attending Yeshiva High, he came to me and said, "Dad, I need some tefillin for school."

"Oh, do I have just the thing for you! Come with me..." I took him into my bedroom and opened a drawer. "Please use these. Grandpa Harry gave me this set of tefillin at my bar mitzvah."

Then I called my mother. "Mom, you're never going to believe this. Drew is using the tefillin Grandpa gave me at my bar mitzvah!"

She was delirious with happiness over this news.

On Sunday, I went with Drew to the Orthodox synagogue and watched him walk into the mikvah bath. As he emerged from the water spiritually cleansed, the rabbi said some prayers over him before drawing blood. Then Drew got dressed and went to the rabbinic court, comprised of Rabbi Cohen (the headmaster of the school), Rabbi Estricher, and another rabbi.

I had to sit that one out. It was a very private proceeding that Drew was not allowed to share with anyone—not even his father. They gave Drew the go-ahead, although not without some struggle. It came to light later that Rabbi Cohen had to twist the arm of the third rabbi in order to get him to sign off on Drew's conversion.

A week later was Drew's graduation.

"Where are my tefillin?" I asked him.

"Oh, I had to bury them in the back of the school."

"What?" I said, incredulous. "You buried my tefillin in the back of the school?"

"The rabbi said I *had* to bury them because they weren't kosher anymore. The material was frayed. He said to bury them so they would become purified again." I never would get them back. Ironically, they remain buried under the foundation of the gym I built for the school.

Janie threw a graduation party for Drew and used a kosher caterer. She was inviting all the rabbis—Rabbi Cohen, Rabbi Estricher and the two Orthodox rabbis who had koshered our house. The third rabbi from the rabbinic court was not someone with whom we were socially acquainted and so we hadn't invited him. We had told everyone, "Come celebrate with us. We're having a big kosher buffet dinner and kosher wine."

The party got underway and we noticed that the rabbis that koshered our house were not eating. I went over to them. "Rabbis, why aren't you having something to eat?"

"Well, we don't know whether the house is still kosher."

"But you were here two weeks ago and you koshered our kitchen yourselves! And you know the caterer and you know he's kosher."

"Sure, but I don't know whether *you* followed all the regulations on how to clean the dishes." They were not about to put themselves in the position of eating something that might not be kosher.

An Orthodox Jewish friend of mine who was a guest at the party overheard the conversation.

"Bob?" he said.

"Yes?"

"If you tell me it's kosher, that's good enough for me," he said with a smile, helping himself to the buffet.

Drew had now graduated and become an Orthodox Jew. Scott also underwent a conversion to Conservative Judaism. He was not considered by the rabbi to be learned, so he could not undergo an Orthodox conversion. Like his brother, Scott had to go through all the same steps, including entering the mikvah bath, the subsequent drawing of blood, and the appearance before a rabbinic court.

We continued to keep a kosher home for many years. In year six following Janie's diagnosis, I started to have help for her come into the house. I couldn't expect these ladies to keep the kitchen kosher. So, I had no choice but to abandon the practice of keeping a kosher home.

Twenty-Nine

A year after Drew's graduation, Yeshiva High School honored me with a dinner for building the new gymnasium. Two of my best friends got up to the microphone and introduced me. It was a huge honor for me and an opportunity for them to raise money from new followers. After all, they knew I wasn't an Orthodox Jew. Ipso facto, my invitees likely wouldn't be either and would therefore represent a group of potential new donors for the school.

I had invited plenty of friends to the dinner in my honor but not one person from my family was in attendance. (Interestingly, these days they honor both the husband and the wife, believing that the person being honored gave up their time with their husband or wife to do whatever he or she did for the school).

I had sent an invitation to my brother, sister and mother and told them all about it. I felt that my dad would have come but, by that time, he had already passed. The fact that no one from my family felt compelled to attend the dinner remained a thorn in my side.

A year or so after that dinner, Janie and I were on a Las Vegas getaway with two other couples. Over dinner, the conversation turned to the subject of the honorary dinner for the gymnasium I built. I talked about how upset I was that no one from my family showed up to celebrate with me. Then the subject was forgotten as the conversation turned in another direction.

Later that night, the six of us went to see a Vegas show. One of the guys in our party had an injured leg. So, when we got to the venue and found the row where our seats were located, I said, "I'll go into our row first and take one of the inside seats. This way, Raymond can sit on the aisle and stretch out his bad leg."

When I sat down, the man seated next to me turned and looked at me. His eyes were exactly like my dad's in every way—and he looked to be about the same age as Dad was when he passed. It was the strangest thing that has ever happened to me in my entire life. During the entire show, I was frozen in my seat. I couldn't even tell you one thing about the performance.

Later, while Janie and I were lying in bed, I was thinking about the conversation at dinner and how I had told the group how upset I was over the absence of my family at the honorary dinner for my work on the gymnasium. I had also said that I was sure my father would have been there if he had been alive. Then it hit me: Las Vegas was the last town Dad had visited before he became sick and passed. It was part of the forty-state road trip he had taken with my mom.

I figured that having a man seated next to me who looked back at me with my father's blue eyes must have been Dad's way of letting me know that I was right. I felt like he was saying, "You're right, son, I *would* have showed up at your honorary dinner if I had been alive."

I hadn't even connected those two things until I was lying in bed that night—me being in Las Vegas and Dad having been there on the tail end of his road trip with Mom. I now believe in the hereafter, thanks in no small part to that incident and a few others many years later.

Life was going along smoothly and then catastrophe hit in the form of The Tax Reform Act of 1986. This bill threw the entire real estate industry into a tailspin, and my business right along with it. It eliminated the ability to accelerate depreciation on real estate. Worse than that, when it was signed on December 14th, it was made retroactive all the way back to January of that year.

This retroactive aspect of the bill hit us hard because 1986 was a very busy year for us. We had already done four deals by the time the bill passed at the end of that year. (We had been averaging about four deals a year for many years.) In putting an end to accelerated depreciation, the Tax Reform Act created a domino effect that threatened to put us under. For starters, it meant that the investors would not be receiving the tax benefits that they had anticipated when they originally invested with us.

Our deal with these investors was set up in such a way that they funded their investment over two or three tax years, in thirds. Once the ramifications of the Tax Reform Act were understood by the investors' accountants, they told them, "Whatever you do, don't make the next payment!"

"We know you had nothing to do with the piece of legislation that passed," the investors' accountants told us, "but unfortunately, that doesn't change our course of action."

This left us in a terrible position because we had literally been banking on their promise of payment. We had been going to the bank and borrowing against the second and third installments, and doing so with total confidence in the investors' promise of the remainder of the funds. I suppose we could have sued the investors for the remainder of the funds, but we were too busy down at the federal courthouse, trying to salvage the properties from foreclosure.

As a result of the investors withholding their second and third payments, my business partner and I now had obligations we couldn't possibly meet. For one thing, we were unable to repay the banks from whom we had borrowed against the second and third installments we'd been expecting from investors. We were also unable to pay the vendors who had provided labor and materials to us for renovations with the expectation that the money would be forthcoming. So, we had to stall the renovations.

We had to go to court on many of our single-asset-partnership properties. Our job was to convince the court to make the lender back off. In order to agree to do so, the judge made us come up with new money. That was the take-it-or-leave-it deal he offered: either we come up with a viable plan for obtaining fresh money and thereby working our way out of the problem, or the court would decline to force the lender and the vendors to step back.

My business partner and I didn't know whether to laugh or cry. "Should we try to get a space by the month down at the federal courthouse?" we said, only half joking. "We're going to have to put a lot of these deals into bankruptcy."

Many of our deals ended up in Chapter 11 bankruptcy reorganization proceedings. We were very lucky to have a judge who understood; there were certainly those who did not. In every case but three, we were given time to reorganize and come up with new money for these single-asset-partnership deals. Then, the judge modified the terms with the bank and let us go forward.

All in all, we managed to salvage seven or eight deals. We lost three properties in foreclosure because we could not convince the judge to tell the lender and vendors to step back. The same judge told me years later that we had taken more single-asset partnerships successfully through Chapter 11 reorganization than anyone at that time in history. Once things started to turn around in the early 1990s, we built the business back up again.

The real estate industry eventually bounced back but it took six or seven miserable years. In the meantime, going to work was like putting on my helmet every morning and going to war. I had to fight for the survival of my business. Thankfully, the Chapter 11 bankruptcy reorganization process we underwent related to the properties had nothing to do with my personal financial situation. I never had to declare personal bankruptcy.

Between 1986 and 1993 when things finally turned around, I sent two kids off to college—Drew to the University of Colorado in 1989 and Scott to the University of Florida in '92. It was a case of the worst possible timing, financially speaking.

Thirty

In 1992, as Scott went off to college, Janie was still full of energy. She had been volunteering with the Jewish Federation adoption agency through which we adopted both our boys, but she was not as busy as she liked to be. So, when she was approached by a woman and asked if she would like to go into partnership with her, she agreed.

The business revolved around taking authors to T.V. and radio publicity appearances as well as book signings. So, Janie made a trip to New York, met with a bunch of publishing companies, and got contracts with them. Unfortunately, not long after joining with her business partner in this endeavor, Janie realized that the woman was only interested in the fun part of the business—taking authors around to their appearances. She tried to delegate the actual running of the business to Janie.

The woman Janie was in business with happened to be the wife of Drew's boss at the construction company where he worked. So, there was a lot at stake.

"Look," I said to my wife, "the relationship is too close. End this relationship now before it starts to go south, and start over by yourself."

So, Janie went out on her own and was doing very well. In the mid-1990s, there was a literary convention in New York that Janie needed to attend for her business. We saw it as a chance to be in New York together, so I went with her. We were joined by a friend of ours who owned a book store, and her husband. While Janie was busy with meetings and other convention activities, I met up with college friends around town. I also went and saw my mom.

The convention was held outdoors in a park behind the main library on 42nd Street. All sorts of luminary authors were in attendance. One night, we were attending a dinner function with the other couple who had come with us. A bunch of us were seated around a big table when a woman who was by herself walked up and asked if we minded if she took the empty seat at the table.

We all got to talking and went around the table introducing ourselves. When it was my turn, the woman asked, "And who are you?"

"Nobody important," I joked, "just arm candy." Everyone had a good laugh over that one.

As for the woman, she gave us quite a surprise when she turned out to be Helen Gurley Brown, the editor of Cosmopolitan Magazine.

Then, in 1996, the Olympics came to Atlanta and Janie decided to volunteer. My wife had always had tremendous energy, so balancing her volunteering and business responsibilities was easy for her.

In 1997, while Janie was busy with her work and volunteering activities, I started renovation of an old one-story brick warehouse near the West End Mall in Atlanta. This time, I entered into the project without the involvement of my business partner. A couple of years earlier, he had decided that he wanted to do something on his own.

The project involved the conversion of an old-brick, thick-walled building with wood beams holding up the roof. The ceilings were over twenty feet tall. I designed and built concrete elevated platforms with stairs leading up to them in each unit. I sold a total of nineteen condominium units comprised of twenty-five-thousand square feet. Fortunately, the units sold out quickly and the venture was successful.

Then in 1998, a friend of mine named Bob called me and wanted me to come look at a building he co-owned. He was aware of my success with the old brick warehouse near the West End Mall in Atlanta and that's what led him to call me. He approached me with the offer to enter into a partnership on a conversion of the property with him, his brother, a friend of his brother's, and a parking-lot company out of Cincinnati.

I agreed—with the caveat that they would all agree to give me the autonomy I needed to work without anyone breathing down my neck.

This property was a combination of two-and-three-story buildings, totaling three-hundred-fifty-thousand-square-feet on eight acres. It was built in the 1920s and had originally been a mattress factory. (That's what it was still called by the local community:

The Mattress Factory.) It was deemed an historic building due to its unique architectural characteristics.

Part of the property had been turned into apartment units. The units were separated by nothing more than screen doors, and rented out to Georgia State University students. At the time I purchased the building, it had been tagged by the city for code violations. The owners were forced to have all tenants vacate the building when the city inspectors saw the existing conditions.

This project would take me years to complete. The entire first year of the project entailed plenty of red tape, as I tried to get the city to rezone it, and tried to put financing in place. I attended community action and neighborhood boards. Eventually, between a combination of city bonds, historical tax credits and financing from one of the main banks in town, I was able to proceed.

After I had spent an entire year putting together the deal, Bob and his three partners refused to provide financial statements to the bank for approval of the loan. Their logic was, "We don't give financial statements to anyone."

I was really aggravated. I said, "This is insane! I have been working on putting this deal together for the past year! No one will loan us money without seeing our financials. So, look, guys...if you don't want to do it, just sell the property to me."

After some verbal wrestling, I got them to agree. I ended up buying it for $2.5 million. I paid pennies on the dollar value of the property and it was a hell of an investment.

Then I went straight to Eric, the attorney who had been handling all of the legal aspects of my and my business partner's real estate deals for the previous twenty-five years.

"Eric," I said, "get in the car and take a ride with me. I want to show you something."

I drove him to the property and said, "I want you to join me in this investment."

He looked at the neighborhood and then looked at me like I'd lost my mind. That was the same reaction I got from just about everyone who found out I had bought the Mattress Factory, due to its location not far from the entrance to the historic Oakland Cemetery.

"Are you crazy?" he said.

Before I could respond, two spectacularly beautiful models exited the back door of the property, as perfectly timed as if I had hired them myself to prove a point.

"You set this up!" he said, suspiciously.

"No, I swear I didn't!" I said, laughing. "They're probably headed to the Marta station to catch a train."

"Well," he said, still a bit suspicious, "if these girls don't mind being here by themselves..."

After giving Eric a tour of the building, I took him up on the roof. I had been up on the roof myself when I became sold on the project. Despite the sketchy neighborhood, the building had a spectacular view of downtown, the expressway, and Buckhead, seven or eight miles north of Atlanta. I envisioned putting in a rooftop deck and knew it would end up being a major selling point for the apartments.

I was able to convince Eric to come in on the deal with me. He then brought in two guys he had done some deals with, and the four of us formed a partnership for the property. We were then able to finally get started on phase one of the renovations. I used an architectural firm and was heavily involved in the plans.

The property was comprised of eight acres, and we bought another adjoining acre for additional parking. The main building was three stories, brick with massive metal windows and wood-beam ceilings. It was an early example of poured-concrete construction with poured concrete columns. The early poured-concrete construction and the fact that it was over fifty years old were the features that had made it possible for the building to become eligible for historical tax credits.

The downside of the historical tax credits (which we sold to a local bank) was that they were restrictive as to what we could do physically to the building exterior. We had to maintain the look of the place. We had more creativity with the interior.

After four years of design and construction, The Mattress Factory building eventually became 228 rental apartments, with some retail space in a separate building. We wound up with a very attractive historical building which enjoys high occupancy to this day. The entire surrounding area has since been redeveloped and is a very attractive in-town neighborhood. (Given how well the project worked out, people no longer think I've lost my mind.)

Meanwhile, Drew and Scott—both of whom were in their early to mid-thirties by then—went into the real estate business together. Thanks to having me as their dad, the boys had already witnessed some of the downturns and pitfalls of the business. They remained undeterred. They formed a company, called M&M2S (I came up with the name Me and My Two Sons). They did the work and I provided the needed seed capital and advice when asked.

The three of us went down to the courthouse steps and bought some houses in foreclosure. Unfortunately (or fortunately, depending on how you look at it), their partnership was short-lived.

Drew was the one to state the obvious. "I just want you to know, Dad, it's not working out with me and Scott."

"It's not good for you two to work together anymore? Does Scott think so too?"

"Yeah...and the only way I'm going to be able to keep loving him as a brother is if we put an end to being business partners."

Thirty-One

It was 2003 when I began to notice that Janie was having problems with her speech and insisted that she see Dr. Leaderman. It was in 2004, after getting confirmation from specialists, that Janie was diagnosed with frontotemporal dementia. By 2005 when we began to plan Drew's wedding, Janie was still functioning but had lost much of her ability to speak.

I didn't approve of the girl Drew was marrying. She was smart and had a good job in the software business which required her to travel quite a bit. But I just couldn't see her and Drew making a lasting marriage. She had too much going against her.

For starters, she wasn't Jewish—but that wasn't the only thing that made me uneasy. Janie and I spent some time over dinner with her and Drew and, the more I learned about her family, the less it added up for me. Because I felt so strongly that Drew was making a mistake, I couldn't keep my reservations to myself.

When I talked to Drew about what was on my mind, he listened.

Then he said, "I appreciate you sharing your thoughts, Dad. But I'm a man now and I know what I want. I'm getting married."

So, I said, "Okay...but I want you to know I have serious misgivings. And I am not going to do anything more than I absolutely have to do for this wedding." On principle, I declined to pay for the liquor, the band, and the flowers.

Scott, meanwhile, didn't seem to have strong feelings one way or another about the girl his brother was marrying. At the time of Drew's wedding, Scott was dating the woman who would become his wife, and traveling a lot on business. In fact, he met his wife while on a business trip.

Drew went full-steam ahead with the wedding plans, despite my words of caution. On the wedding weekend, the festivities began on Friday night with the rehearsal dinner. The wedding ceremony itself was on Saturday evening. Then on Sunday morning before all of the out-of-towners headed home, a brunch was held.

Janie looked gorgeous at the wedding, as always. The fact that she was speaking very little was the only indication that she wasn't quite herself.

The wedding came off well enough, but I didn't care for the bride, the rabbi, or the venue. The venue was a nightclub, donated to Drew as a wedding gift from the owner who was a friend of his. It was a strange setting for a wedding—but it fit the oddness of the pairing.

As for the rabbi, he was ultra-Reform. (No Orthodox rabbi would have married people of different faiths). I found him to be too theatrical, drawing the spotlight away from the bride and groom, where it belonged, and onto himself.

By the time Drew got married, he had left orthodoxy behind him and was now a Conservative Jew. He attended the synagogue for services on the high holidays, and yahrzeit services for the saying of kaddish prayers on the anniversaries of the deaths of family members. (Yahrzeit services are a part of daily synagogue services. Anyone present who is there to honor a deceased loved one stands and repeats the kaddish prayer along with the rabbi. I say the kaddish annually in remembrance of my parents, my sister, my wife, and even my brother, despite our distant relationship.)

It broke my heart to see Drew marrying a girl I felt certain was wrong for him. I was also heartsick over the fact that my mother had been too ill to attend. Knowing that Mom wouldn't be able to make it to the wedding, I arranged for a workaround. I hired a videographer and sent him to Mom's apartment in New York. He set up the equipment necessary for Mom to watch the wedding live from her rocking chair, as it was taking place in real time.

Drew had written on a piece of paper he held up for the video camera, "Hi Grandma! Love and miss you!"

My mother had been living with breast cancer and enduring various treatments for eighteen long years. By the time of Drew's wedding, she was near the end of her life. Her doctor once explained to me that the first two rounds of chemotherapy are done by the book.

But if the first two rounds of chemo fail to completely arrest or eradicate the cancer, the rest of the patient's treatment entails a bit of creativity on the part of the oncologist.

One day, Mom's oncologist invited me into the area where he blended the drugs he was using to treat my mother.

"You know your mom should not be with us today," he said.

"Yes," I said, "I know that's true."

"I'm a pretty good mixologist, so to speak," he said, "but frankly, I'm amazed that she has survived for so long!"

"Well, that's a tribute to you."

"I think it has more to do with your mother than with me. I honestly feel like I could spit on your mother's tumor and she would react positively," he said, smiling.

That was my mother—a tough lady with an indomitable spirit. She had strong morals, a strong character, and was strong in every way. Both my mother and my wife had those traits in common, despite their very different personalities. As you know by now, my mother was quiet and reserved and Janie was very outgoing—a tornado.

One night in the mid-1980s, we were talking on the phone when Mom started crying.

"Lizzie, what are you crying about?"

She said, "I can't tell you."

"I promise you can tell me."

"I'm afraid I'm not going to get Medicare."

"Why wouldn't you get it? You get Social Security, don't you?"

"Yes, but I'm worried I might not get Medicare because I'm not a citizen."

I was stunned. "You mean to tell me you never got your citizenship papers?"

"No, I never got them."

"I remember you talking about this around the table when I was ten years old! You still never got your papers?" I asked, incredulous.

"No," she said.

"Listen," I said, "I'm going to take it upon myself to get you your citizenship papers! I know you were born in Minsk, Russia. Now all you've got to do is give me power of attorney and I'll get the ball rolling."

Once my mother gave me her power of attorney, I started the long process of collecting the necessary documentation. I wrote to the Bureau of Records in Albany, New York. I requested and received a bunch of information on her father, Grandpa Harry, and his arrival on American shores in 1921. I filled out the citizenship forms, attached the documents, and sent them in to the citizenship office.

Six months later, they wrote back requesting more information. Once again, I was at square one, assembling the paperwork they had asked for. Six months later, another request for more documents. Over two years, I got three different requests, six months apart, and then the final letter. It stated, in essence, "We are having trouble identifying your mother. We cannot find a birth certificate for her."

They had my parents' marriage certificate and my grandma's death certificate but my mother's family did not leave Russia with birth certificates. I suspect that Russians were not issued them at the time.

To make matters worse, my grandfather's naturalization papers listed my mother, Elizabeth, as Liza on some of the forms and as Lizzie on others. So, the citizenship office was left questioning whether this person was actually my mother, Elizabeth.

An unlikely person ended up saving the day and providing just the thing we needed to tip the scales. Inna was a friend of Janie's and mine—and she was one of the Jews who left Russia when they opened their borders in 1990 for Jews who cared to leave the country. She wrote a letter for me to give to the citizenship office, stating her own Russian name and her occupation as a translator and teacher at Georgia Tech University. She explained that the Russian root of the name Elizabeth is Liza or Lizzie. (More about her and her family later.)

At last, we got the long-awaited call from the citizenship office, saying, "Okay, we have everything we need. Now we need your mother to come down for an interview."

One morning, I flew up to New York City and took my mother to the citizenship office on Wall Street.

At one point, the woman interviewing my mother said, "Okay, please stand up and raise your right hand..."

As I watched my mother being sworn in, I felt tears come to my eyes. To this day, I get choked up when I think about it.

"...And do you swear to defend the United States against all sworn enemies?" continued the woman swearing in my mother.

"Hold on a minute," I said.

My mother knew that nothing good was going to come out of my mouth. She started shooting daggers at me with her eyes.

I couldn't resist. "Do you realize, Mom," I said, "that if you agree and sign those papers, we will need to go right from here to the draft board?"

If looks could kill, I would have been dead that very minute.

The lady doing the swearing-in procedure with my mom thought this was hilarious.

My mom was not amused by my joke but nothing could detract from her elation. She was so happy, she would not have traded that citizenship paper for a million dollars. She had waited her entire life for this moment. Mom got her picture taken and walked out onto the street with me. She was carrying her citizenship papers, backdated to 1928. The expression on my mother's face was beatific.

"See, Lizzie? I was right!" I said. "When Grandpa became a citizen in 1928, you automatically became one." (That system has since been abandoned, and now everyone must apply for citizenship individually.)

"...And," I went on, "after all the work I did to get your papers, you've got to promise me you're going to vote in the next election."

"Don't worry," said my mother, "I'm going to vote! I promise."

"And promise me one more thing..." I said, "that you'll vote Republican."

She gave me a serious look, paused, and then handed me her citizenship papers. She was letting me know that she was not going to do what I asked and, if I insisted, she was willing to relinquish her citizenship. I'm sure my maternal grandparents were socialists. Coming from Russia, that's more than likely. And coming from socialist parents, my mother was naturally leaning in the direction of a liberal democrat.

Mom got her citizenship papers about ten to twelve years before her health began failing. Her breast cancer had metastasized and she had already had a double mastectomy. She was constantly undergoing different forms of chemotherapy and it was finally taking a serious toll on her body.

In early 2006, she was transported to the hospital. By that year—which would end up being the final year of my mother's life—I refused to allow her to live by herself any longer.

"Lizzie," I said, "that emergency alert button isn't enough anymore. I'm going to hire someone to come in and be with you during the day."

She had used the alert button twice. Once, she fell and couldn't get up. Thank goodness, the alert system included a speaker in the room. The system representative was able to stay on the line with my mother until help could arrive. Mom found it very comforting.

In 1972, when my mother moved from Great Neck to Manhattan, she had gone to work in the apparel industry. (Once my father passed, she left the beauty business.) She rented an apartment at 24th and 3rd near Gramercy Park. Living in a place where it was easy to walk everywhere was perfect for her since she never drove.

Mom was living in a rent-controlled apartment but it still went up two or three percent per year. When it went co-op, I stepped in and bought the apartment in my own name so we could keep the overhead at an even level.

"That's fine," said my independent mother. "But I still want to be the one to pay the maintenance costs!"

So, every month, my mother sent me a check, which I deposited. Then I sent my own check to cover the maintenance. When the maintenance costs went up, I increased the amount of my checks to the building but intentionally kept quiet about it.

My mother was none the wiser until one day when she was checking her mailbox. She started chatting with a neighbor who lived in the same apartment, one floor up or down.

"Can you believe how much the maintenance costs have gone up?" said the neighbor. "It's ridiculous!"

My mother looked at the woman, stunned. "What do you mean? Mine haven't gone up at all. How much are you paying now?"

When Mom heard the woman's response, she marched back into her apartment. Then she called me and read me the riot act. She was not touched or moved by the fact that I had kept her monthly bill at a manageable level for her. She was furious with me.

"I never lied to you, Lizzie! You never asked and I never said..."

"You know perfectly well that you misled me!" Mom said. "You knew I wanted to at least be responsible for the maintenance costs."

That was my mom—strong and fiercely independent. When her disease progression began to accelerate and she started losing control over her body, it was very hard for my strong, independent mother to take.

As she got sicker, she had to be taken to Lennox Hill Hospital.

I hopped a flight to New York City. Janie was still ambulatory at this point but couldn't speak much. She could still be left alone for short periods of time, but I would ask one of my kids to come stay the night when I went to New York.

I got to my mother's bedside at the hospital around noon—the very hospital where I had been born sixty-three years previously. I said, "Geez, Mom, they haven't changed this place in years!"

Once again, my mother did not appreciate my humor. She gave me a look.

I took a seat in the chair in her room. In walked my mother's oncologist and the oncologist's father, also a doctor, who had initially treated Mom. Neither one was on staff at Lennox Hill but both wanted to check on my mother and see how she was doing. (The two of them were the only doctors to ever receive a thank-you note from me.)

The elder of the two doctors leaned down and whispered to me, "Where are you going to take your mom when the time comes?"

"I don't know...I haven't thought about it yet." I understood that he was referring to hospice care.

He handed me a piece of paper. "Take a look at this place."

"Where is it?" I asked.

"In the Bronx."

"In the Bronx? I can't do that to my mother. That's where she grew up before moving to Long Island and it would be too depressing for her."

"You need to go take a look at it. It's where I took my wife."

I knew that the Bronx had changed over the years and wasn't the best neighborhood. Then again, I took seriously the fact that this doctor had taken his own wife there. So, I took my sister and brother with me and we checked out the place. One of the social workers showed us around, and we were all very impressed. It was an absolutely magnificent facility.

When I commented to the social worker that it was one of the nicest hospice-care facilities I had ever seen, she looked me square in the eye and said, "This is not a hospice. We are a full-service hospital for the terminally ill."

They avoided using the word hospice to refer to their facility, as it evoked images of death. And she was right about the hospital-like nature of the place. If I took you there and showed you around, you would think you were in a hospital. You would see a nurse's station as well as rabbis, ministers, priests and loved ones, all milling around and visiting the patients.

My siblings and I decided to move Mom there.

In the handful of days Mom spent at Lennox Hill Hospital, her health started swiftly declining. When it was time for her to be released from the hospital, I talked to her about moving to Calvary Hospital, the hospice facility.

I got no objection from my mother. In fact, she was more than ready to go. "I know I'm not long for this world, and I'm okay with it. I just have one question... what are you going to do with the apartment?"

"The apartment?" I said. "I haven't even thought about it."

"I don't want you to lose any money on the apartment when I'm not living there."

"Don't worry about it, Lizzie, I'll take care of it."

Typical of my mother, she worried that it would be a financial hardship for me to continue to pay for the apartment once she was gone.

(When the time did come after my mother's passing for me to consider what to do with her apartment, nearly everyone I talked to gave me the same advice. "Oh, you have to keep it! That way, you'll have a place to stay when you go to New York. It will be so much cheaper than staying in a fine hotel."

Common sense would lead me to sell. I simply wasn't in New York often enough to warrant keeping the place. It was purchased, after multiple offers, by a woman who had already bought the unit next door and wanted Mom's unit too so she could combine them and end up with a larger space.

The sale was filled with aggravation due to the laws governing co-op buildings. Still, I ended up making a great profit on the sale. I had bought it in the early 1980s for $37,000—the insider price offered to the existing tenants. After Mom's passing, I sold it for $700,000. It was one of my better investments.)

It was reassuring to know that Mom was in such good hands at Calvary and would be getting her own private room. (All the patients there had private rooms.) There was only one problem: above the bed in every room hung a crucifix.

When the staff realized that our family was Jewish, they said, "Would you like us to remove the crucifix from the room?" Other facilities I had been to would usually just ask if we wanted them to cover it.

"Yes, I would really appreciate it," I said.

On March 12th of 2006, I got to Calvary around nine o'clock in the morning to be at my mom's bedside. She was in and out of a coma by then so there was no conversation. I just held her hand. The sun set and the evening passed and I was still there, holding her hand. I knew she didn't have a lot of time left.

At eleven o'clock, the nurse came in. "You know, Bob," she said, "some people won't leave while their loved ones are here with them. Why don't you go back to the hotel and get some sleep?"

I had been there for thirteen or fourteen hours by then and was utterly exhausted, so I agreed.

I made the forty-five-minute drive to my hotel in Westchester and got into the shower. As soon as I got out of the shower and lay down on the bed to take a nap, the phone started ringing. I looked at the clock and it was one-thirty in the morning.

"I'm sorry to tell you, Bob, but your mom just passed," said the nurse.

"Can you keep her there until I get back?"

"Yes, absolutely," said the nurse.

I threw on my clothes and drove all the way back to the Bronx. By the time I got back to Calvary Hospital in the early morning hours of March 13th, 2006, the ambulance had already been called and I had instructed them as to where to take my mother's remains. But the hospital promised me that they would not let the doctor pronounce Mom dead, and they would not move her body until I got there.

As I walked into my mother's room, I saw her lying there looking peaceful, calm and serene. The staff at the facility had combed her hair and groomed her to preserve her dignity. This was in keeping with the loving care they gave my mother during her brief time with them.

Suddenly, I realized something. "Wait a minute," I said to the nurse. "It just hit me! It wasn't that I was here last night...that's not what was keeping my mom from passing."

"What do you mean?" asked the nurse.

"Mom didn't pass last night because it was my father's birthday! That's why she waited. She had to make sure March 12th was over before she went."

Later that same year, I was talking with the lay president of a nursing home here in Atlanta called The Jewish Home. He offered his condolences on my mom's passing.

I told him about Calvary Hospital and the wonderful services they gave my mother in her last days of life. "The place is absolutely terrific!" I said. "They treated my mother so well."

"I can only imagine how much it must have cost to have her in a place like that," he said. "How much did it cost per month?"

"Nothing," I said.

"That's impossible," he said. "I know how much it costs to run this place!"

"No...they took Mom's Social Security check and not a penny more. They're owned by the archdiocese in New York and they're ridiculously wealthy. A lot of philanthropists give money to Catholic Charities and I'm sure that helps fund it."

Thirty-Two

Jewish tradition dictates that a person be buried within twenty-four hours of their death. There are only three exceptions—a person cannot be buried on Shabbos, Yom Kippur or Rosh Hashana. It is also interesting to note that, from the time of death until the time of burial, the body is never left unattended. Assuming the family of the decedent used a Jewish funeral service, a Chevra Kadisha member—a secret committee of people affiliated with whatever synagogue the decedent might belong to—stays with the body until the time of burial.

There is a reason for the quick burial: Jews do not believe in being embalmed because they hope to be resurrected whole when the Messiah returns. When you're embalmed, all the blood is drained from your body and replaced with embalming fluid. So, a person wouldn't be considered resurrectable. Along these same lines, the decedent is wrapped only in a shroud and placed in a simple pine box with doweling rather than nails so as to aid in the resurrection process.

By the time I got to the hospital after my mother had passed, I had been up half the night. I hadn't wanted to wake the boys too early so they still didn't know. I dreaded breaking the terrible news to them, and I certainly didn't want to wake them up to do it. They had both been close to their grandmother and knew she was very near death.

"I hate to tell you this but...Grandma's gone," I told my sons when I finally called them around seven-thirty in the morning, "She passed last night."

After the boys and I shed some tears together on the phone and offered each other condolences and comfort, I said, "I need you to go get your mom and bring her up here for the funeral."

Janie wasn't in the best shape and had lost all ability to speak. She was losing her essence, little by little. But she was still able to get around, and I was grateful to have her with me at my mother's funeral.

The services were held in a funeral parlor in Westchester near Calvary Hospital. Many of my parents' friends had already passed by then. Those who were still alive were in attendance. There were also some cousins at the funeral, as well as a lady who worked for my parents for many years.

I felt badly that I could not get up to the podium to speak about my mother but I was feeling too emotional. I knew I wouldn't be able to pull it off without breaking down.

My sister Randee did speak. Following is an excerpt of her speech:

My mother, Elizabeth Fischbach, known as Betty, was truly a beautiful woman, and not just physically. Friends and relatives would describe her as always a lady, dignified, proper, sincere, a good person who always did the right thing. Wonderful wife, balabusta, wonderful hostess, excellent cook. She was loyal and a good friend, always showing compassion for others. She was the most honest person I know and had the highest level of integrity. I stand here today to tell you Betty Fischbach was an excellent mother and grandmother... Life for Betty Fischbach was about family and loyalty... She was a truly loyal and kind person and that will be her legacy.

Randee and I had maintained a great relationship over the years and were even closer than when we were young. Her son, Alex Harrison (who was given my father's name as his middle name) and my mother had a very close bond and spoke every day. They were both big Yankee fans and, from time to time, Alex would pick up Mom and take her to games.

Danny got up at the funeral and spoke—but the words he shared were written by his wife. Unfortunately, my brother and I were no closer than when we were young. Even on the day of our mother's funeral, my brother was his usual stoic self. I never saw him broken up or particularly emotional. There I was, so emotional I couldn't even say a few words about our mother. And there was Danny, as cool as a cucumber.

I was shocked when my brother had said that he wanted to speak at Mom's funeral. He was barely on speaking terms with Mom at the time of her death, and things were strained between them.

Thanks to my brother's refusal to get on good terms with our mother before she passed, my relationship with him had also become strained. The proverbial straw that broke the camel's back between Danny and me came on Mom's birthday about ten years before her death. It was in 1998 while Janie was still healthy.

My mother was celebrating her eightieth birthday. She was the youngest of eight siblings. Diane, one of my first cousins (the daughter of one of Mom's sisters), hosted a birthday luncheon at her New Jersey house in honor of my mother's eightieth. It was going to be a surprise party for Mom.

Randee called and told me about the party. "All the New York cousins are coming."

When I told Janie about the party, she said, "It sounds great. I'd love to go up and surprise your mother. And you'd better also call your brother and tell him about the party."

Danny and I certainly didn't have a close relationship but we spoke from time to time. So, I called and told him about the party. I was calling partly out of deference to my wife and partly out of deference to my mother. Mom would ask me, "Why won't Danny talk to me?"

So, I had tried to talk to him about it. "You've got to be on speaking terms with Mom! She's your mom! I don't know what's wrong between you two but you need to be an adult and deal with it."

When I told Danny that we were going to Diane's for Mom's surprise birthday party, he said, "That's great but I'm not going."

"Well, that's your decision," I said, sighing deeply. "I just wanted you to know Janie and I are going."

Janie and I stayed at a hotel in Manhattan. I called Randee and told her, "Look, on your way to Diane's, drive up Sixth and look on the corner of 59th. I'll have my thumb out. You can pick up Janie and me on the way." And that's exactly what she did.

About a dozen of us showed up for Mom's party, including all my first cousins and their spouses still living in the New York area. It was not a particularly formal or fancy birthday luncheon, but it was a lovely way of celebrating Mom, the last living member of the Fishkin clan.

The next time Mom spoke to my brother after his no-show, she asked, "How come you didn't come to my party? Bob and Janie flew up from Atlanta. All you would have had to do was drive down from Boston!"

I don't know what Danny said in reply. All I know is that this conversation led to a two-year period during which my mother and my brother didn't speak at all. The guilt from Mom was the straw that broke the camel's back as far as Danny was concerned. It prompted him to declare, "That's it! I'm not talking to her anymore."

Mom would say to me, "Please try to talk to Danny! Have him call me."

I was really upset with my brother for refusing to speak to our mother. I knew how much it hurt her. I tried to get him to see reason, saying, "Look, you don't have to be best friends with Mom. Just pick up the damn phone and talk to her!"

Time and time again, Danny refused to make things right with Mom. I was completely unable to convince him that it was important that he mend fences with her. I couldn't have a relationship with my brother while he was being hurtful to Mom, so I cut off all contact with him. My feeling was, "You're sixty-five years old! You're not a child anymore. Be a man!"

Eventually, they got back on speaking terms but just barely.

After Mom's funeral, we all went to a cemetery on Long Island for the burial. Among non-religious Jews, the seven-day shiva is a thing of the past. So, we sat shiva at Randee's house for one day only. I was anxious to get Janie home because I knew how agitated she could become in unfamiliar surroundings. Thankfully, we got through the funeral trip without any incidents or scenes.

For a few months or so following Mom's funeral, Danny and I had no contact. Then on May 5th, 2006, my phone rang.

"It's me," said Danny. "I wanted to tell you I was just diagnosed with esophageal cancer."

I didn't know what to make of the call from my estranged brother. He didn't bother to apologize or try to make amends. He simply informed me of his diagnosis and left it at that.

"Well," I said, "I hope everything turns out alright."

(Prior to that call from Danny, I had been diagnosed with Barrett's Esophagus where the esophageal cells begin to change. I had a lot of acid indigestion and reflux for quite a while and that's what led to the diagnosis. The condition can be a precursor to cancer so it has to be closely monitored.

My gastroenterologist, the doctor who performed the endoscopy on me that led to the diagnosis, told me that he wanted me to come back in a year for a checkup. When I returned a year later, he told me that the condition had stabilized and I didn't need to be checked again for five years.

As soon as I got off the phone with my brother that evening, I got right on the phone with my gastroenterologist who also happened to be a good friend.

"I will be in your office in the morning," I said. "Make some time to see me."

I had been taking Prilosec for years for my condition. When I saw my gastroenterologist the following morning, he left my Prilosec prescription unchanged. He did, however, also do an endoscopy on me to check me for cancer. Thankfully, the endoscopy did not reveal cancer. But, considering my brother's esophageal cancer diagnosis, I changed the frequency of my checkups to an annual schedule. In those doctor's visits each year, the doctor does a biopsy. Prior to that visit, I had been seeing him at five-year intervals.)

After nineteen years of marriage to my brother, Danny's ex-wife, Judy, came out of the closet and announced that she was going to be living her life as a lesbian. Despite their divorce, she and I remained close over the years and always spoke to each other on our birthdays.

Judy was now married to a woman who happened to be a doctor. Judy's wife was able to get Danny in to see one of the experts at Women's Brigham Hospital in Boston. The treatment plan for my brother involved an initial round of chemotherapy and radiation to shrink the tumor, followed by surgery to remove the affected part of the esophagus. Then, the stomach would be pulled up and attached to the esophagus.

My brother made it through the chemo and radiation treatments. Then in November of 2006, he underwent surgery. Unfortunately, when the surgeon opened up my brother, he discovered that both lungs were compromised by cancer. So, he closed him right back up. Danny smoked a pipe and that may or may not have anything to do with it.

What I don't understand, I thought, *is how those scans of his esophagus, which sits right between the lungs, could have missed the cancer in his lungs!*

To this day, I don't understand how his doctors, who were excellent, could have missed it.

When I heard what the surgery had revealed, I took Janie and we flew up to Boston. It would be our last plane flight together. My wife was very sick at this point and she knew it. She was steadily losing functionality. I was having to help her when she went to the bathroom, and I was bathing and dressing her, as well as taking her shopping and to her errands and appointments.

It was time to make peace with my brother—not that we were suddenly going to become close at the end of his life.

When we went to see Danny, he was at home. I said, "We wanted to come see you and wish you well..."

Janie was sitting by my side.

"...and I want you to know, I'm sorry we haven't been getting along the last several years, but you know why."

"Yeah," said Danny, "I'm sorry. Maybe I should have made up with Mom. I just couldn't make myself do it. And then it was too late."

It made no sense at that late juncture for me to once again question my brother about why he had been mad at our mother in the first place. I didn't want to get into all that nonsense.

Danny passed on December 13th, 2006, exactly nine months to the day from the date of Mom's passing.

It was a great feat of self-restraint to keep from saying to my brother before he passed, "I am sorry for you if there's a hereafter. If Dad sees you, he's going to beat the living shit out of you for not talking to Mom!"

Although my brother was, of course, Jewish by birth, his spiritual life was mostly non-existent and fell somewhere in the realm of atheism or agnosticism. I'm not sure even he could have articulated exactly how he identified in terms of his faith or lack thereof. In any case, it was his wish to have no funeral.

His second wife, Ginny, with whom I had never forged a real bond, called and let me know there wasn't going to be a service for Danny. In light of that, it made no sense for me to make another trip up to Boston.

Even though my brother died at the end of December, 2006, it wasn't until January of 2007 that I got a call from Ginny, letting me know that there was going to be a celebration of life for Danny. It was held in a rented space that was some sort of informal museum combined with a community social hall.

I decided that attending would be the right thing to do. So, I talked to Drew and Scott and asked them to stay behind and look after their mom, who was no longer functioning well enough to travel. I also had a nurse come in so the boys could be spared from some of the more gruesome aspects of looking after their mom—things like bathroom duty.

I flew from Atlanta to Boston, and Randee drove up from New York and picked me up at the Boston airport. Before we left, I made a call to Danny's son, Steven. (My brother also had a daughter, Heidi, whose

"H" name was given in remembrance of our late father.) I asked Steven to give me the name of the cemetery where Danny was buried, and to try to describe to me the exact burial spot. He did his best to point me in the right direction.

When Randee and I got to the cemetery, we wandered around, trying to find our brother's grave. We couldn't find it. After a while, I got a bit punch-drunk and started going down the rows whispering, "Danny, are you in there?"

Randee was in hysterics. We were both tired from traveling and from wandering around aimlessly. To this day, I don't know where in the cemetery Danny's marker might be, or if there even is one.

When we reached the venue for Danny's celebration of life, there was a big crowd gathered. At the table where I was sitting with Randee and her son, Alex, we were joined by Danny's first wife, Judy.

There was a microphone at a podium at the front of the room. Ginny was guiding the procession of people who wanted to get up and say a few words. One by one, my brother's friends and loved ones took the mic and spoke about him as if he were a king.

I sat there listening as everyone talked about how wonderful Danny was, and how filled with humanity. One woman even had the audacity to take the microphone and talk about thoughtful, wonderful Danny, who was amazing with our mother while she was sick.

Danny? I thought to myself. *The very same guy who had refused to make peace with Mom before she died?*

I could feel my blood pressure rising by the second.

Randee was sitting next to me and could tell that I was about to blow a gasket. "Calm down...calm down," she was whispering to me.

Next, somebody took the microphone and introduced themselves as Danny's "little brother" from the Big Brothers of America organization. This young man also launched into a heartfelt dissertation on the wonderful qualities possessed by my brother.

"Bob, are you going to get up and say anything?" whispered Judy.

"I'd better not," I said, trying to exercise restraint.

"I totally understand," said Judy.

It didn't end there, unfortunately. One after another, people continued to make their way up to the mic to sing Danny's praises.

I was beside myself at this point and about to come off my chair. Right at the moment that Ginny was getting ready to wrap things up, I sprung out of my chair and went up to the microphone, unannounced.

"May I say a few words?" I said, without waiting for her reply. "My name is Bob Fischbach and I was Dan Fischbach's *real* little brother. I have been sitting here for the last hour and a half listening to so many of you talk about the virtues of my older brother and share how wonderful he was to you. Well, I lived with him in the same room until I was fifteen and he was seventeen and went away to college. I'm truly glad some of you knew him the way you knew him, as a wonderful guy, but I never knew Dan Fischbach that way."

With that, I handed the microphone back to Ginny, walked off the stage, and returned to my seat. I turned to Randee and said, "Did I just blow this whole thing? I held back as much as I could..."

In the nicest way I could pull off, I tried to let those in attendance know that I knew a completely different side to my brother, and could not relate at all to the picture they were painting of him. I knew that my sister was in the same boat as I, and had never experienced the Danny people were speaking of that day.

After my brother's passing, my feeling was, *Thank G-d he didn't die before Mom. It would have killed her... even though they weren't getting along.*

For that I was thankful. I also felt badly for his family, his kids, and all the people who knew him so well and spoke so highly of him. Apparently, despite being his brother, I didn't really know him that well.

As for my own feelings about my brother's death, I felt badly to have lost my brother. I had already experienced enough loss that year. And I was sad that he and I had never managed more than a barely cordial relationship between us.

Thirty-Three

By the time of my brother's December, 2006 death, I had been sleeping with one eye open for about six months. In the summer of 2006, Janie started declining at an accelerated speed. It was startling how quickly she started to go downhill once she hit the two-year mark in her illness.

Janie would throw fits from time to time. She would yell and scream—or, more accurately, she would make screaming and yelling noises but no words would come out. She was also occasionally throwing things at me and hitting me. Knowing that Janie could go off at any given time, I had to stay close to her and hold onto her so she wouldn't strike out.

I will never forget the first time Janie got physical with me. It left me with a scar on my wrist that's the exact shape of Janie's mouth. I got this scar one day when Janie was sitting on the side of the bed and I walked by her to get something from the nightstand. As I reached toward the nightstand, Janie grabbed my wrist and bit a chunk out of it. Other times, she would haul off and smack me.

One time, she got so mad over something, she reached for the wooden bowl filled with wooden apples that sat on our kitchen countertop, and started hurling them at me. During most of these incidents, I was able to keep from getting angry with her. I reminded myself that these outbursts were manifestations of her disease, and that prior to the disease beginning to rob Janie of her personality, we had enjoyed a decades-long, wonderful marriage. That's the terrible thing about frontotemporal dementia—it alters the patient's personality in profound ways and eventually steals it altogether.

More than once, she was so out of hand, I had to physically pick her up and deposit her on the bed in order to get her to stay put. "Don't you move! Stay right there!" I said, exasperated.

So, in September, a few months before Danny's December, 2006 death, I realized I had no choice but to retire. It was the only way I could keep my promise to Janie that I wouldn't put her in a facility. Janie was sixty-two at the time and I was sixty-three.

When people asked me why I was retiring so young, I said, "Because I can. And because I want to spend time with Janie and we both want to travel." Even though both of those things were true, neither one was the reason behind my early retirement.

I ran the numbers, asking myself, *If I retire now at sixty-three, do I have enough money to last until I die? If I'm going to die at seventy-two, no problem. If I don't die until I'm eighty-two, we may have a problem!*

I didn't like those odds. So, I said to myself, *Okay, I've counted up all my money today, and I'm going to count it again a year from today. I'll watch the money I have in the stock market and see how it's performing. I can always go back to real estate if I have to.*

One year after I retired, I would indeed run the numbers again. I was happy to see that I had more money than I'd had the year prior. That told me that things were going in the right direction and I could keep going with my retirement plan. I was determined to do everything in my power to honor the promise I had made to my wife not to put her in a facility.

I was still getting a monthly check from my business partner for the buyout. In order to retire, I'd had to negotiate with him to buy me out of the business. He came up with the final offer—an offer I knew was too good to be true. (More on that later.) The deal was that, instead of paying me a lump sum to buy me out, he would pay me over time until we sold the last property we jointly owned.

I was also doing well in the stock market. And The Mattress Factory was producing cash. Thankfully, my former business partner had never been a part of that deal. The checks he was sending to me were separate from my Mattress Factory income.

Retirement was initially very strange after being in business for so long. It took a bit of time to adjust to the fact that I no longer had to wake up at a certain time in the mornings to go to work—although "wake up" might be overstating it.

At night, once I knew that Janie was deep asleep, I would doze off. But I had to have an alarm set for every half hour or forty-five minutes so I could wake up and check on her. Doing this night after night, year after year for several years would end up taking a serious toll on my health and well-being. I gained weight and looked horrible.

After barely sleeping at all the night before, I would drag myself out of bed in the mornings, make breakfast, do the shopping, take care of the laundry and do anything and everything else Janie might need in the course of the day or night.

Because my wife was, by this point in time, radically different than the Janie everyone had known, I wasn't interested in having her friends see her in that condition. Occasionally, some of them did come by.

By this time (the end of the second year of Janie's illness), when friends did come to visit, I controlled and limited the visits. Even during the first year and the first part of the second year, before I started discouraging people from visiting Janie, many of Janie's friends backed away on their own. People tend to shy away from loved ones who have medical conditions that trigger their fears. When you're diagnosed with a catastrophic illness, you quickly discover who is and is not a true friend.

The limited visits I allowed from friends of Janie's were usually comprised of the person bringing food over, and standing at the door talking with me for a few moments. If Janie happened to be sitting in the living room at the time, I would permit the visitor to wave at

Janie. That was about the extent of it. By the time that Janie passed after declining for eight and a half years, most of her friends hadn't seen her in five and a half or six years.

In 2007, it became clear that it was time to take Janie's car away from her. Breaking this news to her was heartbreaking. I had to sit her down and explain to her, "Bunny, I don't feel safe with you driving anymore. You haven't had an accident yet but the whole thing scares me to death. I am willing to drive you anywhere you need or want to go but I don't want you to drive your car anymore."

Not surprisingly, she took this badly. She got very upset with me, and made screaming and yelling noises.

Now that I was retired, I was there to take care of her and take her the places she needed to go. In my efforts to preserve Janie's dignity, I took her to the department store to shop, to the nail salon and to the hairdresser. I told Janie's hairdresser about Janie's medical situation. "I'll be bringing her to her appointments," I explained. "But I want you to know she is having trouble with her speech. So, please keep that in mind during her appointments with you."

Janie's hairdresser could not have been more gracious or caring. I liked her so much, I started going to her for haircuts myself. Years later, after Janie's death, her hairdresser would see me walking by the salon and come out to express her condolences to me.

(Later, when Janie's disease had progressed to the point where she could no longer go to the hair salon, I would end up bringing in a former hairdresser friend of Deanna's, a caregiver who had joined our household by then. My years spent in Dad's salon paid off as I bought the haircolor Deanna's friend Deedee would need for Janie. Deedee referred to hair styling evenings as "Janie's spa evenings." She would color, cut and style Janie's hair. I gave Janie her manicures.)

In 2007, Randee informed me that her cancer had returned and spread to other parts of her body. My sister had first been diagnosed with cancer three or four years before Mom's death. We were hopeful about the prognosis because our mother had been diagnosed in the mid-1980s and lived for two decades with her breast cancer.

Randee downplayed her medical situation. She said that the doctors had caught it early and it was under control. She underwent a lumpectomy and radiation and seemed to come out of it really well.

Then, in 2007—after the deaths of both my mother and brother—Randee's cancer returned with a vengeance. My sister kept her diagnosis from Mom because she worried that our mother would feel guilty and believe she had given it to my sister via heredity. Randee was right. There was no question that Mom would have felt responsible.

It was hard for me to keep this secret from my mother. One time, for example, I was in New York visiting my sister at the hospital for her lumpectomy, and I was four blocks from Mom's apartment. I felt terrible that I couldn't visit my mother, or even leave the hospital for fear of bumping into her.

Over Fourth of July weekend of 2008, shortly after Randee's son, Alex, graduated from high school, they moved to Atlanta and into an apartment fifteen to twenty minutes from Janie and me. That fall, Alex would be attending college and majoring in criminal justice.

By that time, Randee's two best friends had died and our mother and brother had passed. My sister knew that she didn't have much time left. So, she wanted to move to Atlanta and have family around, to support her and be there for Alex after she was gone.

My sister had never married but she was engaged twice. Sadly, both weddings were called off within two weeks of the wedding date. In the early 1980s after the second of her two engagements fell apart, Randee had gone through a difficult time emotionally. She wound up in Bellevue Psychiatric Hospital to get the care she needed.

After just a few weeks, I had Randee moved to a private New York hospital through the connections of a doctor friend I had in Atlanta. Thank goodness, after a few weeks, Randee bounced back and returned to her old self. She never had another episode and the mental health imbalance never recurred.

Since marriage didn't seem to be in the cards for my sister, she had decided to adopt a child and become a single mom. When Randee was ready to adopt, she consulted Janie, who had volunteered with the adoption agency through Jewish Family Services in Atlanta. (We adopted both our boys through Jewish Family Services in Cincinnati.)

It didn't make sense for Randee to adopt through the Jewish Family Services agency because, by that point in time, fewer families were putting children up for adoption. Those who *were* lucky enough to get a child often had to endure interminable wait times.

"Why don't you put an ad in USA Today?" suggested Janie. "I know it sounds crazy but I've known people who came through the agency trying to adopt, were unsuccessful, and found their children by putting an ad in the paper. It actually works!"

"Seriously?" said Randee. "It really works?"

"It really does! And I have one more suggestion," said Janie. "When you run the ad, get a separate phone number and put a designated phone in your house for that number. Then forward the number so it rings directly to an extension at your desk at work. This way, if somebody calls the house while you're at work, it will automatically be transferred to your desk."

Randee figured it was worth a try and placed an ad in the paper. It stated simply that she was a single, Jewish woman with a college degree, looking to adopt an infant.

The ad worked. Randee got one phone call that didn't go anywhere. The second phone call led to her adopting Alex. The call was from the baby's biological grandfather. (The family was Gentile.)

As it got close to the birth time, Randee and Mom drove out to eastern Ohio to meet the family. The meeting went well and Randee got the ball rolling by hiring an attorney to handle the adoption.

By this point in time, the system had changed. The days of the closed adoption were gone. So, Randee was at the hospital as the biological mother was giving birth. The bio-mom was very young—a fifteen-year-old girl. The biological father was also very young and was out of the picture by then.

As soon as Alex was ready to leave the hospital, Mom and Randee checked into a hotel in Columbus, Ohio. They had to remain in the state for a ten-day waiting period, during which all legalities were handled. Only at the end of that time period could Randee and Mom leave Ohio with the baby and take him home to New York.

Randee agreed to keep the family updated on Alex's well-being for a year, via letter.

"Are you nuts?" I said when I got wind of this promise. "Trust me, when you leave the hospital, you don't ever want to see those people again! All that you're required to do with an open adoption is meet them. That's it."

Randee disregarded my warning and kept up her end of the bargain. She sent the biological family letters about Alex for the first year. Then she stopped and never heard from them again. I knew that Alex was very much on Randee's mind when she made the decision to move to Atlanta.

Meanwhile, in the fall of 2008, just a few months after Randee and Alex moved to Atlanta, Drew came to me and said, "You were right, Dad. This marriage was a mistake. We're getting a divorce."

The marriage had lasted only three years. Thankfully, my son and his wife had no children between them and didn't have to deal with custody issues. So, it made sense for them to handle the divorce themselves. Everything seemed to be going smoothly and harmoniously between them. Then one day in early December, a sheriff walked into Drew's office and handed him divorce papers. So much for handling the divorce themselves.

Thirty-Four

By 2009—five and a half years after Janie's 2004 diagnosis—being her full-time caregiver had finally caught up with me. I was so exhausted physically, emotionally and mentally, I was starting to feel my life force ebbing away. Between the missed sleep, the constant caregiving, and the emotional devastation caused by watching my beloved wife of decades slip beyond my grasp, the entire ordeal had taken a serious toll on me.

I had actually begun to feel the toll being Janie's caregiver was taking on me much earlier. At the two-year-point of Janie's illness, I happened to have my annual checkup with Dr. Adam Leaderman, my internist.

Dr. Leaderman had known me for twenty years by then and was aghast at my appearance. "Bob," he said, "I've got to say, you look terrible! I know you're looking after Janie, but are you taking care of yourself?"

Having been involved in the diagnosis of Janie's condition, Dr. Leaderman was aware of the promise I had made to my wife. He knew that I had committed to looking after her myself.

After trying to reassure the doctor that I was doing my best to look after myself as well as my wife, I said,

"Now, I need you to promise *me* something, Adam. If you find anything alarming during my checkup, you've got to treat me very conservatively. I can't die before Janie!"

Watching my wife die slowly over several years was the scariest, most lonesome experience I have ever endured in my life. For about the last seven years of her illness, we couldn't even converse. In the early stage, she could still communicate by shaking her head, but even that faded over time. By the end of the second year of her illness, the Janie I had known and loved since we were young was, for all practical purposes, gone.

Yet, Janie was still there physically—and someone had to look after all her physical needs. It had gotten to the point where she needed me for the most basic functions, such as helping her after she went to the bathroom, and showering and dressing her.

These tasks were in addition to the usual tasks I was doing for her—including shopping, cooking and handling basic cleaning. (Annie only came to clean twice a week.) I was still giving Janie her manicures myself and having someone come in to do her hair. Preserving Janie's dignity remained of the upmost importance to me.

Even though both of my boys were busy—Drew with his divorce, and Scott with his dating life—they visited their mom often and were always happy to come by and stay with her any time I needed to leave the house for a short period of time. I don't know what I would have done without them.

From time to time, the boys would come to me and ask, "Dad, do you know how much more time Mom has? What's coming next?"

I had been candid with them from the beginning and they both knew that their mom was suffering through a terminal illness.

"Well," I would say, "We don't really know. Mom's hanging in there and I'm taking care of her. In terms of what to expect timewise, all the doctors really told me was that patients with Mom's illness typically live between seven and fifteen years after they're diagnosed."

We knew that, and we also knew that unlike Alzheimer's which affects the memory, Janie's illness affected her speech, personality and cognitive function.

Janie was on medication to slow the progression of the disease. In the years following my beloved wife's passing, I've given a lot of thought to that approach. As the patient slowly becomes a vegetable and loses their capacity to comprehend even the simplest things, it is the family that suffers.

I can honestly say that if I had it to do all over again, I might not give her the medication. I would ask myself, *Toward what end am I giving her this medication? It's not going to change anything! And not giving it to her might end her suffering sooner.*

There were more than a few times over the eight-and-a-half-year progression of Janie's illness where I questioned whether or not I would be able to keep the promise I had made to her. I often found myself fielding questions from people who would ask, "Why did you do it? How did you do it?"

My answer was always the same: "I never thought about not doing it. I put on blinders and did it. Period."

I didn't even think twice when Janie asked me to promise to not put her in a facility. I loved her and I married her. When we took our marriage vows, I signed up to love my wife in sickness and in health. I had seen my parents take care of each other, no matter what. We had been married for thirty-eight years by the time of her devastating diagnosis. I didn't think twice about making or keeping the promises I made to my wife on my wedding day and then after her diagnosis.

Unfortunately, Janie's sister, Gail, never exhibited anything close to the same level of devotion to Janie or stepped up to help me with her care. This was shocking, considering that she lived only fifteen minutes from us when Janie became sick, and was perfectly aware of Janie's diagnosis.

Gail only visited Janie about every four months. When she was ready to visit Janie, she would plan her visits on a day when Annie was going to be at the house. Gail would arrive with lunch for Annie, spend some time visiting with her, and then spend maybe five minutes with Janie.

Then, Gail would announce, "I can't take it! It's too hard on me."

Then she would get up and leave. This went on for the entire eight-and-a-half years that Janie suffered through her illness. Gail's husband, meanwhile, never visited once, and neither did their children. Not even Janie's niece, Elizabeth, despite Janie's devotion to her since she was young. (In fact, Janie practically raised Elizabeth.)

The best part of me tells myself that Gail cautioned the kids against visiting Janie, with a warning along the lines of, "Don't go over there! You'll find it too shocking to see Aunt Janie like that." The worst part of me says that the kids were no better than their mother.

As I mentioned earlier, some twist of fate had led to Gail and her husband moving to Atlanta four months before we did. Once both Janie and Gail were living in Atlanta, their parents followed, wanting to be close to their girls.

Since everyone was living in Atlanta, the entire family got together for the holidays. Either we would host the gathering at our house or Gail would host at theirs. It was wonderful for Janie's and Gail's parents to be able to spend so much time with family. They moved to Atlanta around 1975, part-time, and eventually moved here permanently. (I moved to Atlanta in 1974.)

Then, in a case of unbelievably insensitive timing, Gail declared, *right after* the funeral of their mother, "I'm not going to be involved in any more holiday dinners. They're too much trouble!"

I had never been fond of Gail and this feeling was reinforced over and over again by her actions—and inaction.

Thirty-Five

When I decided to devote myself to becoming the full-time caregiver for my beloved ailing wife, I did so without reservation or hesitation. And I did so without all the information—information I could not possibly have known until it was too late.

Here is the missing piece of critical information that no one told me beforehand, and that I only discovered along the way: the world was not going to stop, and the rest of my life was not going to suddenly vanish, while I gave my all to Janie and took on the role of her caregiver.

I couldn't have foreseen the immense burden it would put on me. I will never know what decision I might have made had I been able to see into the future and know what was in store. There was the physical burden of course, but there was also the heavy psychological and emotional weight. To try to continue to show up for my work (prior to the time I retired), and to be there for my family and loved ones while carrying such a heavy weight became harder and harder the longer Janie's illness dragged on.

Between the time Janie's illness was first diagnosed in 2004 and my retirement, her illness had a profound and disruptive impact on the daily functioning of our lives. Then in 2006 when I retired to become Janie's full-time caregiver, her illness began taking nearly *all* my time, energy and internal resources.

Meanwhile, the rest of my life continued on unabated. Life was in session regardless of my wife's declining health, and it continued to show up every day with its usual demands. There was only so much I could mitigate or delegate. The rest of it fell squarely on my shoulders.

I was still a brother to my sister and brother and a son to my mother, until they began to pass away, one by one. I was still a parent to my children. None of these roles were set off to the side just because my wife required so much of me. It wasn't like I could lock the rest of my family out of my life so I could focus on Janie.

As I tried my best to show up for all my loved ones and be a good son, brother and parent while also looking after my wife, I was becoming a zombie. By the time I brought in caregivers in mid-2009 to help, I was so physically and emotionally drained, I honestly didn't know how much longer I would live.

When I realized I might actually expire before Janie did unless I brought in caregiving help, I reached out to a female friend who was active in the operations of The Jewish Home Auxiliary.

"Would you see if you can get me some names of people that they recommend as in-home caretakers?" I asked my friend.

My friend called me back within a couple of days and gave me some names.

I called them one by one and met them at a coffee shop. The first two that I met with were an obvious mismatch for us.

I arrived early at a coffee shop and waited for the third woman to arrive: Thelma. She was an African American woman of seventy-two.

She walked in the door and smiled at me, and brightened up the whole place. She had a glow about her.

I introduced myself and we sat down together. I noticed that she was missing part of her right arm, just below the elbow. I instantly fell in love with her and felt I had found the perfect caregiver for my wife.

We discussed the terms of employment, including the fact that she was a live-out rather than a live-in caregiver. That sounded perfect to me. Then I asked her for a couple of references.

Thelma gave me the name of someone and said, "I took care of his mother for several years."

I called the number Thelma had given me for a reference. Once I had introduced myself to the gentleman who answered the phone, I explained, "I understand that Thelma took care of your mom for many years, up until a few years ago."

"Oh, yes...Thelma!" he said. "She was like a gift from G-d!"

Well, I thought to myself, *you can't get a better reference than that!*

"And don't worry," he continued, "it's not a problem."

I didn't catch on right away. "What's not a problem?"

"Have you met Thelma yet?" he asked.

"Sure, we met at a coffee shop and talked."

"Well, then you know what I'm talking about. I'm telling you, it's not a problem."

The lightbulb went on in my head. And I would discover that he was right. Even though Thelma was seventy-two, she could handle Janie with an arm and a half as well as I ever could with two arms. Not only that, but she turned out to be an absolutely wonderful person with a warm, caring, maternal way about her. She became so dear to our family, I have maintained a friendship with her over the years, and take her to lunch regularly.

Before I introduced Janie and Thelma, I needed to make sure that Annie and Thelma hit it off. If the two of them didn't get along, I wouldn't have even introduced Thelma to Janie.

Annie is very southern, having grown up in Montezuma, Georgia, about an hour and a half south of us. She is the mother of eight children and once worked as a laundress in New York.

Six of Annie's eight children went to school and got master's degrees. Three or four of Annie's sons had their college educations financed by a childless couple who lived next door to them. Annie's boys used to help the couple with groceries and lawn care, and the couple became very fond of the children. When the time came for them to go to college, the couple wanted to give them the gift of a college education—something otherwise beyond their reach.

Annie would end up becoming such an integral part of our family, her "first lady" nickname for Janie would appear on Janie's grave marker.

"You'd better handle Janie with kid gloves," Annie told Thelma, "because I'll be here watching. And remember, she's the first lady in this house!"

This cautionary note was touching but unnecessary. Thelma was golden. Not surprisingly, Annie immediately liked Thelma and they became fast friends.

I had a set routine with Janie, one that had become more involved than ever. I would get her up in the morning, take her in to use the bathroom, clean her up afterwards, put her in the shower, get her dressed, and put her into her wheelchair. Then I wheeled her out into the living room.

I always parked Janie's wheelchair next to the couch and turned on the T.V. To this day, I have no idea how much of what was happening on the T.V. was actually grasped by Janie. I do know that, whether it was the colors, the movement, or the sound, there was something about it that seemed pleasing to her.

Meanwhile, our dog Sidney, a Bichon-Shih Tzu mix, nicknamed Pookie by Annie, would hop up on the couch and put his head on Janie's leg. He stuck by Janie's side for the entire day, except for those times when Annie took him outside to do his business. He was the most faithful, loyal companion ever. (When Janie finally passed away, Pookie stood in the bedroom for two weeks, staring at the bed. I believe that if he could have talked, he would have said, "Where did my mommy go?" It was horrible.)

The day that I brought Thelma over to the house to meet Janie (after Thelma and Annie had hit it off), I told Janie, "I want to introduce you to Thelma. She's a caretaker and she's going to come over and help me on those days when I'm tired and worn out...if you two get along. I'm sure you will. She's a lovely lady."

Thelma went over to Janie and wrapped her arms around her in a hug, and then moved around to the back of her and began rubbing her shoulders.

Janie's delight was written all over her face. I felt like she wanted to say, "Oh, this is so nice!"

Thelma and Janie both shared that same high-wattage luminosity. They truly lit up the room wherever they went. The only difference was that, before her illness, Janie's was more of the raging-ball-of-fire variety whereas Thelma's was more of a calm and quiet sunbeam.

I left the two of them to have a little chat, and went to sit outside for a while. Thelma took a seat on the couch and talked to Janie for an hour, bonding with her. When it was time for Thelma to leave, she turned to Janie and said, "See you tomorrow...if that's okay."

Janie smiled. In fact, she was beaming. She was clearly happy knowing that Thelma would be returning to be with her.

Annie, meanwhile, was a short distance behind Janie during all of this, keeping a protective eye out. Janie may have been first lady but there was no question that Annie was the boss of the household. Thelma would have been shown the door if Annie felt that she got out of line in any way.

Both Annie and I were thrilled to see how warm and kind Thelma was to Janie and how Janie lit up in Thelma's presence.

Initially, I would only have Thelma's help on Mondays. Later, I added Wednesdays and Fridays. I would continue to take care of Janie on Tuesdays, Thursdays, evenings and weekends.

(For those of you looking after your loved ones with dementia at home, I want to note that the state provided zero assistance when it came to bringing a caregiver into the home. I would be paying for it entirely out of my own pocket. They do provide financial assistance for hospice, when it gets to that point. For the first year the patient is in hospice, you have to recertify the patient every six months. At the end of the first year, if the patient is going to continue, they have to be recertified monthly.)

One day during the years that Thelma was Janie's caregiver, Thelma came to me and told me that she was being honored that Sunday as a mother in her church.

I asked her to clarify exactly what that meant and then expressed my regrets. "I'm so sorry, Thelma, but on Sundays I have Janie by myself. I wish I could get there but I don't see how."

Thelma let me know that she understood and we left it at that.

Then, I called my boys. After talking it over with Drew, he agreed to provide coverage for that Sunday. On the morning of the event, I wasn't sure what to wear. Drew said, "A tie and a jacket, Dad. You're never overdressed for church."

So, I donned a sports jacket and tie. I drove to the church and, as I pulled into the parking lot, I noticed Thelma's car. I was happy to see that she had already arrived.

I walked up to the front door of the church, and told a man in a wonderful robin's-egg-blue suit, who was greeting at the door, "I'm Bob Fischbach and I'm here to see Thelma honored as a mother of the church."

"Oh, come on in!" he said. "The service hasn't started yet." He couldn't have been more welcoming.

Then he called over an usher and told him that I was there to see Thelma. The usher said, "That's Thelma down there in the first row in the big hat."

Sure enough, I spotted Thelma in a big festive hat with a two-foot-wide brim. I started walking down the aisle toward her. As I got close, Thelma's husband saw me and nudged her.

Thelma swung around, saw me, and let out a squeal of delight. She came up to me and gave me a big hug and then said, "You're sitting with me!"

As the service began and the congregation started singing, I was stunned. The quality of the singing was so excellent, I felt like I was listening to a recording or the radio.

Then the pastor started honoring Thelma. After speaking for a little while, he invited her to join him onstage.

In the course of her remarks onstage, Thelma talked about Janie and me and said how wonderful we had been to her. It was very moving. When she finished speaking, she received a plaque from the minister. The congregation even made financial gifts to Thelma. The envelopes all went into a designated cardboard box, covered in wrapping paper.

I walked up to the minister and said, "Do you mind if I say a few words?"

"No, not at all!" he said.

So, I took the microphone and started telling a story about Thelma and Janie.

"What a wonderful human being," I said. "I've never known anybody like her. She takes care of my wife, who has a terminal illness, like her own child. I can't imagine how I got this lucky."

I also talked about how I found Thelma, and recalled the day she walked into the coffee shop and lit up the place with her smile. As I spoke, I became emotional and tears started to flow.

As I finished speaking, the preacher spoke in my ear. "Young man, you can preach in this church any time you like!"

A year or two later when Thelma's daughter-in-law passed away, I made a surprise visit to the funeral. The service was held at a different church this time. I went inside and found a seat off to the side. Once again, I was the only pale face in the crowd.

When the service wrapped up, as everyone started to file out, Thelma saw me.

She came over and hugged and kissed me, saying, "You're not walking out of here alone! Hell, no! You're walking out of here with me." Then she had me walk out with the rest of the family.

In 2010, six years into Janie's illness, I would realize that the time had come to bring in someone to help me with Janie occasionally in the evenings. Since my wife and I could no longer communicate at all, and she was no longer really present in terms of her personality, I craved the company of adults. I also needed to get out of the house from time to time to preserve my sanity. By having someone come over and relieve me on occasional evenings, I was able to meet up with friends.

The evening caregiver was a thirty-two-year-old woman named LaDeanna (but she went by Deanna, which was pronounced Dena). She too was absolutely wonderful—another gift from G-d. She worked days for Weinstein Hospice. She had taken care of a dear friend's father before his passing. So, I had a great reference on her.

Thankfully, Janie took to Deanna just like she took to Thelma. Had Janie not been so comfortable with these caregivers I had brought into the house, I'm not sure what I would have done.

One day, I was talking to the director of Weinstein Hospice, and she asked me, "Who do you have looking after Janie?"

When I told her about Thelma and Deanna, he said, "My, G-d! How did you put together that all-star cast?"

"I don't know," I admitted. "I just got lucky, I guess."

Over the years, I would come to understand that being a caregiver is truly a calling. In order to take care of perfect strangers, and do so with your whole heart, you have to be a very special person.

Having such caring, wonderful caregivers to help me was an immense blessing. Yet, it didn't really alter my basic reality. I was still living with, and caring for, a wife who was slowly dying of a hideous disease, and was for all practical purposes, already gone. And at the same time, I was trying to be there for my loved ones and deal with the challenges of life and loss.

Within a year of retiring, both my mother and brother died. Two years after that, Drew got divorced and my sister moved to Atlanta to get ready to die. Before Janie's illness finally reached the end, I would also bury my sister and attend the weddings of both my sons.

As Janie's illness progressed, and her personality and essence steadily receded, I became more and more disillusioned and started questioning G-d.

I knew that Janie was not a bad person, and I didn't think I was a bad person either. I would ask myself, *So, why is G-d punishing us? And why the hell does Janie's illness have to be going on for so many years?*

My unanswered questions festered until they turned into anger. When Janie first got sick, I would ask G-d, "What is this all about? Are you punishing Janie for something she did? Or, punishing me for something I did?"

Then when my brother, mother and sister got sick and passed, I asked G-d, "Did my *entire family* get involved in something you don't like? Are you taking your anger out on us for some reason? What the hell is this all about?"

I still haven't reconciled all of this. And, to this day, G-d and I are not exactly on speaking terms, although I study with an Orthodox rabbi and attend annual kaddish services for my entire family.

Questions about whether and why G-d was punishing Janie, me and perhaps our entire family sometimes led me back to the Holocaust. I wondered about the thousands of Jews who were killed, and thought about the hideous way they died.

I asked myself, *What in the world is G-d doing, exactly? What's the game plan? I don't get it.*

My situation with Janie really threw me for a loop and threatened my faith. I understand that people die. And, G-d willing, when it's my time to go, I will fall asleep and simply not awaken the following morning. But I have never understood the purpose of protracted suffering and the grief it brings, both to the person suffering and their entire family.

Speaking of protracted suffering, it was becoming more and more clear to me that the medications the doctors were giving Janie were just prolonging her suffering. Of course, they were prescribed with the best of intentions—but they were prolonging her suffering nonetheless.

In the early stages of Janie's illness, her doctors were giving her the exact same medications they had been giving people for twenty-five years prior. There had been no advancements in all that time. These medications were ostensibly given to slow the illness long enough to allow for the possibility of a miracle cure. Hopefully there will be one soon, as there is an increase in the number of people with all forms of dementia.

As I mentioned earlier, if I had it do all over again, I would have elected not to give Janie medications that simply prolonged her suffering—and mine. Over the years of caring for my beloved wife, I developed a strong belief that euthanasia should be given as an option to terminal patients. I believe that everyone should have the right to end their life.

I would watch my wife suffering, feel the life draining out of me, and think, *Janie's got a death sentence here. So, what are we doing, exactly? What's the purpose of keeping her alive once she's lost all cognitive ability? Where is Dr. Kevorkian when we need him?*

Thirty-Six

Thankfully, both of my sons were wonderful during the many years of their mother's long illness. They went above and beyond what was expected, and were there for me for whatever, whenever. Even when I didn't really want company, they were there anyway, making sure I got the support I needed and didn't get too isolated.

I couldn't have asked for two greater children. It was ironic that I had initially tried protecting them from the realities of their mother's illness, and then they turned the tables by becoming protective of me.

Drew began dating a woman named Nina. I felt that things between them were moving a little too fast so I had a talk with my son and aired my concerns. It wasn't that I objected to Nina on any personal basis. At the time, I had not yet spent enough time with her to form an opinion one way or another. I just felt that it was awfully soon for my son to be getting serious with anyone.

"Why are you doing this so fast after that horrible experience you just got through?" I asked, referring to his divorce. "Play the field a little bit!"

Obviously smitten, Drew said, "Dad, it's different with Nina. This time, I'm really in love!"

Every year in the spring or summer, I rent a house at the beach for the family. We go down for a week and spend some time relaxing and enjoying the beach and the company of each other. That particular year, I even managed to get Janie in the car. By the time of our annual family trip, Drew had been dating Nina for six months and he brought her along. I had gotten to know Nina a little bit by then and had a good feeling about her.

While we were there, Drew and Nina announced that they were planning to marry at the beach in six weeks. It would be the second marriage for them both. I had already given my blessing on the marriage under the condition that any children that came from the marriage would be raised Jewish.

Nina is an incredibly organized girl, so as we were all sitting around discussing wedding plans, she went online and did some research. She quickly discovered that the house we were renting and the one next door were both going to be available for their wedding six weeks later.

Nina reserved both houses for the wedding—one for her family and one for mine. (They were planning a small wedding with forty-eight guests in total, comprised mostly of a few close friends and family.) Six weeks after our annual trip to the beach, everyone returned for the wedding.

The wedding day, October 24th, 2009, dawned cloudy and rainy. The weather was so miserable, we were in the midst of making plans to move the ceremony to an indoor hotel with a banquet facility. (Or, I should say that Nina was making the plans, as she was the one organizing everything.) Suddenly, the clouds lifted, the rain stopped and the sun came out. It turned out to be the perfect day for a wedding.

If you'll recall, the first time that Drew got married, I had a very bad feeling about the union. Thankfully, I had a good feeling about this wedding. Over time, it would become obvious that Drew had chosen his second wife well. Their romance and engagement had been short but they have been happily married ever since. They have one child of their own and a daughter from Nina's former marriage. And they just celebrated their ninth wedding anniversary.

Somewhere along the line—perhaps thanks to the love of Nina!—Drew matured into the ultimate husband and father. He left his wild days behind him. It warmed my heart to see my oldest son embrace his new role as a husband and father.

Since I had a good feeling about the woman Drew was marrying, I wanted Janie to be present and decided to bring her along. In so doing, I was committing myself to taking care of her grooming and dressing, just as I had been doing for her at home. I did not bring a caregiver with me to help with Janie, so I definitely had my hands full.

When it was time for us all to head down to the beach for the ceremony, I managed to get my wife on her feet. She was not moving very fast but, with my help, she was able to walk. I had her portable wheelchair with us just in case, but Janie would have thrown a fit if I'd tried to put her in the wheelchair for the wedding. Thankfully, the two houses we had rented were right on the beach. It was a short walk down to the area where the ceremony was being held.

Drew's wedding to his second wife was along semi-conventional lines, thank G-d. Whereas the first wedding had been held in a nightclub, this second wedding was a beach wedding—but they had a rabbi, a chuppah and the whole nine yards. Thanks to my dear friend, Rabbi Phil Kranz, I found a local rabbi to officiate the wedding.

The wedding came off beautifully with glorious weather as a backdrop. Everyone was dressed up but barefoot in the sand—the men in suits and ties, and the women in gorgeous dresses. Janie and I walked Drew down the aisle with him between Janie and me. Scott was the best man.

After I had walked Janie down the aisle, I circled back around and walked Nina down the aisle. To my great surprise, Nina had asked me if I would do the honors.

"I would be honored to do it," I told her, "as long as I wouldn't be upsetting anyone else in the family who might be expecting to be asked to walk you down the aisle."

She said, "Absolutely not. There's nobody I want to walk me down the aisle, other than you."

The reception was held in the second of the two houses rented for the occasion. It was a lovely affair, with music and dancing on the patio. The highlight of the reception for me was seeing my sons dancing with their mother for the last time.

Thirty-Seven

Once Drew and Nina were married, they moved into Nina's house—a lovely house in North Gwinnett County with a backyard overlooking the lake. They invited the entire family over to their house for Mother's Day of 2010, several months after the wedding.

At the time of that invitation, it had been about a month or so since I had seen Randee. When I saw her at Drew and Nina's for Mother's Day, my heart sank. She was very sick and getting worse by the day.

The fact that she was dying was clear from looking at her, and yet she persisted in keeping her medical condition a secret from her son, Alex. My nephew was witnessing the deterioration of his mother. Since Randee refused to talk to him about it directly, Alex was left with only his impressions of what was happening.

I had just buried my mother and my brother, and was enduring a daily nightmare with my declining wife. To see my sister dying, and know that I would soon be burying her as well, added a lot of grief to my already heavy burden.

We were all scheduled to head to the beach in June. The Monday before we were to leave, Randee called me. "I'm not going to make it to the beach. Do you think maybe it's a good idea for me to check into hospice for the week you're gone so I won't be alone?"

Right away, alarm bells went off in my head. My sister never asked for my opinion (or anyone else's) on anything. She was an extremely headstrong and independent person and didn't feel she needed help from anyone. So, I knew that her situation had to be dire for her to be asking me such a question. I wondered if it was an indication that she knew she only had a few days to live.

"That's a great idea, Randee," I said. "That way you can be sure to be taken care of."

At that point, I realized that there was no way I could leave Randee and go to the beach. We cancelled the trip and none of us went. We were all due to leave that Saturday. On Monday evening, Randee went into hospice.

During the weeks prior to my sister going into hospice, I kept trying to convince her to tell Alex that she didn't have long to live.

"Randee, you've got to tell Alex!" I said. "It's not fair to keep it from him. He's a grown man and he can take it. He needs to know. It's just not right. You're leaving him in my care and it's not fair to me either."

"I can't do it. I can't tell him," she said. Randee was afraid to tell her son that she was dying. In admitting she was dying, it would become real for her. And yet, she was freely using the word hospice.

"Okay, well, if you're not going to tell him," I said, "I'm going to tell him myself. One of us has to tell him... and now! I'm not going to be left dealing with this situation after the fact." (At the time of this conversation, Alex was twenty years old.)

Randee didn't argue with me. She realized that Alex needed to be told and she couldn't get up the nerve to tell him herself.

I left Randee in the apartment and took Alex outside. "Let's take a walk," I said.

"Okay, Uncle Bob," he said.

"Alex," I said, "I want to make sure you realize that your mom is really sick. She's not going to live very much longer. She doesn't have the strength to tell you but you need to know. So, I'm telling you."

He looked at me and said, "I thought so but Mom never said anything to me."

"...I want you to know," I continued, "that we're all here for you. In fact, that's one of the main reasons your mom moved down here. She wanted you to have family close by. We are your family and we are here for you. Never forget that."

As Alex and I parted, he was teary-eyed and I was miserable.

My sister passed away on Thursday, June 16th, 2010, only three days after she entered hospice. Randee's memorial service was attended only by our family and a few close personal friends. By the time of her death, my sister had only been living in the Atlanta area for a couple of years and had not made any new local friends. She did have one friend from Great Neck, Laurie, who happened to live in Atlanta with her husband. Laurie and Randee had been best friends since elementary school.

Afterwards we had shiva, mostly in the evenings for three nights. Since Janie was bed-bound and wheelchair-bound by then and in no shape to receive guests, our house wasn't suitable for shiva. A very good friend of mine who was aware of Janie's condition, kindly offered her house.

Of course, I mourned my sister long after the three-day shiva. We were close at the time of her death, just as we had always been. Other than Randee's reticence to ask my opinion, and the fact that she was a dyed-in-the-wool liberal while I am a conservative, we had a great relationship.

As an interesting side note, a couple of months ago, Alex was contacted on Facebook by someone claiming to be his biological half-brother. All signs pointed to it being true. He was also contacted by his biological half-sister. (Oddly, Alex's name on Facebook is Alex Harrison, not Alex Fischbach, so it's anyone's guess how they found him.)

"Look," I told Alex, "this is not an emergency. You don't have to decide today. Take some time and think it over. Decide whether you want to find out who they are, what they are about and, whether you want to enter into a relationship with them. It's a big decision."

Ultimately, Alex decided that he didn't want to pursue meeting his biological half-siblings—or finding his bio-parents. He had a serious girlfriend by then and good solid ground under his feet, and didn't feel like there was a void he needed to fill.

Sometime after Randee's death but prior to Alex's biological half-siblings reaching out to him, I had said to Alex, "Look, if you want to find your biological parents, I will do some discreet inquiries for you. You don't want to show up on someone's doorstep and ruin their family's life by blindsiding them, or get the door slammed in your face."

What I didn't reveal to Alex was that I had the phone number of his biological grandfather—the one Randee had met with before Alex's birth.

With the death of Randee came the dawning awareness that every single member of my family of origin was now gone—and all of them had died of cancer. It was a lonely and spooky feeling. About that time, I started glancing over my shoulder to see if I could catch a glimpse of the grim reaper sneaking up on me. He had already caught everyone else in my family.

I would think to myself, *Thank goodness my boys aren't my biological kids. Hopefully they'll be spared. But if they do end up getting cancer someday, it won't come from my genes! And if, G-d forbid, either of the boys were to get FTD, it won't come from Janie's genes!*

In the years following Janie's diagnosis, I would often wonder if maybe G-d had his hand on our family when he guided Janie and me toward adoption. New research shows that frontotemporal dementia may be hereditary. I would not wish that fate on anyone, and least of all my own children.

Thirty-Eight

Randee passed in June of 2010. A couple of months later in August, the checks I had been routinely receiving from my former business partner for his buyout of my share of the business suddenly stopped coming. So, I called my former partner at the office.

"What happened? Where's the check?" I asked.

"Listen," he said, "I need to renegotiate this deal. It's not good for me anymore."

"What do you mean you need to renegotiate?" I asked, incredulous. "I have a signed document with your signature on it!"

"Well, that's too bad."

"But that was our deal and you signed a contract with me! And if you'll remember, it was you who came up with the last offer on the negotiation."

"I don't care. It's not working for me anymore. So, you can either negotiate, mediate or litigate," he said.

"I'll take litigate," I said and hung up the phone.

As I hung up the phone, I thought, *He knows the position I'm in with Janie slowly dying, and he would do this to me now?*

So much for being amicable former business partners! That's all we had ever been—business partners.

We had never been close friends or socialized as couples. We sent each other those strippers on our fortieth birthdays but that was about the extent of our social interaction.

Business partnerships can be just as bad or worse than marriages when they go bad. I knew I was going to need legal counsel. So, I immediately went out and retained an attorney to handle the matter. We conferred, I showed him the documents signed by my former business partner and me, and then I told him, "I want to bury that miserable S.O.B.!"

My former business partner and I had formed a limited partnership to purchase the properties we bought, and also formed a limited partnership for the management company that operated those properties. I happened to be the president of both.

I called a meeting of the board of directors of the limited partnership. My partner was out of town but he joined the meeting by phone conference. We had a vote to remove him as vice president, with him not only listening but voting on his own behalf.

After winning the vote two to one, I wrote a thirty-day-termination letter to the management company, terminating the management agreement between the two companies. Thirty days later, I went to the office, changed all the locks and took over everything. I also went to the bank as one of the signatories on the account, and paid myself all the money owed to me from the time my former partner stopped paying me through that day. From then on, I took the management fee and paid myself out of that going forward.

I filed a lawsuit against my former partner for stealing my money and as a way to prevent him from any further shenanigans. Yes, I had already paid myself back from our joint bank account, but I felt he still needed to be held accountable.

I then brought in my son Scott to run the business. We locked my former business partner out of the business. At last, the partnership was severed, and I couldn't have been happier about it.

I received a letter from my former partner's attorney stating that he had moved his office into the apartment complex and would like all of his personal belongs returned—his desk chair, files, everything.

Through my attorney, I responded stating that I would be happy to return his personal belongings if he could show me a bill of sale proving that he had purchased the items he was requesting.

There was one property my former partner and I still owned between us. The property mortgage was coming up for refinance in June of 2013, about eight or nine months from then. I was either going to have to sell or refinance the property. I decided to pursue both tracks, selling and refinancing, and see where I got traction before the deadline.

As it turned out, I got a contract offer to purchase the property. Prior to the June, 2013 closing on the property, I had asked my former business partner to sign the listing agreement for sale with the agent and look over the refinancing document. He refused to do either and even made a point of leaving town just before the closing of the sale.

He was operating under the assumption that by failing to be present to sign the closing documents, he would stop the sale from closing. He had no particular reason for trying to sabotage the deal. He was simply being an ass and trying to make a point—that I couldn't do anything without him.

He was essentially throwing a tantrum. He wanted what he wanted. In order to get it, he was willing to take advantage of me when I was in a very weakened position, thanks to caring for my dying wife. I was not about to stand for it. (Thanks, Dad, for teaching me to stand up for myself and never let anybody push me around!)

My former partner was mistaken in his belief that his signature was required. I had the authority to handle the closing on my own.

On the day of the closing, my former partner would call in to the office of my attorney, Eric, where the closing was being held.

Eric told his secretary to say that he was too busy to get on the phone. Then, turning to me, he said, "He needs to learn that when he steps off the globe, it keeps spinning."

The sale on the property closed as planned and I distributed the money as provided for in the documents. My former business partner got everything he had coming to him. So did the limited-partner investors. And, so did I—no thanks to him!

Thirty-Nine

One day not long after the debacle with my former business partner began in 2010, one of my sons said to me, "Hey, Dad, let's all have lunch—just the three of us."

I said, "Sure. Where do you two want to go? I'll pay." That was nothing new; I liked to treat the boys and pick up the check whenever we went out to eat.

As we were sitting over lunch, talking, Drew said to me, "Dad, what are you going to do with the rest of your life? It's been over six years since Mom's diagnosis."

I looked at Drew, not understanding the question. "Well, between cooking, cleaning, shopping, and taking care of Mom at home, I don't have time to think about the rest of my life!"

Drew said, "You look and think young, you're active, and you need to start thinking outside the box."

Drew was doing all the talking and Scott was nodding in agreement.

Finally, I said, "Thinking outside the box? What do you mean?"

Those words were hanging in the air and I was trying to grasp their meaning. Then it hit me. "Are you guys giving me permission to start *dating*? Is that what this is all about?"

I couldn't imagine what else the boys could be talking about with the whole thinking-outside-the-box line of conversation. I knew they couldn't be talking about bringing in caregivers to help me. I had already done that.

"Well, not really, Dad..." they said in unison, "but we wanted you to know that whatever decision you make, you'll get no judgment from us."

I have always had a very good relationship with my kids. I can say anything to them and they can say anything to me. What they said about withholding judgment was probably the most loving thing they could have said to me.

At the time of this conversation, Janie was in really bad shape. It was becoming more and more obvious that the end was coming on fast. I was hyperaware of this fact and the kids knew it too. We would turn out to be right. Janie only had another couple of years to live.

My sons saw me heading toward my own demise as a result of giving everything in me to take care of their mother. They were watching me go down the drain, and they knew that something had to be done. They were both crazy about their mother and were heartbroken over slowly losing her—but they didn't want to lose me too.

In saying what they said to me, the boys were letting me know that they recognized what was happening to me, and completely understood if I needed some support to help me through the miserable nightmare of the end stages of Janie's illness.

Before the boys brought up the subject, the thought of bringing another woman into my life for support had never occurred to me. In every way, I remained devoted to the care of my beloved wife—and we *were* still married. But Janie had long ceased being able to connect with me on any meaningful level.

As we finished lunch, and walked to our cars, I was blown away and my head was spinning. Although I knew there was merit and wisdom to my sons' suggestion, the thought was almost more than I could fathom. I had been married to the woman I dearly loved for my entire adult life. It seemed outlandish to start dating other women.

I thought to myself, *I don't know where on earth that idea came from! It really came out of the blue.*

It took me six months of grappling with it before I could even consider it. During that period, I would go back and forth internally. I would think, *Maybe that's not such a bad idea. Maybe I should start dating. I am exhausted and worn out from going it alone.*

Then, I would ask myself, *Would I be cheating on my wife if I started dating? Do I even have a wife anymore? Or am I just a nurse to someone who is barely existing?*

One day around that time, it finally hit me, *She's still here physically but she's barely existing. She's not living anymore.*

In the final analysis, I concluded that while my wife was quickly disappearing, I was still alive. And, for all intents and purposes, I was living without a wife. She wasn't there any longer, except in the most basic physical sense.

Once I had made an uneasy peace with the idea of dating, another thought occurred to me. *I have been with Janie for forty-eight years, including dating and marriage. Can I even talk to another woman at this point? And will I be able to find a woman who wants to go out with me?*

I decided that my best bet would be to try to reconnect with women I had dated in high school and college. I figured that way, I wouldn't be starting from scratch, trying to break the ice with strangers. It would be easier to talk to people with whom I already had a history. I wasn't even thinking about romance at that point. I simply wanted to have a social life again, and to enjoy a woman's company.

One night after I had put Janie to bed and finished cleaning up the kitchen, I sat down to relax and started thinking to myself, *Well, if I'm going to do this, I guess I'd better get started. Delaying isn't going to make things any easier.*

I got my bearings by briefly reconnecting with a couple of women from my past, starting with my high school sweetheart. These encounters were not disastrous and in fact went fairly smoothly. They brightened my eyes and restored my confidence enough that

I felt ready to dip a toe into the local dating pool. I had proven to myself that I hadn't lost my ability to connect with a woman, despite how strange it felt to do so after being married for so long.

In March of 2011, I got an invitation from Jeff, my best friend since fourth grade. He and his wife Judy were celebrating their forty-fifth wedding anniversary jointly with her sixty-fifth birthday. Both Janie and I had attended their daughter's wedding. Typically, I would not have left Janie and flown to California for this type of event. In this case, though, I desperately needed to get away and spend some time in a different environment.

I arranged caregivers for Janie, took a flight to San Diego and went to the party. I knew almost everybody there, including Jeff's brother and some other members of their family. I had known them all since Jeff and I were kids. Despite the ease that came with being around people I had known for so long, I felt more miserable than I'd ever felt at a social gathering. To be at this party without my wife left me feeling unbearably lonely, and drove home the reality of my situation.

I left the party early and went back to my hotel. I was supposed to return to their house the following morning for brunch but I couldn't bear it. So, I called when I woke up and told them that I wasn't feeling particularly well. It was true—I was miserable. Then I called the airline.

When I got back to Atlanta, I thought to myself, *That trip was a preview of what awaits me when Janie's gone! Maybe I really am doing the right thing by starting to date. If I don't, Janie's going to pass someday and I am going to be facing an awfully lonely future by myself.*

Forty

Shortly after my trip to California, Scott, who was thirty-four at the time, told me that he and his girlfriend, Jaime, had gotten quite serious and he was getting ready to propose marriage to her.

The two had met in Seattle while they were both there on business. Jaime worked for a marketing and advertising company that was doing some work for the real estate company that employed Scott. She is an attractive redhead from Baltimore, with a strong mind and heart, and one sibling—a sister.

Jaime also happens to be a warm, caring Catholic girl but she's not very observant. Her sister is an observant Catholic but is married to a Jewish guy whose last name is Epstein. The girls' parents are both observant Catholics.

Scott and Jaime seemed to be a good match. When she began coming over to visit Janie, I knew that my initial gut instinct about her was right. She is a wonderful person. I was glad that my son had found such a substantial, caring woman. I had only one concern.

"I approve of this marriage," I told them, "on one condition. I want a promise that any grandchildren will be raised Jewish."

"I understand what you're saying," said Jaime. "And, I promise. If and when we have children, they will be raised Jewish."

When they agreed, I was relieved. I could now give my full stamp of approval to the marriage.

Thinking about Scott proposing to Jaime got me to thinking. Over the years, Janie had acquired quite a collection of jewelry from yours truly. Our long marriage had been filed with life milestones—holidays, birthdays, anniversaries—and I often gave her jewelry as a gift. I can't remember the occasion, but on one special occasion, I had a cocktail ring designed for Janie. It was white platinum with several diamonds in it.

I told Scott, "Here...I want you to have Mom's ring. The big diamond in the middle was from her original engagement ring. Use that diamond and have it reset. Feel free to use the side diamonds, as well. My dad gave me the diamond and I am giving it to you. '*L'dor, v'dor,*' as they say. From generation to generation."

"But, Dad," said Scott, "Mom loved that ring...and you made it for her! I can't take that ring apart."

That was classic Scott. He is one of the sweetest human beings G-d ever created. But, while I appreciated his hesitation to accept Janie's ring, I really wanted him to have it. I knew that his mother would have wanted it too if she had been in any condition to weigh in on the subject.

As I watched Janie's health decline, I had been asking myself what I was going to do with her jewelry collection. It made me happy to know that her cocktail ring would have such a meaningful second life as Jaime's engagement ring.

"I'll tell you what," I said to Scott, "why don't you just give the ring to Jaime as an engagement ring, and let her decide what to do with it. Remember, it's a cocktail ring, not an engagement ring. So, she may want to have it made into an engagement ring. In any case, if you give her the ring and let her decide, you won't have to feel like you're taking your mom's ring apart."

Scott was often in Washington, D.C. on business. One night he and Jaime were out to dinner in D.C. when he asked her to marry him. Scott gave Jaime the ring and she loved it. To this day, she has not altered the ring in any way.

Scott's engagement took me back to Drew's 2008 engagement to Nina. It was an event I will never forget. Drew invited Janie and me to a restaurant to meet him and his soon-to-be-fiancé, Nina, for dinner.

"Dad, could you pick up Nina's engagement ring for me and bring it to the restaurant?" he asked. "It will be ready but I'm not going to have time to get it."

"Sure," I said. "I'll ask you to come out to the car to sign some documents and slip it to you that way."

I picked up the ring during the day and had it with me when Janie and I arrived at the restaurant. We all got a table, had a drink or two, and enjoyed some conversation over cocktails. Then, I casually said to Drew, "Oh, I almost forgot. I have some documents in the car

I need you to sign. Come out to the car with me. It will only take a minute."

When we got to the car, I gave Drew the ring.

"Dad, I can't figure out where I should propose!" he said. "The beach? The top of the Empire State Building? I just can't make up my mind."

I said, "We'd better get back inside if we don't want to raise any eyebrows. You can decide later. At least now you have the ring."

When we got back into the booth in the restaurant, I could see Drew visibly shaking. His entire body was vibrating under the effect of the ring he had hidden in his pocket.

"I can't stand it anymore!" he said, producing the ring from his pocket. "Nina, I want to ask you to marry me..."

So much for Drew's ideas about proposing at some historic or exotic location. He was so anxious to get that ring on Nina's finger, all his plans for the proposal went right out the window.

Nina was shocked when she heard the proposal and started to cry tears of happiness.

Drew later explained to me, "I couldn't stand it, having that ring in my pocket and not proposing!"

The fact that Drew felt completely comfortable proposing in front of Janie and me was a testament to the close relationship between Janie and me and both of our boys.

After the proposal, the happy couple excused themselves so they could go into the parking lot and have a few private moments to kiss, hug, and celebrate their engagement. After a few minutes, they returned to the restaurant and we all had dinner.

A couple of months after Scott proposed to Jaime, he came to me and said, "Dad will you come to D.C. and help me pick out a place for the rehearsal dinner?"

The wedding was to be held at the W Hotel in Washington, D.C. Scott and I flew up there, arriving around lunchtime.

Scott told me that he was taking me to the restaurant where he and Jaime had their first date, and that she would be meeting us there.

When we got there, a surprise guest was waiting for me: Chaim. He was a member of a family of Russian Jewish immigrants that Janie and I had sponsored in May of 1990. That was the period of time when there was a mass exodus of Jews from Russia to the United States and Israel. Russia finally permitted these refuseniks, as they were called, to leave the country rather than permit them to openly practice Judaism. This was shortsighted of the Russian government; when they lost their Jews, they lost some of their most skilled and talented citizens.

As a side note, I had spent eight days in Russia in my capacity as a representative of the Atlanta Jewish Federation. It was 1986 and I was there on a missionary trip of sorts. We were visiting Russian Jews who wanted to leave the country but were not permitted to do so. We met with them one on one, had dinner in their homes, and brought them medicine. We also brought them copies of a magazine containing an article about a journalist who had been arrested in Russia the previous week. The story had gotten a lot of attention in the media.

Before we left for the trip, a woman who represented The National Conference of Soviet Jewry told us, "Once you've arrived and checked in with the American embassy, we lose all control of you. You're on your own. There will be people there who will be trying to intimidate you into not talking to any of the refuseniks."

As we went through Customs when entering Russia, we were instructed to form three lines. The Customs agents dealing with those in my line rifled through our suitcases, took the magazines, ripped out the article, returned the magazines and our luggage to us, and ushered us through. Those in the second line had the magazine confiscated. And those in the third line were allowed to pass through with the magazine intact.

I never did understand the criteria the Customs agents were using to make these determinations. It all seemed random to me. They never even stamped my passport. When I arrived, they put a piece of paper inside my passport and when I left, they removed it. There is no evidence I was ever even there.

Anyway, in 1990 when Russia finally permitted Jews to leave the country, these immigrants were relocated all over the United States and Israel, and many came to Atlanta. I was very involved with the Jewish Federation in Atlanta at the time, so I was asked if Janie and I would sponsor a family of Russian Jewish immigrants. This entailed helping them get settled into American life and learn their way around Atlanta. It did not involve financial sponsorship.

We agreed, and went to the Atlanta airport to meet them as they got off the plane. Four generations of the family had arrived. Among them was the grandmother, Babushka, who was in her mid-seventies. She had all silver teeth and was in a three-hundred-pound wheelchair. Babushka had spent the previous twenty-five or thirty years in Siberia, where she had to visit her husband in prison. He was imprisoned for being one of the original refuseniks. Sadly, he passed away while behind bars.

Then there was Avina, Babushka's daughter. She was a brilliant woman and a physician for the Bolshoi Ballet. Inna, the granddaughter of Babushka held a Ph.D. in languages. She was the one I mentioned earlier—the Russian woman who helped me secure my mother's citizenship papers.

Inna's husband, Leonid, had a Ph.D. in geology. Leonid would become a tenured professor at Georgia Tech within three years of starting to teach there. Leonid and Inna had two children—a daughter from her first marriage named Anna and a son between them whose given name was Gene. These were Babushka's great-grandchildren.

I gave Gene the nickname Chaim as his Jewish name, and it stuck. When he became a bar mitzvah, he took the name of Chaim. I became very close with the entire family. I helped them find an apartment and get settled. They also had their hearts set on getting an automobile, as cars were scarce in Russia and few Russians owned one. So, I told them that I would help them find a used car.

One day when I was visiting them, they pulled me over to the window of their apartment and excitedly pointed to a car parked outside. The car didn't run but they loved knowing it was theirs. I helped them find a car that actually ran.

Chaim was nine years old when he arrived in the U.S. He would become one of the students in the first graduating class of the New Jewish High School in Atlanta. In college, he earned his bachelor's degree from Georgia Tech in three years, and his master's from Georgetown. He was working as a government contractor at the time of this lunch visit, and happened to have an office in the Pentagon, in a role with a high security clearance.

I like to tease Chaim, saying, "What were they thinking letting you into the Pentagon, Chaim? Don't they know you could be a Russian spy?"

When I saw Chaim waiting for Scott and me at the restaurant, I was surprised and delighted. I had remained close to the family over the years but it had been a year or more since Chaim and I had seen each other. Since he lived in D.C., it was the perfect opportunity for all of us to catch up.

After a wonderful lunch, Scott, Jaime and I looked at restaurants for the rehearsal dinner. We chose a nice Italian restaurant a couple of blocks from the W. It was convenient for the out-of-towners coming in to stay at the hotel. Then Scott showed me the site at the W Hotel where the wedding would take place.

I had decided that as long as I was on the East Coast, I would go visit my folks and my grandfather at the cemetery. I also planned to meet an old girlfriend for dinner—someone I had known from Cincinnati and dated before Janie and I got together. When Scott flew home to Atlanta, I boarded a train from D.C. to Manhattan.

While I was in the city, I met up with friends and visited the gravesites of my parents and Grandpa Julius. I also had a pleasant dinner with a woman from my past. The fact that this went well reinforced my confidence.

As I returned home to Atlanta, I had a new comfort level with the concept of entering the Atlanta dating pool. The whole idea seemed less outlandish, now that I knew I could still speak to a woman without feeling completely awkward and out of my element. (I still had it!)

Forty-One

A couple of months after returning home from my trip, it was time for Scott's wedding. His wedding date of August 19th fell between Janie's August 17th birthday and our August 21st anniversary. Sadly, Janie was just barely existing by that point in time. I was having to help her to the bathroom, bathe her, dress her and feed her.

I knew that taking her to the wedding was out of the question—and I also figured that she wouldn't have absorbed what was happening around her, even if she had been up to going. The last family event Janie had been well enough to attend was the family Mother's Day gathering during Randee's last days.

I didn't want Janie to miss our son's wedding and I started thinking about a possible workaround. That's when it hit me—a way that she could be present, physically anyway.

I called Rabbi Phil Kranz. "Would you do me a favor?" I asked, and then went on to explain what I had in mind.

He readily agreed.

Then I called Scott and said, "I know how disappointed you are that I'm not going to be able to bring Mom to D.C. for the wedding. So, I had an idea. I'm thinking of doing kind of a make-believe wedding at the house."

He said, "What did you mean, Dad?"

"We'd do it for Mom's benefit, before going to D.C. for the real wedding. I talked to Phil Kranz and he's agreed to come and perform a wedding ceremony at the house. I don't know whether Mom will realize what's going on but I want to try, just in case. I thought I would put a chuppah in the living room and then separate the furniture to create sort of an aisle I can wheel her down..."

After I explained what I had in mind, Scott liked the idea. He realized that his mom couldn't make it to D.C. for his actual wedding.

Rabbi Kranz and I had known each other for over forty years by then. Our friendship had begun in Cincinnati, continued through his early years as a rabbi, and only strengthened with time.

Phil Kranz is an amazing human being. As you might recall, I have known him since we both lived in the dorms of the Hebrew Union College in Cincinnati. I first met Phil thanks to a friend of mine from Louisville named David, whose friend Bruce Kranz came to visit him during those years. Bruce introduced me to his cousin Phil, we became good buddies and we've been friends ever since.

As he mentions in the Foreword to this book, Phil was very ill and couldn't find anyone to diagnose him while he was a student living in Cincinnati. Janie's pulmonologist cousin diagnosed, treated and cured him. It was remarkable when, through pure happenstance, Phil Kranz ended up becoming the rabbi at Temple Sinai, the synagogue to which our entire family belonged.

The fact that Rabbi Kranz had been a longstanding friend of both mine and Janie's, bar mitzvahed both my boys, and would now be officiating Scott's wedding (or the at-home simulation of it, anyway) was very meaningful to me.

I knew that the chances were slim that Janie would even know what was going on, but I wouldn't have been able to live with myself if I hadn't at least made the effort.

I brought a chuppah into our living room, and rearranged the furniture to create an aisle. I knew that I would be able to guide Janie down the aisle in her wheelchair.

By the time of Scott's make-believe wedding, Janie and I were no longer living in our dream house. I loved the house, but with the boys off and living their lives, Janie decided it was more house than we needed. So, we had sold it and now we were living in a three-bedroom house, two miles closer to downtown Sandy Springs.

Drew and Nina came to the make-believe wedding, and so did my nephew Alex. I pushed Janie down the makeshift aisle in her wheelchair. Drew and Nina, Janie and I, and Scott and Jaime were all together under the chuppah with Rabbi Kranz. The ceremony was brief and lasted no more than half an hour.

I couldn't say whether Janie was aware of what was happening or not, but it made me feel good. And who knows? On some level, Janie may have understood that her son was getting married. It's not impossible.

Once we had the home wedding for Janie's benefit, it was time to head to D.C. for the actual wedding.

As I prepared to travel to Washington, D.C., I felt very heartsick. Scott's wedding date fell two days after Janie's birthday and two days before our anniversary. And yet, Janie had no idea that either of these two milestones were taking place, much less that Scott's D.C. wedding was happening. I hated knowing that I would have to attend our son's wedding without her, the staged living-room wedding notwithstanding.

I left Janie in the capable hands of our wonderful caregivers, and went to the wedding. By this point in time, I had Thelma helping me four days a week, Deanna a couple of evenings a week, and another warm, caring woman named Peaches filling in on occasional Saturdays. I was still in charge three full days a week and all nights.

The wedding was being officiated by a female rabbi and a priest from the church that Jaime's family attended. The priest was a very nice, friendly guy, and looked like a character out of a Robin Hood movie.

As I was signing the ketubah, the rabbi and I started chatting.

"Where are you from?" I asked her.

"Long Island. And, you?"

"Oh, my, G-d! That's *my* hometown!"

When we compared addresses, we discovered that she was born and raised four blocks from my childhood home.

The wedding was lovely, just as Drew's beach wedding had been. Scott's was much more formal than Drew's but every bit as warm. The bride looked gorgeous and Scott was beaming. We had a nice father-son moment as I was tying his bow tie for him.

During the wedding festivities, there were many details to consider as father of the groom, and I had my hands totally full. It wasn't until I returned home to Atlanta after the wedding that I finally had some time to feel my emotions over being there without Janie. Her absence was a harsh reminder of how much her disease had progressed.

Scott and Jaime left for their honeymoon and I got back into my normal routine, not that there was much normalcy left to my routine by then. My life remained centered around and was consumed by Janie's illness, with only brief moments of reprieve when the caregivers stepped in and gave me a break.

Forty-Two

In addition to looking after Janie, I was also focused on my nephew, Alex, who was now nineteen years old. After Randee passed, Alex became my third son.

As my sister was preparing to move to Atlanta with Alex during the end stages of her breast cancer, she had told me, "I am moving down to Atlanta because I want Alex to be around family. I am leaving him in your charge."

The thing was, my sister and I differed greatly in our methodology of raising children. Randee had raised Alex to be somewhat sheltered.

I'd told her, "Randee, you've got to let the rope out a little and let him fall and skin his knees. The world is not a piece of cake and you're not going to be around forever to take care of him..."

Now that Alex's mom was gone, it was up to me to make sure he learned how to safely navigate the ways of the world. He attended Georgia Southern, a very nice smaller college near Savannah. Alex had to contend with ADHD learning challenges. Drew had also been tested for, and found to have, learning disabilities when he was young. In looking back now, I'm pretty sure I suffered from ADD although there weren't tests for it at the time.

So, I spared no expense in bringing in tutors. I was bound and determined to give Alex the best odds at excelling in college. He and I spent a lot of time and effort. Thankfully, it paid big dividends. Helping my nephew do well in college and graduate with his degree was one of the great accomplishments of my life.

In addition to being there for Alex and caring for my dying wife, I revisited the thought of dating in Atlanta. I had already talked to Drew and Scott and told them that I thought I was going to start dating.

Given that they were the ones who had prompted me to start thinking about dating in the first place, I knew they would be fine with it. So, about a month after Scott's wedding, I arranged a date with a divorced lady who attended Temple Sinai. (A mutual acquaintance had suggested that I might want to take her out.)

In my phone conversation with the woman, I told her that I had previously belonged to Temple Sinai, and that Rabbi Kranz and I were old friends. After we hung up, the first thing I did was call Phil Kranz, who told me that the woman was a nice woman, and in fact had already called him to check *me* out.

There wasn't much between us, so that first date didn't lead anywhere. In all fairness, I'm sure I couldn't have been much fun on the date. I was too mentally, physically and emotionally exhausted at the time. Given that she was the first woman I had dated with whom I had no history, it was a bit awkward and strange getting my feet wet.

I was only getting an average of two or three hours of sleep a night, and maybe a bit more when I was lucky. Since I did not have live-in help, I was still the one taking care of my wife every night starting around ten or eleven o'clock when Deanna went home. I was also taking care of Janie all day on Tuesdays, Thursdays and most weekends, unless I had something to do.

By the time of Scott's wedding and in the months afterward, Janie was well beyond the point where she had the ability to get up and walk. So, I was no longer afraid she might wake up and wander off somewhere.

During the period of her illness when she *was* still mobile, she had wandered outside the house. One incident in particular was extremely disturbing. I had dozed off one day while sitting in a chair in our bedroom. When I woke up, Janie was gone. This was in 2007, right after I took away Janie's car. I was petrified.

When I went looking for her, I found her about four blocks away in a shopping-center parking lot. She had apparently gone into a restaurant and the staff, seeing the state she was in, called the police. A great deal of confusion ensued as a police officer tried to determine what was causing Janie's distress and what my role in it might have been.

"Officer," I said, "I completely understand if you feel you need to take my wife to the hospital. I will follow you there."

He was not sure who I was and didn't know whether to believe that I was her husband, or perhaps a part of the problem. I could see that he was in an awkward position. He asked Janie, "Is this your husband?"

Janie shook her head to indicate a "no" response.

"Do you want to come home with me?" I asked her in front of the police officer. "If not, this policeman is going to take you to the hospital. That's fine with me. I'll go with you."

When Janie heard this, she started clinging to my arm. The fact that she was going to have to go to the hospital if she didn't come home with me must have sunk in a little bit.

By this time, the police officer had observed enough of my interaction with Janie to be reassured that I was telling the truth.

I repeated the two options to Janie, saying, "So those are your two choices. Do you want to come home with me? Or go to the hospital with the policeman?"

She started pointing toward my car.

"Okay," said the policeman. "I'll let you go home with her." But he took down our address and phone number and did check on us a few days later.

Needless to say, with Janie completely unable to walk on her own at this point, there was no chance of a repeat of that situation. I would have almost welcomed a repeat of it, just to know that my wife could still walk and perform basic functions. Sadly, those days were long over.

These days, I was concerned about her potentially falling out of bed. I knew how much upset this would cause to both of us. So, I slept with one eye open, and was constantly getting up to check on her.

It was very odd to get into bed with my wife at night, knowing she was no longer my wife—not in any meaningful sense. She was present only in physical body and the rest of her had departed her body. It had been six and a half years since we'd had so much as a conversation. There was no coming home and saying, "Oh, honey, I had such a good time tonight." Or, "I missed you. It feels so good to be home at last."

There were plenty of nights I didn't even get into bed with Janie. I slept in a chair because I was afraid to fall into a deep sleep. I would spend the night alternating between nodding and waking up to check on her. Deanna suggested that I put a pillow under the cover at the edge of the bed to keep her from rolling off. That helped a lot.

I never did get a hospital bed for her, something Medicare would have provided at no charge. I wanted to sleep in the bed with her. (They did provide me with a wheelchair for her at no charge.) I also used a shower chair when I showered her in the morning because she couldn't stand up. I bought that myself at the drug store. I also had a hose attachment put on the shower so I could use the hose around her and wash her down without the water raining down from above. That way, she didn't have to have the water coming down on her head all the time.

Forty-Three

Despite being utterly exhausted, I moved forward with dating. I knew that time was ticking down and that Janie was in the final stretch of her illness. Being without her was an unbearable thought—but for all practical purposes, she was already gone. And, I knew that if I didn't make myself available to meet a woman (as strange as that thought might have been to me), it was totally feasible that I might find myself living the rest of my life alone.

Someone recommended the dating site JDate. I found online dating to be a strange way of meeting women. First of all, this form of dating did not exist when I was a young man. I would meet girls at college and sometimes at a bar.

I decided I would try it on a limited basis and took the shortest membership they offered. In order to use the site, I was required to create a profile and checkmark one of the following categories: single, divorced or widowed.

I hesitated, thinking, *Now, what? I don't fit any of these!* So, I left that part blank.

Once I had joined, I was able to search for possible matches. I found a few potentially interesting women on the site and went on a few dates here and there. Nothing amounted to anything.

If the online interaction with someone led to a phone call and the conversation was pleasant enough to warrant an in-person meeting, I would always say, "Pick a place you feel comfortable and we will meet there. If we don't click, you're free to go home and you never have to worry about seeing me again. No pressure."

The handful of dates I went on ran the spectrum from uneventful to downright bizarre. The only thing that was consistent was this: I felt it was important to tell a woman my story right away. It wasn't the sort of thing I wanted to share over the phone but I felt it should be the first topic of conversation once we'd met in person. I needed the person to know what they were getting themselves into if we ended up continuing to date. I would open the conversation by saying, "I've got a story to tell you," and then take it from there.

After a handful of dates with women, I met Michele. She saw me on JDate, messaged me to say hello, and requested a conversation.

When I got the notice on JDate from Michele and first looked at her profile, I saw that she was born the year I graduated from high school.

What in the world would I be able to talk to her about? I asked myself. *We're from two different eras!*

When I got a second message a week later, it was short and sweet—something along the lines of, "Hi, I haven't heard back from you..."

Again, I ignored it. *We're from different generations,* I said to myself. *We won't have anything to talk about.*

I ignored three messages from Michele. When she sent me a fourth, I decided to go out with her.

At some point early in our relationship, she asked me, "By the way, Bob, why did you not answer the three earlier times I tried to get in touch with you?"

"Honestly, it was because of the more-than-slight difference in our ages," I said. "That, and the fact that you're a midget! I'm about a foot taller than you."

To this day, I tease her, saying, "You were annoying me so much, I knew that taking you out was the only way I would ever get rid of you!" We always have a good laugh over it.

It would come to light that she was persistent because she had her heart set on meeting a Jewish man who was tall. At five-foot-eleven, I fit the bill. Apparently, most of the men she had been meeting on JDate were on the shorter side and stood no more than five-foot-six or five-foot-seven. It is interesting and funny to note that she herself is pint-size. She claims to be four-foot-eleven but I don't think she's a speck over four-foot-ten.

When I finally called Michele, the conversation flowed easily, so I suggested that we go out for dinner and drinks.

"You pick a place you feel comfortable," I said, "and I'll meet you there."

"No," she said, "you can pick me up outside my condo."

So, one night in September of 2011, I pulled up in front of Michele's condo. I was wrapping up a phone call as I saw this cute little lady approach my SUV.

"Bob?"

"Yes!" I whispered, covering the phone receiver.

Michele got into my SUV, leaned over, gave me a kiss on the cheek, and said, "Hi! How are you?"

We chatted a little bit on the way to dinner.

Somewhere down the line, I would ask her, "Since you let me pick you up outside your condo on our first date, is it safe to assume you checked me out in the Jewish community and confirmed that I wasn't a serial rapist?"

"Yes," she said. "I started calling people I knew in the Jewish community and asking everyone if they knew you. Eventually I found someone who did."

I found out that Michele had been born in Atlanta and knew a huge circle of people. Interestingly, none of the people she talked to mentioned that I was still married to a wife who was terminally ill.

Any fairly intelligent person with a heart would have understood the situation I was in and refrained from holding it against me. I was shocked when I discovered over time that not everyone was so understanding. I appreciated that I had the chance to tell her the whole story before someone else told her their version of it.

When we arrived at the restaurant and were seated and enjoying cocktails before dinner, I said, "I've got a story to tell you."

"Well," said Michele once I had finished telling her about the situation with Janie, "I've heard a lot of stories from men in my life, but I've never heard one like that!"

We were at a French restaurant that is one of my favorite Atlanta restaurants, seated on the outside covered patio. Despite the extreme age difference, the conversation between us flowed naturally and beautifully. As we talked, we shared about different aspects of our lives.

I found out that she, too, had two boys. It also came to light that she had matured early, thanks to a difficult childhood. She lost her mother when she was ten. Meanwhile, her father was a traveling jewelry salesman who spent most of his time on the road. (Her father would die right after she graduated from high school in 1978 or '79.)

"Once your mom died," I asked, "did your father stop traveling and stay home to take care of you and your brother?"

"No, he stayed on the road most of the time and was usually gone for a couple of weeks at a time. Sometimes he would come home on Friday nights. Mostly, we had housekeepers and neighbors who came in to help look after us."

I couldn't believe that Michele's mother's death had no impact on her father's travel schedule. Since he wasn't around to take care of his children, ten-year-old Michele became sort of a surrogate mother to her seven-year-old brother. Michele cooked for herself and her brother, took him shopping for clothes for school, and took over all the duties of the mother of the house. The fact that Michele was so mature for her age helped shorten the distance between our ages.

We had a lovely evening on our first date so I asked her out again, and then again. For our fourth date, I asked her to join me at the fundraising gala held every other year by the Jewish Home.

"The gala is coming up in October," I said. "I have these two tickets, if you'd like to go with me. But you have to understand, this will be the first time since Janie's illness that I've been in public with another woman. And there's going to be a parade of people at this thing. So, we're going to be under the microscope of every Jew in the city. They're all going to want to know who you are...and they're probably going to talk. So, I'll totally understand if you don't want to go. No hard feelings."

"I'd like to go," said Michele, without hesitation.

"Okay, great. But just remember, if you change your mind, just let me know."

I was fine with the scrutiny, myself. I didn't much care *what* people thought, as long as my children and I were okay with it. Over the six months it had taken me to reconcile myself to the concept of dating, I had come to accept the fact that people were likely to have opinions about me starting to date while Janie was technically still alive. Sadly, by then, that was about it—technically still alive.

On the night of the gala, I picked up Michele and we drove to the Atlanta hotel where the event was being held. I was wearing a suit and tie and Michele was wearing a pretty cocktail dress.

Before we even entered the banquet room, I noticed the chairperson of that year's gala and went over to say hello to her and introduce Michele. Right at that exact moment, a reporter with the local Jewish paper approached us, camera in tow.

"Stand together, you two," he said, "I'd like to take your picture."

"I'll just step out of the picture," said the chairperson.

"The hell you will!" I said, laughing. "Nice try but you're staying right here."

The chairperson was hoping to avoid being the subject of gossip, but I wasn't having it. I knew that a photo of the three of us would attract a lot less attention than a photo with just Michele and me in it.

I whispered to Michele, "I sure hope we don't make the cut on the photo for the newspaper!" Thankfully, we didn't.

We found our table assignment, and approached a table in the middle of the room, where six other people were already seated. I was friends with all three couples at our table and introduced them to Michele. As we were all chatting away, I looked around the room. It was filled with eight hundred attendees. Before long, people began approaching our table and a crowd gathered.

I leaned over to Michele and said, "Look around at what's happening here. If you want to get up and leave, we can. No problem."

"No, I'm fine," she assured me.

"I guess there's something to be said for breaking the news that we're dating to everyone at the same time," I joked.

Since Michele had been born and raised in Atlanta and was active in the Jewish community there, and since I too was active in the Jewish community, there were probably an equal number of people who knew me and were curious about my date (a woman other than my wife), and who knew her and were curious about me. Then there were those who knew us both.

One person who approached our table was the first woman I had dated after the couple of ex-girlfriends from my past—the woman who had called Rabbi Kranz to check me out.

She came and stood by me. Then she leaned down and whispered into my ear, "I really had a nice time with you when we went out. I'd really like to see you again if you're not serious with this young lady..."

I was sitting with Michele on my right, and a close female friend on my left. Michele didn't hear what was said but my friend to my left did. We exchanged a look and then my friend said, "Wow, what a set of balls that lady has!"

I had to laugh over my friend's characterization of that woman. She certainly had chutzpah—there was no question about that.

Later, I teased Michele about it, saying, "Looks like you've got some competition, lady!"

After the gala, the news that we were dating quickly spread. Nasty comments started making their way back to us, and they were mostly about me. People were saying things along the lines of, "How could he do this? How could he have an affair on his wife when she is sick and dying?"

I would be out in public somewhere and see women whispering. It didn't take a rocket scientist to understand what was going on.

The rumbling among friends and associates of mine and Michele's continued and grew louder. It really started to get under my skin. I had a pretty good idea of the identity of one of the women who was perpetrating the spread of gossip. One night when I'd finally reached the end of my rope, I called her.

When I got her on the phone, I said, "Who the hell do you think you are, anyway? Your husband is healthy and you're judging *me* and telling *me* what I should do with my life? Until you walk in my shoes, you have nothing to say about it. As long as it's okay with my kids and myself, that's all I care about. So, I would shut my damned mouth if I were you! I don't want to hear you saying another word about it."

By the time I had finished with her and hung up the phone, she was in tears—and I had no regrets. This woman had no idea how much of myself I had given to my wife during her protracted and hideous illness. I felt that she had a lot of nerve to judge me for trying to get out there and have some kind of a life.

Forty-Four

As Michele and I continued dating, I noticed that many of the people whom Janie and I counted as close friends began drifting away. The real close ones stayed around but the rest slowly backed away.

Maybe they felt awkward because they had known Janie and me as a couple for so long and couldn't adjust to me being with a new woman. In any case, I do know that the woman in the relationship often is the one to approve or disapprove of another couple, in terms of their suitability for socializing. Michele is certainly the social director in our relationship.

After we had gone on four or five dates, Michele invited me up to her condo. Both of her sons, Evan and Eric, were grown and long since out of the house by then. Evan had an infant son, Robert, with his first wife. They had been split up before the baby came and were in the process of attempting to reconcile. Ultimately, the reconciliation didn't take and Evan would eventually remarry.

One day, Michele said, "My boys aren't happy we're dating."

"Why not?" I asked, somewhat startled by this announcement.

"Because Janie's still with us."

I thought about it for a minute and then said, "It's more important to me how *you* feel about it. If you don't feel comfortable with it, then c'est la vie. If you're okay with it, then I suggest we have brunch with your boys on Sunday morning and get the issue out on the table."

My boys knew that I was dating but they had not yet met Michele. She and I had only been on five or six dates by that time.

Michele let me know that she herself was fine with dating me while Janie was still technically with us, so we decided to go ahead and set up a brunch with her boys.

When we met at the restaurant for brunch, I got to meet Michele's older son, Evan. He was twenty-seven at the time and had his wife and son with him. Eric, who was twenty-three or twenty-four at the time, couldn't make it. We met at a later date at a family function.

After the introductions and a bit of small talk, I got right to the point. "Evan, let me explain something to you. My wife is dying. She has a terminal illness and she is going to die. I can't tell you when...nobody knows... but she is going to die in the not too distant future. Your mother and I have met and we enjoy each other's company. All I can promise you is that, whether or not the relationship endures, I will never hurt her. More than that I can't promise."

I expressed what was on my mind and we had a nice breakfast—but I can't say that Evan totally bought into the idea of his mother and me dating. Not then and not immediately afterwards.

As Michele and I got more serious and I spent more time around her boys, I got to know baby Robert. When he was still a tot and first starting to speak, everything he pointed to was referred to as "Da," posed in the form of a question: "Da?"

So, Da became my nickname for him. Later, when Da's dad, Evan, remarried and he and his new wife had a little girl, I came up with a new nickname for Da.

"Well, Da," I told him, "it's time for a new nickname. I'm going to start calling you Bro since you're now an older brother."

Michele and I continued to date, casually at first. Then, after a couple of months or so, things grew more serious between us.

Eventually, Michele gave me the code to her parking garage. Late one evening, I came out to find my car booted.

I thought to myself, *What on earth? I had permission to park in Michele's guest spot!*

I called the number I found on the nasty note slipped under my windshield wiper. It stated something to the effect of, "You're in violation. Don't let me catch your car here again!"

I was irritated and annoyed as I called the number on the note and explained that I had come out to find my car booted.

"Well, sir, you didn't have a sticker on your car showing you to be a resident. You've got to have a sticker."

"But I am *not* a resident, as I explained...I'm the guest of a resident."

The person was not swayed by my logic. "Sorry, but it's going to cost you seventy bucks to get the boot off."

The guy met me at the garage and I paid the ransom to have the boot removed. I handed him a hundred-dollar bill, got my thirty bucks in change, and walked away.

The next day, I got a phone call from the guy. "Mr. Fischbach?"

"Yes?"

"The hundred-dollar bill you paid me with is counterfeit!"

"What do you mean it's counterfeit? How can you be sure you got that from me?" I said.

About ten days earlier, I had been having lunch at a Chinese restaurant with a friend, and paid with a hundred-dollar bill. It turned out that the bill was counterfeit. I could have argued with the restaurant owner and asked him how he knew that the hundred came from me, but I knew him to be an honest guy. So, I replaced the hundred-dollar bill and took the counterfeit one back from him.

Then I went to the bank where I had gotten the counterfeit bill, and explained the circumstances.

"We're very sorry, sir, but we have to confiscate this bill from you and send it to the Treasury Department."

"You're not getting this from me unless you replace it!" I said. "You're the ones who gave it to me!"

"I'm sorry but it's against regulations."

"If you'll check your records, you'll see how many years I've been a customer here!"

When all was said and done, they refused to replace the counterfeit bill and I refused to turn it over. I left with it in hand. When I paid for the boot removal the following day, I did pay with a hundred—but no one can say whether it was the same hundred.

Anyway, that was the end of me parking in Michele's guest spot in her garage. Although my relationship with her was slowly becoming more serious, marriage was the last thing on my mind. On a sheerly practical level, I was thinking about the finances of blending two lives at such a late stage of life.

I was thinking, *I'm not sure I want to get married again at this stage in my life. What would be the point?*

Once I had become exclusive with Michele and we had gone to brunch with her son Evan so I could explain the situation, it was her turn to meet my boys. We planned a dinner at Michele's house and she cooked. She used to own her own catering business and is an excellent cook, so it only made sense that she would do the honors. (In fact, she is *such* a good cook that she has a way of turning leftovers into a brand-new meal. I never liked leftovers until I tasted Michele's. And, everyone knows the old saying about the way to a man's heart.)

Janie had also been a great cook, as was my mother. Mom passed her recipes down to Janie, just as Mom's recipes had come from Grandma Sadie, Mom's mother-in-law. They had been passed, *l'dor, v'dor*, from generation to generation.

In advance of the dinner, I talked to Drew and Scott and said, "I understand that this is going to be a bit awkward, after seeing your mom and me together for all these years. And I'll respect your feelings, whatever they might be. But I wanted you to meet the woman I am dating."

I was right—it was a bit awkward at first, as the boys tried to get used to Michele's presence in my life. Over time, they really came to like her.

Michele's great qualities won me over, and I'm sure my boys appreciated them too. I liked both her looks and her personality and I appreciated that she wasn't pushy, demanding or high maintenance. Perhaps most importantly of all, she was very respectful of my boundaries. She kept her distance relative to my relationship with Janie, and everything I was going through in caring for her.

Michele's approach to this aspect of my life made all the difference in the world. I truly do not think I could have maintained a dating relationship with a woman who had tried to dictate how I handled the last stages of Janie's life and the resulting end of our long marriage.

Forty-Five

Michele and I had started dating in October of 2011. A few months earlier in the summertime, Drew and Nina had been struggling to get pregnant. Nina had one child from her first marriage when she was in her very early twenties, but she was around forty by this time.

Being so close to my kids, there was no subject that was off the table. So, I said to them, "Have you two thought about adopting? It worked out pretty good for us. Or, have you thought of something like IVF or one of the other methods for conceiving a child? Your mom and I didn't have those options back then."

"We've thought about IVF, Dad, but it's really expensive..."

"I'll tell you what. You go talk to the doctors about it. If it makes sense to you and Nina, I'll pay for it."

So, they started investigating their options. After two or three IVF shots didn't work, the doctors determined that an egg donor was in order. So, we found a donor with the same characteristics as Nina.

Many thousands of dollars later, Drew and Nina got a little boy and I got a grandson. To this day, Drew and Nina are constantly thanking me for little Max, who is six years old. For his middle name, they gave him Robert, after me. Actually, he was technically named for Randee, who passed in 2010. Jews don't name after someone who is still living. But in my heart, I know who he was really named after.

The amazing thing is that Max looks just like Drew, even to the point of having the same little cowlick Drew has just above his right eye. Max's hair at birth was not quite as red as Drew's had been when he was a baby, but he does have light reddish-brown hair.

Max was born in July of 2012. Seven months earlier, on or about New Year's Eve of 2012, Scott's wife, Jaime, had turned up pregnant.

Scott and Jaime asked me to go with them to one of the sonogram appointments. I knew by now that I was going to have a granddaughter.

I was watching the doctor measure the baby, in utero. I knew the doctor, so I felt comfortable joking, "Hey, doc, while you're at it, could you do me a favor? Measure her for a chastity belt so I can have it ready when the time comes!"

The baby was about to become my little girl, and I was already worried about the guys who might be pursuing her. It turns out that my granddaughter truly is precocious and is already quite a handful. In fact, Annie thinks that personality-wise, she's a carbon copy of Janie.

Jaime experienced a lot of nausea during her pregnancy and swore that, once she gave birth to this baby, that was it. No more pregnancies for her. She was set to deliver on a certain date by C-section.

When the day came and Jaime went into labor, Scott called me. I couldn't leave Janie alone until the caregiver arrived to stay with her. So, I sent Michele to the hospital ahead of me and told her I would meet her there as soon as I could. (We were dating pretty seriously by then.)

The baby, Olivia Jane Emilia Fischbach, was born on September 23rd, 2012. She looks just like her father, Scott. When I arrived at the hospital, I was told that mama and baby were just fine and there had been no complications. The baby was adorable and I immediately fell in love with her. As I said, even though I love Olivia to death, I also recognize what a handful she is going to be when she hits her teen years.

Within a couple of months of the births of my grandchildren, I experienced a big shock related to my health. It all started a couple of years earlier in 2010 at my annual physical.

"Your PSA number is a bit high," the doctor had said to me at that time. "But it could be just a urinary tract infection causing the number to be high. Let me give you an antibiotic and see how you do."

When I returned for a follow-up a couple of weeks later, the PSA number had gone back down to normal. Then in early 2012—before the birth of my two grandchildren—I returned to the doctor for an annual checkup.

"Your PSA number is high again," the doctor said. "It could be another urinary tract infection. Let's give you another dose of antibiotics and see if we can bring it down."

The PSA number did come down—but not all the way.

"I think it's time to send you to the urologist," said the doctor.

In between waiting for the births of my grandchildren and watching Janie get worse by the minute, I chose a urologist from the couple of choices the doctor had given me.

"We're going to need to do a biopsy," said the urologist.

When the results came back, I went in for the news.

"Well," he said, "the numbers aren't bad, but the biopsy was positive."

Being a Doubting Thomas by nature, I asked the doctor to have the results sent to another lab. I wanted to see if their interpretation matched that from the first lab. When the finest lab in the country came back with the same interpretation, I decided I needed to get a second opinion.

The first urologist had said to me, "Look at it this way, Bob. There are nine different ways of treating prostate cancer. First, there's active observation where we don't do anything and you come back in six months and we see where you're at with it then. There are also several different radiation options. The variety relates to *the means of delivering* the radiation—freezing, frying, injecting seeds with radiation in them. There's also bent-ray radiation, otherwise known as proton treatment. There are also two types of surgery—open surgery which is exactly what it sounds like, and robotic, also known as microscopic."

There was a vast range of options, depending upon one's diagnosis and the severity of the cancer.

"...And lastly, there's a new treatment that's not yet approved by the FDA. You'd have to fly to Bermuda to have the procedure done there." That procedure would have cost me twenty-five-thousand dollars.

I went to see one of the doctors recommended to me for a second opinion. I fell in love with this doctor right away. He was a no B.S. kind of guy.

I was in the exam room when he came in wearing blue scrubs. He looked at my medical file.

"Drop your pants," he said in a matter-of-fact tone.

When he was done with the exam, he said, "Okay, I'll meet you in my office after you get dressed. I'm going to give you an education on prostate cancer."

When I met the doctor in his office, he pulled his chair up alongside mine and drew me a diagram. "Here is prostate cancer," he explained. "It's slow growing, but the problem is, it gets bad when it reaches a certain point. Obviously, you don't want to let it reach that point."

"Let me ask you something, doc. What course of treatment would you suggest if I was one of your own relatives?"

"Well, funny you should ask. It just so happens my father died of it, my brother had it, and when I get it, I'm going to do the seeds."

I really liked the doctor. But when I investigated further, I discovered that the bulk of his income was derived from the radiation-seeds treatment. So, I thought to myself, *Well, naturally he's going to be pushing me in that direction.*

Now, I felt I needed one more doctor to weigh in before I made my decision. As it turns out, a longtime friend of mine had been diagnosed with prostate cancer not long before I did. And, Dr. Steven Frank, his son-in-law (his daughter's husband) happened to be the head of radiation oncology at M.D. Anderson in Houston, Texas. I had known my friend's daughter since she was knee-high to a grasshopper.

A phone call was arranged and on Saturday morning, my phone rang. "Why don't you come out here to M.D. Anderson," said my friend's son-in-law, "and I will work you up. Afterward, I will get you appointments with doctors that do all the various procedures. You can meet with the doctor that does the freezing, the doctor that does the frying, the doctor that does the seeds. And then you can make your decision from there."

I liked this idea a lot. I felt that the guidance I got from the salaried doctors on staff at M.D. Anderson would be a lot less biased than the guidance given to me by a private physician doctor—however likeable—who made the bulk of his income every year on the procedure in which he specialized. (Salaried doctors collect the same paycheck each month regardless of the procedure they perform.)

I made plans to fly to M.D. Anderson in Houston the first week of October, 2012.

This time of my life was an emotional roller-coaster. I had the joy of two brand-new grandchildren who were the spitting image of their fathers.

I had lovely new daughters-in-law in Jaime and Nina.

I had the horror and grief of caring for a wife who I knew would be gone very soon.

I had the loving comfort and companionship of a new woman in my life with whom things were getting serious.

And I had prostate cancer.

Forty-Six

Very early in the morning on October 2nd or 3rd, 2012, I got a disturbing phone call, letting me know that the brother of a very close friend of Janie's and mine in Chicago had passed.

The last thing I wanted to do was leave Janie when I knew that I would be leaving her again mid-month to go to M.D. Anderson in Texas. At the same time, I knew that going to the funeral was the right thing to do. So, I immediately booked a flight to Chicago, attended the funeral, and returned the same day.

Then, somewhere between the 10th and 15th of October, I flew to M.D. Anderson. It was evident immediately that I had arrived at an incredible, state-of-the-art facility—someplace truly special.

If, G-d forbid, you ever get presented with a diagnosis that necessitates a visit to a cancer treatment center, you can't do better than M.D. Anderson. It's considered one of very top cancer hospitals in the world. There's not much you can do about the horrors of the diagnosis itself, but M.D. Anderson does everything within their power to make the experience of being there as pleasant and comfortable as possible.

It is located in downtown Houston, attached to the University of Texas, and comprised of a collection of twelve thirty-story buildings. At the top of each building is the name of a major donor that helped make that building possible.

I was delighted and relieved to discover that all the buildings were connected by an enclosed walkway. On the interior walkway between buildings on the second floor are golf carts for the use of anyone who needs them.

Houston in the summertime can be humid to the point of feeling uninhabitable. Years prior to this visit, I had been to Houston on business and was stunned by the humidity when I exited the plane onto the tarmac.

When I remarked on the humidity to a colleague who had come to pick me up from the airport, he said, "It's actually nice today. You ought to be here when it's really humid!"

Attached to, and owned by, the hospital is a hotel called The Rotary, managed by Marriott. There is even an on-site medical library in the hotel lobby, and it's available to guests who wish to read up on their condition, the facility and treatment options.

When I arrived, I went to the front desk of the hotel. I was presented with my room key for my hotel stay and an envelope containing my appointment itinerary. I was also told that there was a van available to take me anywhere I wanted to go within a five-mile radius.

The first order of business for every patient checking into M.D. Anderson is to give blood. To make this more convenient for patients, they have a lab in the lobby, open evenings.

On one of my visits to the lab to give blood during my stay, I said to the phlebotomist, "I've got to ask you a question. Every patient here has some sort of issue with cancer. And yet, all the medical personnel have smiles on their faces. If I was an employee here and all I saw all day long was patients worried about their condition, I think it would wear on me. How do you all keep such a good attitude?"

"It's interesting that you observed that," she said. "It's all part of our training to maintain a humanitarian culture and make the patients' stay as pleasant as possible."

Their humanitarian culture is the brainchild of the founder, and explains why the center is usually voted number one in the nation for cancer research and treatment. It is truly exceptional.

I had arrived in the afternoon on the day before my appointments because I hadn't been able to find an early morning flight the following day. I hated leaving Janie at home without me any longer than necessary, knowing that she was getting worse by the day.

My wife was back in hospice after a period of having been removed from the program due to the fact that she was no longer visibly declining. Janie had first entered home hospice in the fall of 2009. She stayed in it for a year until she appeared to stabilize and was removed in the fall of 2010. (The hospice facility evaluates patients every six months during the first year and monthly from then on. In order to remain eligible for hospice, the patient must be visibly declining.)

As Janie began to again go downhill and get worse and worse, she was put back into hospice in the fall of 2011. So, this was her second time under the care of Weinstein Hospice, a private nonprofit that was part of The Jewish Home community. They primarily do in-home hospice and only have two or three beds for inpatients. As I said, I paid only for the caregivers I brought in to help with Janie. All other expenses including hospice care were covered by Medicare.

When I met Dr. Steven Frank for the first time the morning of my appointment, I liked him right away. He was the doctor that would be overseeing my treatment.

"I'm going to have a nurse get you ready," he told me, "and take you and work you up."

Whatever that means! I said to myself.

I was taken into an exam room that resembled a surgical room. Once undressed, I quickly gained an enhanced appreciation for what women go through during a gynecological exam. It was a real affront at first but I quickly learned that exams and treatment for prostate cancer required me to check my dignity at the front door.

During my workup, there was a knock at the door.

"Bob," said the doctor, "you know this is a teaching hospital. Some interns would like to come in and observe."

I was lying there in a very compromising position and figured I'd already relinquished all my privacy anyway. "Sure," I said, "what the hell. Have them come in. I don't care."

In walked three people, including a very attractive female doctor in a white coat. She walked over, introduced herself and shook my hand while the rest of me was completely exposed. I was embarrassed to say the least, and shocked to see a female doctor. I didn't realize what I had agreed to.

I was thinking, *Oh, stupid me...I assumed they were male doctors.*

After the sonogram on my prostate, the doctor told me to get dressed and meet him in his office. Sitting there together, he explained, "There's something called a Gleason score, Bob. It's an indicator of the number of bad cells found in the blood samples. Yours is a seven..."

"So, is that a good or a bad thing?" I said.

He went on to explain that yes, it was a good thing, because my seven was comprised of a two and a five. That is apparently better than a five and a two.

"I have you set up for appointments tomorrow," he said. "You'll start at eight in the morning with several doctors on staff here, and see the last doctor at one. Tonight, I will be sending all of them your info. They will have looked it over by the time they see you tomorrow."

Seeing several doctors in one day could have been cost prohibitive if not for the fact that the cost of my stay at M.D. Anderson was all-inclusive. The only thing I paid for was my airfare, hotel bill, and food. Medicare covered the doctors' bills, medical facility bills and any and all other medical costs.

I was facing a long day of appointments the following morning so I went back to the hotel room to get a good night of sleep. I talked to Michele, who was naturally worried about me, and talked to the caregivers to see how Janie was doing.

In the morning, I began my series of appointments. In the afternoon, Dr. Frank and I met so we could go over the results of all the consultations, exams and tests. The other doctors I had seen that day were also present and spoke up. But, by now, Dr. Frank had conferred with them all and was the one guiding the course of my treatment.

To recap everything that had been discussed, Dr. Frank told me, "Okay, the surgeon said you absolutely do not need surgery. They also don't believe you should simply do active observation. You need to be more proactive than that. Any of the other possible treatments would work with your condition."

Then he talked me through the upside and downside of every available treatment option. Many of the options required me to be in Houston at M.D. Anderson for extended periods of time, ranging from a multi-day process, to a multi-week process, to five-days a week for eight weeks.

"...but with the seeds," he continued, "you would be in one day and out the next."

"Let me think about it and I'll call you back."

As I had been undergoing this workup in Houston, I was painfully aware that Janie was swiftly going downhill in hospice care back at home. To be dealing with my prostate cancer while also dealing with Janie's impending death was almost more than I could handle.

I didn't have the same level of attention from either of my boys during this time, understandably. They were now parents and needed to give their children the lion's share of their focus. Thank G-d I had—and have!—Michele in my life.

I returned home to Atlanta, gave the radiation-seed treatment some thought, and talked it over with Michele. Then I called Dr. Frank and asked him a couple of questions. He helped me make up my mind to do the seed treatment.

After telling him that I had decided to move forward with the radiation seeds, I told him that I could not schedule the treatment right away.

"Janie's sinking fast," I explained. "In the next couple of weeks, I want to try to make her aware that she's a grandmother."

Forty-Seven

I invited both Drew and Scott over to the house, along with their wives. Then I took Janie's grandchildren one at a time, put them in front of her and introduced them. I stuck the kids' feet in Janie's mouth to ensure that the introduction registered. (Olivia was five weeks old at the time and Max was three and a half months old.)

I watched Janie carefully, looking for any expression that might let me know that she understood that she was meeting her grandchildren. I can't say for sure how much she understood, but I was happy I had done it.

Perhaps Janie was waiting to meet her grandchildren before she passed. In any case, from that point on, Janie's decline accelerated at a surprising rate of speed. During the last two weeks of her life, I requested Deanna from Weinstein Hospice, and she became my overnight hospice attendant. She never left my side. In the past, she had always gone home at night.

It was a brutal two weeks—a dark, foreboding and dismal stretch of time in which I realized that the end really was imminent. I watched Janie's breathing get weaker and more labored. I looked at Deanna with a question in my eyes.

"It's getting close," she affirmed. "Her system's starting to shut down."

My wife had been on morphine to dull the pain and gently ease her into death. Since we don't have legal euthanasia in this country, morphine is used in hospice care.

As I said, Janie and I slept in the same bed until the night she passed away. I never brought in a hospital bed for her in all those years. At 3:00 in the morning on October 31st, 2012, as I was lying in bed holding Janie's hand, she took her last breath. Deanna was present in the room with me at the time.

It somehow made perfect sense to me that Janie would die on Halloween. I had always called her a good witch, with a knack for predicting upcoming events. There were many other-worldly things that had happened throughout her lifetime.

We once chartered a sailboat for a cruise around the British Virgin Islands with a captain and a crew. We slept on deck every night under the stars and woke up to seagulls and birds flying overhead. We were with another couple.

Janie turned to the wife, Sally. "When we get home, you need to see the doctor," Janie said. "You have Graves' disease."

Sally's husband was a cardiologist. When he heard this, he took a close look at his wife. Then he turned to Janie and said, "You're crazy! There's nothing wrong with my wife." Sadly, he was mistaken.

As I mentioned earlier, a handful of years after that when Janie was in her late forties, she had another moment of prescience. She declared, "I'm going to have Alzheimer's when I'm older."

Despite the long eight and a half years of preparing to lose Janie, her death hit me like a tidal wave. I felt overwhelming grief mingled with a palpable sense of relief. The force of my grief was tremendous. Right alongside it was terrible guilt over my sense of relief. I felt so conflicted.

What's the matter with me? I asked myself. *Why would I be feeling relieved? Janie just died!*

The truth was, there were many reasons why I was feeling both devastated and relieved at the same time. For starters, my beloved wife had spent too many years suffering through an illness for which there was no cure and no hope. Then there was the fact that her agonizing, protracted decline nearly put me in the grave beside her. By the time of her death, I was feeling like I was not long for this earth. I had been pushed to the very brink on every level of my being.

In the bedroom we had shared, with Janie now finally peaceful, there was the most profound stillness. It was both wonderful and terrible all at the same time.

Deanna called Weinstein Hospice and had them send over the doctor to pronounce Janie's official time of death and fill out the necessary paperwork.

It was time to call Drew and Scott. When they got to the house, we all hugged and cried together. Then Scott went into the bedroom, sat there beside his mom, and didn't leave until she was taken to the funeral home. Drew was equally devastated but couldn't bring himself to enter the bedroom and see his mother like that.

They both dearly loved their mother. But they are such different guys in the way they experience and express their emotions. As I mentioned earlier, it has always been that way with them. Even when he is deeply sad, Scott is very stoic. Drew is more outwardly emotional.

As is customary in the Jewish tradition, Janie would be buried within twenty-four hours of her death. The weight of the grief I was feeling was nearly overwhelming in and of itself. I was suddenly so grateful that I had given myself the gift of making Janie's arrangements in advance. All I had to do now was go to the cemetery.

I thought back to when my dad died. I remembered how hard it was on us to have to make all the arrangements at the very same moment that we were trying to process our grief. I'd had to go to the funeral home, pick out the casket and make all the other little decisions that accompany laying a loved one to rest.

When my father-in-law died, I discovered the value of making advance funeral arrangements. (May he rest in peace.) By making his arrangements in advance, it had made things so much easier on the family.

Janie died around three o'clock in the morning and we had her funeral arranged for that afternoon.

Getting any more sleep between the time of her death and the funeral was out of the question. I was going to have to face the funeral on whatever amount of sleep I had gotten from the time I went to sleep until the time she passed away in the middle of the night.

I called Sue, Janie's best friend while growing up. They had kept in touch up until Janie lost the capacity to communicate. When I told her the news, she told me that she would fly in from Florida for the funeral. We also had friends in Chicago who would be flying in.

Bad news travels fast and somehow the word spread. When I saw the huge crowd that showed up at the funeral to say their goodbyes to Janie and pay their respects, I was taken aback. All of Janie's amazing caregivers were there—Thelma, Deanna, Peaches, Rose (a woman who filled in from time to time), and of course Annie who was—and remains!—our longtime housekeeper and loved Janie dearly. Each was a true gift from G-d.

I was surprised to see many of my former employees from my real estate syndication business. I was thrilled that they thought enough of me to come. My association with some of my former employees went back thirty-five years.

Kay, the first person I ever hired to work for us in the early days of my real estate career, came to the funeral. I'll never forget hiring her. She had just graduated from Georgia State or was about to, and wasn't yet even old enough to legally drink. I always deeply appreciated her loyalty and expert handling of our day-to-day operations.

One day at our annual Christmas party, after working for us for fifteen years, she came up to me with tears in her eyes.

"What's the matter, Kay?" I asked.

"I don't know what to do, Bob. I've been offered a position with John Portman..."

They are a big firm here in Atlanta that does architecture, as well as real estate development and management.

"...I don't know whether to stay with you guys or go with him."

I didn't even hesitate. "Kay, twenty years from now, you don't want to wonder what would have happened if you had taken that job. Accept the offer!"

At Christmastime in 2017, Kay invited me to witness her induction as President of the Atlanta Commercial Real Estate Board. She was only the second woman to ever hold the position. I was so happy for her. It all started when she left us to accept the position at the architectural firm.

She had come to work for us when she was about twenty years old, and was now sixty. When she got up to the microphone to say a few words, she quoted a passage from a book to the effect that it takes many trees to make a forest. After thanking her husband, she asked me to stand up.

"This is Bob Fischbach, my mentor..."

All eyes were on me.

Then she asked others to stand as well. "See?" she said. "We've created a forest!"

It was really lovely of her to acknowledge me in that way. After the luncheon, I said to her, "See? I was right when I told you to take the job all those years ago. Look at what you would have missed had you stayed with us!"

Kay wasn't the only ex-employee of mine to surprise me by showing up at Janie's funeral. There were eight or nine others there, as well. These included a maintenance man who worked for us for twenty-five years or more, and some subcontractors who had worked for us and with whom I had become very close friends.

There was also a remarkable number of friends and family there, many of whom were surprises. I wish I could have seen all of these people under other circumstances. As it was, I was in a fog, and only half there. I was disoriented, exhausted, and devastated.

I would have asked Rabbi Phil Kranz to conduct the service but he happened to be out of town at the time. So, the honors were done by Rabbi Sandler, the rabbi from the synagogue I attend. Interestingly, his wife happened to be the social worker for Weinstein Hospice, the wonderful facility that took such great care of Janie.

During the graveside service, the coffin had remained above ground. Then they lowered it, and everyone in attendance was invited to place a shovelful of dirt on the coffin. Only once everyone was gone from the burial site did the cemetery personnel fill the grave.

Her gravestone, in addition to her name and the dates of her birth and death, would bear these words: *Vivacious and talkative, she could work a room. A wonderful wife, a doting daughter, mother, grandmother and first lady.*

I went over to the edge of the grave and stood there for the longest time, staring down at Janie's coffin. I don't know how long I might have stood there, unable to move. Mercifully, one or both of my boys came over, put an arm on my shoulder and gently guided me away from their mother's grave.

Forty-Eight

After the funeral, we had shiva at our house, with the rabbi coming every evening at seven to lead the service. Michele told me that she felt it would be best if she bowed out of attending the shiva. She said she didn't feel it was her place to be there. She had also declined to attend the funeral for the same reason.

I had to agree with her on both counts. I so appreciated her thoughtfulness. A lesser woman would have insisted on being by my side, despite the effect it might have had on others in attendance.

I was truly surprised by some of the people who showed up to pay a shiva call, many of whom were acquaintances from the Jewish community. I wasn't sure whether they were coming to pay respects to Janie or to me because of my loss. Either way, I was touched by their presence. I felt that they were going above and beyond the call of duty by being there.

Then there were those who didn't even bother to call me after Janie died. One couple in particular comes to mind. I knew they had to have heard of Janie's death through the grapevine. They could have been away and unable to come to the funeral or the shiva, but they could have called or sent a condolence card—something to show they cared.

As I grieved my wife of many years, conflicting and competing emotions continued to rise and fall inside me. They came in waves, hitting me when I least expected it. Alongside the grief was the awareness that I was suddenly a man without a purpose.

For eight and a half years, my entire life had revolved around looking after Janie. I had somehow managed to keep my promise to her, that I would never put her in a facility. In so doing, I had nearly put myself in the ground with her. Somehow, I got through that dark period, thanks to my love for Janie, my determination to keep my vow to her, and the love of my boys and other family and friends.

Michele was truly my rock during the end stages of Janie's illness, and especially the last six months. And during that entire time, she was very sensitive to my feelings. She took it in stride when I couldn't see much of her because I had to stay by Janie's bedside during the last several weeks of her illness.

I was so grateful to my sons for prompting me to open myself up to dating again when they did. Having Michele beside me during that horrible period of my life, and afterwards, was priceless. I told many people, "Had Michele and I not connected when we did, I doubt I would be alive today."

Even *with* Michele by my side, I was far from whole. I was devastated, run down, drained, exhausted, grieving, and on the brink of undergoing treatment for prostate cancer. I was also plagued by nagging existential questions.

As I mentioned earlier, there had been many times during Janie's illness when I thought to myself, *G-d, why don't you take her already? Why are you making her suffer so long? Is it her you are making suffer or me?*

To this day, I've never felt that G-d justified his actions, so we remain on uneasy terms. As I put one foot in front of the other and began to move forward with Michele, I was left with my questions and my grief.

The day after Janie's funeral, I called Dr. Frank to find out how soon my radiation-seeds treatment could be scheduled. He told me that he had an opening in two weeks, so we scheduled the procedure for that time. I could have insisted on getting more of a reprieve after burying Janie and before returning to Houston to face treatment for prostate cancer, but I wanted to get the treatment over with and done.

I arrived at M.D. Anderson on November 15th, this time with Michele by my side. She wouldn't hear of me going alone. Once again, I was grateful that I was getting my treatment at such a top-of-the-line facility.

"Let me ask you something," I said to Dr. Frank during one of my appointments with him in advance of the procedure. "When you're putting the seeds in this way, what happens if one of them works its way loose from the tissue and gets into my bloodstream? If it hits my heart, I'm dead!"

"Well, you don't have to worry about that! You're right...in the past the seeds *were* free-floating. But it just so happens that a new technique has been developed and we're in a clinical trial with it right now. It involves stringing three or four of the seeds together so they're attached." (I may have been part of the clinical trial for that procedure.)

Now, the time had come. I was lying in the surgery prep room, as Dr. Frank was telling me what to expect. Then he said, "By the way, Ivey wants to know what you want for dinner."

I started laughing. "That's thoughtful of her. Thank her for me. But, believe me, Steven, dinner is the last thing on my mind right now!"

"Well, you know what my wife's going to do to me if I can't get an answer out of you!"

"I really can't imagine eating anything too heavy. So, how about yogurt and berries?"

I was close with Dr. Frank's family and that's how they were treating me—like family. His father-in-law, Jay, and mother-in-law, Elise, were longtime friends of mine and Janie's and are currently friends of mine and Michele's.

After taking my order for dinner, Dr. Frank said, "See you later, Bob!" and left me in the hands of the surgery-prep nurses.

Michele was sitting by my side as the nurses bustled about, and put an I.V. in my arm. Since I was going to be put to sleep for the surgery, the anesthesiologist also stopped by my gurney to introduce himself and tell me what type of anesthesia he was planning to use. After he left, a woman walked in.

"I'm the anesthesiologist's nurse," she explained, "and I'll be in the operating room with you. My name is Janie."

Michele and I exchanged a look as if to say, "Whoa! How bizarre!"

The nurse could have referred to herself as Nurse Smith or Jane Smith—but she used the name Janie.

I thought to myself, *This has to be Janie's way of letting me know she's here with me. My good witch strikes again! I wonder if she's here to make sure I get up off the table after surgery...or to make sure I don't so I can join her.*

The anesthesiologist told me to count backwards from one hundred—and then I was coming to in the recovery room, trying to get my bearings. Michele was there waiting for me. After I had sufficiently stabilized, I was put in a wheelchair and taken back to my hotel room.

I was sore as hell afterwards, thanks to the sensitive area where the seeds were placed, the fact that it was accomplished using needles, and the tiny ultrasound camera put inside me to aid in the placement. On the upside, I wouldn't end up experiencing the extended downtime one often faces after surgery.

Dr. Frank had explained to me, "I am going to want you to stay overnight. I'll need to take a look at the scans before I can release you. In one or two percent of cases, I'll realize after seeing the scans that I want to place one or two more seeds."

The phone rang while Michele and I were finishing up the yogurt, berries and bagels that had been waiting for us in our room after surgery. It was about eight o'clock in the evening. "Okay, Bob, the scans look fine. You're good to go home tomorrow."

So, the following morning, we flew home. I was armed with a letter from Dr. Frank, addressed to the TSA.

"Keep this with you when you go through security and be ready to show it to them," he had cautioned me. "The letter explains that you are under my care and being treated for prostate cancer with radiation seeds. The radiation in the seeds can set off the metal detector!"

As we were on the plane, I was feeling profoundly grateful that my cancer treatment had involved minimal tsuris (a Yiddish word for aggravation). I honestly did not feel like I could have handled much more at that point. Every last drop of my internal resources had been spent on surviving Janie's illness and devoting myself to her care.

On the flight home, I used a special tush pillow provided by the doctor to alleviate some of my pain. Standing up from time to time during the flight also helped with the pain and discomfort. I had prearranged this with the flight attendant. She didn't object once she understood my situation.

Returning home, I felt completely unmoored. In the space of a few weeks, my life had become unrecognizable. I had gone from having Janie slowly receding more and more, even as I lay in bed beside her each night, to having the bed we had shared for so long be entirely empty. I had also undergone cancer treatment, with everything that entailed.

Now it was a waiting game. I ticked off the months and let the radiation seeds hopefully cure me of cancer. I said to myself, *I can't wait for the day I'm given the all clear. Maybe then I can finally take a deep breath!*

Dr. Frank had told me that if all went well, no further treatment would be needed. I was told I would then have to undergo quarterly checkups for the next two years, and then every six months until I reached five years. After my two years of quarterly checkups, I put myself on an annual schedule, rather than every six months.

One year, when I was due to return to Houston for my checkup, I told Dr. Frank, "I love you, Steven, but I'm not coming all the way to Houston just to have blood work done. Adam will take care of the blood draw here and we'll overnight the blood to you."

In November of 2017 after successful treatment, Dr. Frank told me, "Bob, I'm releasing you. It's been over five years. You have no cancer and your PSA is undetectable. You're cured. Tell Adam to check your PSA twice a year. Unless it goes up, we're done."

Those words were music to my ears. At last, I could finally take a deep breath and relax. It had been so long since I had been truly carefree, I hardly knew what to do with myself.

Forty-Nine

Annie had been with us for about thirty-five years by then, and she and Janie had been incredibly close. So, it was devastating for her to lose the first lady. Her love for Janie was evident even in the way she answered our house phone. "Mrs. Fischbach's residence," she would say.

More than once, I'd found myself joking with her, "Annie, you do know I live here too, don't you?"

On her first day back at work after Janie's death, Annie said to me, "I can't do this anymore, Bob. I have to retire."

It made perfect sense that, at eighty-one years old, Annie felt ready to retire.

"I understand," I said, "but who's going to take care of me?"

She thought about it for a few minutes and then said, "Well, I guess you're right! But I need to take a couple of months off to get my emotions back together."

Annie never did end up taking any time off. She was worried about what would become of me in her absence. I too was worried about what would become of me—and Pookie, Janie's dog—if Annie retired.

Pookie had been Janie's devoted companion, her best buddy. Prior to getting Pookie, we had a male dog named Baby who was purebred Bichon Friese. Six months after Baby died, I saw an ad in the paper for a dog that was half Bichon and half Shih Tzu. Bichons are extremely smart dogs. They're also very loyal, as are Shih Tzus.

"Hey, bunny, I found an ad for some mixed Bichons north of here..."

"I don't want another dog," said Janie. "I can't go through that again."

"Why don't we just go for a ride and take a look?"

When we got there, we sat on the floor. Right away, the dog ran over and jumped into Janie's lap. That was all it took for us to end up with another dog. Pookie was a real cutie and the smartest dog we had ever had. I've read that mixed-breed dogs tend to be smarter and healthier than purebreds, and Pookie made a believer out of me.

Pookie followed Janie around all day long, looking up at her with his soulful eyes and tilting his head to the side when she talked to him. During Janie's illness, Pookie never left her side. He would happily spend an entire day, sitting on her leg.

Now, Pookie became Annie's loyal companion and was constantly underfoot as she moved around our house. He was already attached to Annie, and often vacationed at her place.

Janie and I would joke with each other, "Tell Pookie we're going to take him to his vacation house in the city." Then we'd drop him off at Annie's place. The minute Pookie saw Annie, he was as happy as a lark.

It became clear to me pretty quickly after Janie's funeral that I was going to have to move. I was having trouble getting back into the bed I had shared with Janie. I completely understood how Pookie must have felt as he stared at the bed after Janie's death, a mournful look in his eyes.

It wasn't just the bedroom that seemed haunted, either. Every place I went in the house, I was blindsided by a painful memory. I couldn't turn a corner without being stopped in my tracks. The entire house was filled with painful memories.

I put the house up for sale at a price above market, even though I knew that the market was in a slump. I figured that while I was looking for a new house, I might as well leave the price high and see if I got any interest. Then, when I was truly ready to sell, I would lower the price to a more realistic number.

While the house was on the market, I took my time looking for a new house. During that time, Michele was often at my house with me. I knew that it must have felt strange to her to be at the house I had shared with Janie.

I also knew that it must have felt strange to Michele to be involved with me while Janie was still alive. I would go on dates with Michele, kiss her goodnight, and return home to my wife. Not that Janie was anything but existing by the time Michele and I got involved. Still and all, I was dating Michele and then going home to my wife.

Michele continued to be very understanding and sensitive, just as she had always been. She never said a word about the fact that I still had photos of Janie around the house. And, she didn't question me when I went to the cemetery to visit Janie's grave.

About six months into our dating relationship as things started to get a bit more serious, I had told her, "I hope you know there's nothing to be jealous about when it comes to Janie. There's no competition between you two. You're two entirely different women and I don't compare two people."

Michele and I had been spending more and more time together, but Annie was still in the dark about our relationship. The time had come to break the news to her. I knew that if Annie found out from someone other than me, she would be hurt. I didn't know how to tell her. I worried that she would be devastated.

One day, Thelma and Deanna were at the house prior to going to lunch together, and I realized that it was now or never. This was the best opportunity I was going to get. I had a feeling that Thelma and Deanna already knew about Michele and I figured they could help soften the blow for Annie.

Over the years that she had worked for Janie and me, Annie had a certain protocol she always followed when she needed to complain about something. "Sit down," she would say, "I've got something to say."

So that day, with Deanna and Thelma there for backup, I went into the laundry room and said to Annie, "Come in here, Annie..."

I led her into the kitchen dining area, and said, "Sit down. I've got something to say."

The four of us—Annie, Deanna, Thelma and I—took a seat at a small square table. Annie was sitting to my right.

"I wanted you to know," I said, looking down and watching Annie out of the corner of my eye, "a year and a half to two years ago, the boys asked me to go to lunch with them. And they asked me at that lunch what I was going to do with the rest of my life. I answered them by saying, 'What are you talking about? I don't have time to think about the rest of my life. I'm shopping, cleaning, taking care of your mother. That's what the rest of my life is right now.' And they said, 'No, Dad, you need to think outside the box. You're young looking, you're young acting, and you need to think that way.' I looked at them with a squint in my eye and asked them, 'Are you giving me permission to start dating? Is that what this is all about?' And they said, 'Well, no, Dad, not really. We just want you to know that whatever your decision is concerning that, we have no judgment about that.'"

As I talked, I watched Annie slump in her chair a bit and her head slowly start to sink.

I was thinking, *Oh, no...*

I kept talking, petrified of Annie's reaction. Then I saw her begin to perk up. I thought to myself, *She prob-*

ably just needed a minute to process what I was saying. It must have come as a shock.

I forged ahead, saying, "Anyway, Annie, it took six months for me to get okay with that idea. Once I got okay with it, I started thinking about it and investigating it. I finally did start to date. And now, I'm dating someone...and it's getting fairly serious."

Finally, Annie spoke. "That's good. You need somebody to take care of you."

I was profoundly relieved that she took the news so well. Over time, Annie and Michele would become thick as thieves. In fact, Annie got to be so comfortable with Michele that she confided in her on some very private family issues.

Even though Michele and I were getting more serious, I wasn't particularly desirous of getting married at my age. I didn't see the point. It wasn't like we had plans to start a family.

Michele's kids had other ideas. "Mom!" they said. "You may be wasting the best remaining years of your life if you continue to date without a marriage commitment."

I asked my boys what they thought of me and Michele living together without getting married. They could have cared less either way.

I was wrestling with the idea of marriage. On the one hand, it didn't really make sense to me. And yet, I knew that it would be meaningful for Michele and her kids.

Before I proposed to Michele, I went to the cemetery to visit Janie. I took a seat on the stone bench which bore a carving of the name Fischbach.

The story of the bench is an interesting one. I was at the cemetery doing some paperwork when I overheard a heated argument:

"That lady ordered this bench and it was delivered in the wrong color stone!"

I saw the opportunity and seized it, saying, "Well, if you'll show me the invoices stating what you paid for it, I'll take it off your hands."

What I didn't tell the woman in advance was that I wanted the name Fischbach carved as large as possible into the bench's backrest.

She agreed to sell me the bench and I now had a memorial bench for Janie. There are no upright headstones in that cemetery, so that became my headstone for Janie. It is the only bench in this entire district that has a back on it.

Anyway, while sitting on Janie's memorial bench, I said to her, "You know, bunny, I'm dating Michele and things are getting serious. I'd really like you to give me a sign that you're okay with us dating..."

The very next day, my phone started flashing every time it rang.

I called Scott and said, "You're never going to believe this. Yesterday, I went to the cemetery to talk to Mom. And now today..." I went on and explained what my phone was doing.

"Oh, Dad," he said, dismissing the notion that anything out of the ordinary was occurring, "you never know what you're doing with your phone! Let me take a look at it. You probably just touched the wrong button or something."

We agreed to meet the following day on his lunch break from work. Sitting across from each other at the restaurant, I said, "You don't believe me? Call my phone!"

He dialed my number and saw the flashing light with his own eyes.

"Okay, smart ass...you tell me. What's wrong with it?" I said.

He looked at the settings of my iPhone and found a function he thought I had inadvertently activated. But then he realized that function was turned off.

"I told you," I said. "Mom's giving me a signal!"

We looked at each other and laughed in disbelief.

For two or three weeks afterwards, my phone blew up with a flashing light every time it rang. *Well*, I said to myself, *I guess I have my answer.*

Janie also played golf with me recently. A butterfly stayed with me throughout the entire eighteen holes of golf, perched on a golf club in the cart. The golf cart kept moving from hole to hole but the butterfly never moved. I also had a butterfly alight on my finger and stay there. This is not in the nature of butterflies, as you know. Janie loved butterflies, and any time I see one coming around, I know it's her.

Another incident that made me think twice involved my money clip. I always keep my money in my front, left pocket in a paperclip made of spring gold. My employees gave it to me twenty or thirty years ago as a holiday gift, and I've used it ever since.

One day, I reached into my pocket and it was gone. I went nuts trying to find it, tearing up the whole house in the process. Even after all that, I couldn't find it. I was so aggravated.

A couple of days later, I was at the cemetery visiting Janie. I was sitting on the bench talking to her when I found my money clip on the bench. I visit the cemetery every ten days and don't remember ever taking my money clip out at the cemetery. I would have no need for money while I was there. This was one more example of Janie being a good witch.

I now believed I had Janie's blessing on my relationship with Michele. I was also coming to a realization that I couldn't shake: I'd lost Janie and the pain was horrible. There was no getting around it. And yet, what choice did I have but to go on with my life? What was the alternative?

As long as I was still breathing, I had to keep moving forward with my life. I had two sons and two grandkids and I had to keep the family together. I had promised Janie I would, shortly after she had gotten diagnosed. I couldn't very well cash in my chips and call it a day. I had to keep moving forward with my life.

Fifty

It took me almost two years to find a new house. This one was also in Sandy Springs, and sat right in between my current house and the dream house I had built. My new house was built in 1983 and needed quite a bit of work. The property was about three quarters of an acre, surrounded by trees. The house was a good size, and the high ceilings made it appear even larger.

When Michele and I first looked at the house, we were thrown by the condition of it. It had been owned by a Persian doctor who had decorated it with bright golds and reds, not at all to our taste. There was also a double archway separating the dining room from the living room and it looked like it belonged in a church, not in my house. Don't even get me started on the mess of trees in the front yard.

Michele and I both liked the house. She reminded me that when I was done with it, it would be unrecognizable. The price was right and, even figuring in what it would cost me to do the renovations, it was still a good deal. We closed on the house in June of 2013 and I started renovations right after July 4th, estimating that we'd be finished within three months.

I did a major remodel that brought it into the Twenty-First Century. I hired subcontractors Drew had worked with in his construction business. "You don't need to come yourself, and I don't need your partner here either," I had told my son. "Just send the workers. I'll do the rest myself."

When the subcontractors came over to redo my deck, I asked them, "Are you the guys who just expanded Drew's deck?"

They were all smiles and clearly proud of themselves. "Yep! That was us!"

"Well," I said, "this one's being done *correctly*. I don't want any two boards butting up against each other, end to end."

"But, patron, it can't be done that way!" (Drew's work crew always called me el patron.)

"Oh, yes, it can!" I said. "Come...I'll show you."

When the inspector came to look at the deck, he was stunned. "Wow! I've never seen a deck done this way before. It's amazing!"

"Thanks," I said. "I designed it myself."

I replaced the rear deck, adding a screened-in porch. I completely redid the master bath, adding a master closet from living space we didn't want or need. I also removed archways and columns to open up the living room and dining room. Michele loved the back yard with a pool.

We lived in the old house during renovations, and moved into the new one in December of 2013. It took me six months rather than the estimated three to bring the house into the current century. The renovated house has worked out really well. We have room for the entire family for dinner, bedrooms for the grandkids when they sleep over, and a pool for them to swim in, which they love to do.

Michele and I were now living together. She had made a huge accommodation by moving in with me while I still had Pookie. She is absolutely not a dog person but she accepted it when I told her that Pookie was not going anywhere.

As I've said, Pookie was devoted to Janie and very attached to Annie. He now took an immediate liking to Michele. What can I say? He's a male and he loves the ladies. He started following her all over the house. Over time, he wore her down to the point that she finally got used to having him around.

Just like I used to do when Janie was still alive, Michele and I would sometimes pack up Pookie for a vacation sleepover at Annie's.

In April of 2015, Michele and I went to Africa on a three-week safari tour. I had made all the reservations for the safari back in 2007 when Janie and I had been planning on going together. After Janie fainted at the funeral of the mother of a good friend of ours and had to be rushed to the doctor, we reconsidered the trip.

"What if I get sick in the middle of the African desert?" said Janie. "It's not like you could just drive me to the doctor."

As disappointing as it was to cancel the trip, we both had to admit that being a continent away in the desert was unwise. Thankfully we had bought trip insurance, so I knew we wouldn't be out any money by cancelling.

With a heavy heart, I called the travel agent and asked her, "Hey, what was your commission going to be on this trip?"

"My commission?" the agent said, incredulous.

"Yes, my wife isn't well and I'm going to have to cancel the trip...but I want to send you a check."

"No," she said, "the insurance covered that too."

Instead of Africa, Janie and I went to the Turks and Caicos and relaxed on the beach for a week. It would end up being our last trip together.

In early 2015, I called the travel agent who had arranged the trip the first time. "Hi, this is Bob Fischbach. Do you remember me, by any chance?"

"Sure, I remember you! In all my years in this business, you're the only person who ever offered to pay my commission when they cancelled a trip!"

I had the agent re-book the trip for Michele and me. She was the ideal travel agent to arrange the trip because she happened to be from Zimbabwe and specialized in safari trips to Africa.

I love animals and nature and knew that the trip would be a wonderful adventure. Knowing that Michele is not particularly an animal person, I was banking on the fact that she would fall in love with the landscape.

Fifty-One

We flew nonstop from Atlanta, Georgia to Johannesburg. Thanks to our business-class seats, we were able to pass the sixteen-hour trip in seats that were fully reclining. We alternated between sleeping, watching movies and eating.

Arriving in Johannesburg, we checked into The Saxon. It would end up being the most fabulous hotel I have ever stayed in. The hotel was situated in a residential area that served the wealthy. It was a magnificent, gorgeous, and very atypical luxury hotel. Being there felt like staying in the most elegant home you could imagine. It was very laid back, with none of the usual hotel rhythms to it.

All the homes in the area had high walls surrounding them, and a guard at the front gate. Not surprisingly, the only access to the hotel itself was through a security gate. That was Johannesburg at that time—all walls and security guards.

While we were there, I wanted to make sure we saw the Soweto and the museums established in honor of Nelson Mandela. Of course, very little of the good attributed to Mandela could be seen in the area. The government in place at that time was corrupt, which led to a lot of civil unrest.

That night, we had dinner and then a massage, which really hit the spot after such a long plane ride. The next morning after breakfast, a private guide took us on a tour of Johannesburg. Seeing the way people were living in Soweto was devastating. Their houses were nothing more than little huts, without floors or electricity. Everyone shared a couple of little port-a-potties and had to walk about half a mile to the water spout to collect water for drinking, cooking, cleaning and bathing.

(Interestingly, the government had built affordable housing apartments for the poor, but they were barely inhabited. The locals did not consider the apartments worth the small stipend the government was charging as rent. They didn't have the money to pay the rent, so they continued to occupy their makeshift huts. Less than a half mile away were million-dollar homes occupied by the wealthy.)

We went to the Mandela museums and got to see many photographs of, and writings by, Nelson Mandela. After a nice lunch and a drive around the business section of Johannesburg, our guide returned us to our hotel in the late afternoon. At dinnertime, we enjoyed another incredible meal thanks to the resident gourmet chef. The food was truly second to none, with exotic spices and sauces.

The next morning, we headed out to meet our guide for the safari—the same lady who had given us the tour the previous day. She took us to a tiny airport where a small plane was awaiting our arrival. The little four-passenger planes on which we would be traveling could not accommodate hard-sided luggage, so our travel agent had given us each a duffel bag. We took what we could comfortably fit in our duffels.

Before leaving the States, the travel agent had given me two options. "You have a choice. Do you want to take a Holiday Inn approach to this trip? Or, do you want to go the Ritz route? If you choose the Ritz, all you have to remember is your name. That's it. Everything else will be taken care of for you."

Considering how far we were from home, and the fact that we had absolutely no idea what we might encounter in Africa, I opted to splurge. I thought to myself, *There's no better time to go all out than when you're in a country where you're truly going to be roughing it!*

I quickly found out that the agent was not exaggerating at all. We were catered to in every way. At every turn, there was someone waiting to look after us. We were treated like a king and queen. We had our luggage picked up, wrapped in cellophane to protect it from thieves, and sent on ahead to Capetown, our last stop. A private guide met us for our safari. And, a car was ready and waiting to take us to the camp.

I didn't mind flying on such small planes but Michele wasn't crazy about it. The travel agent had reassured us that the pilots were all quite seasoned and experienced and we took her at her word. Then we met our pilot, and she looked to be barely old enough for a bat mitzvah! Maybe she really was experienced and had started flying planes when she was quite young. Or maybe she looked much younger than her actual age. In any case, her extremely youthful appearance did nothing to instill confidence in us.

The pilot flew low enough that she was able to point out various animals roaming the plains below. In Africa, the five big species are elephants, giraffes, lions, water buffalos and hippos. As we approached the dirt landing strip, she called down to the guide who was sitting on the runway in an open-top Jeep and said, "Please drive up and down the landing strip. I can see some animals down there. I need you to get them out of the way for me."

I couldn't believe my ears. We definitely weren't in the States anymore. After the pilot made the call, we could see open-top jeeps chasing away the animals.

This was followed by a very smooth landing. Once on the ground, we were met by open-top jeeps from the lodge where we'd be staying during the safari. When I say lodge, I mean the safari camp, which is comprised of tent dwellings. In the entire safari camp, there were only twenty guests (ten couples), occupying ten tents.

Had you told me I could have lived in a tent and been perfectly content, I wouldn't have believed you—until then. The place was incredible. It was the size of a suite and had luxurious furniture. Given that there were only nine or ten tents per camp, very spread out, we had an enormous amount of privacy.

Our room had a solid bottom that was made of either concrete or wood. In lieu of walls, there was tenting held in place by poles. Behind our tent, we had our own swimming pool, as did all guests. The bathrooms at each of the camps where we stayed were incredible, and one of our tents had a freestanding copper bathtub and indoor-outdoor showers.

All that was standing between us and herds of wild animals was a bit of canvas. I couldn't tell you what kept the animals outside the camp but they didn't bother us. We could hear them from time to time, right on the other side of the canvas walls, and that was a bit unnerving at first. But we quickly adjusted to the arrangement, and fear left us for the most part.

After a day or so, Michele too became comfortable. One day, she was getting a massage out in back of our tent when five or six elephants wandered by. She was startled by the sight, and amazed at how close they came to her.

We were escorted by guides to and from dinner, and told in the strictest of terms that we were not to venture out in the dark by ourselves. At dinner, everyone staying at the camp ate together family-style under a gazebo, sharing a community table. Even though we were in an open area in the dining area, the arrangement seemed safe to me—not that I'm a good barometer of such things, as I'm afraid of very little.

When I inquired as to how they could serve such gourmet food out in the middle of nowhere, it was explained to me that a supply truck brought in all their culinary supplies once a week. If they ran out of something before the next shipment arrived, it was flown in.

The safari excursions started around six o'clock in the morning because that's when the animals were awake, feeding and wandering around. After a quick cup of coffee and a muffin, we all went out in open-top jeeps. The seats were staggered stadium-style, with the highest row of seating in the back, so everyone could see.

From six o'clock until ten or ten-thirty in the mornings, we were out in the jeeps, seeing the animals. Around 10 or 10:30, the heat in the bush grew to maximum intensity, and both the animals and the humans were ready to lie down and cool off. So, we returned to camp for a substantial breakfast. We then had a period of time where we were free to lounge around, read, nap, or get a massage.

Lunch was served at 2:00 p.m. Then in late afternoon around three-thirty or four when it started to cool down, we left again for an evening safari. On the evening safaris, everyone was reaching for their jackets. We stayed out until about seven-thirty or eight when we returned to camp to get ready for dinner.

On the very first morning of our safari, we were admonished to remain seated at all times and refrain from standing up in the jeep. We were also told that we must absolutely never get out of the truck unless the guide-tracker gave us permission to do so. That last admonishment went without saying, as far as I was concerned.

In addition to the driver, we had a guide who was also a tracker. He sat in a chair attached to the outside of the jeep. The tracker kept his focus on the ground, looking for footprints and markings that would indicate where we could find the animals. As he spotted signs that animals were nearby, he shouted out instructions to the driver, along the lines of, "Turn right and hurry!"

Neither the tracker nor the driver was armed. So, it's hard to say what would have happened if we had encountered a herd of angry animals that decided to charge the jeep. All staff at the camp seemed to navigate entirely based on their understanding of the animals—an understanding developed with time and experience.

Every morning we spent seeing the animals brought new experiences and adventures I never could have imagined. My favorite was the giraffes with their astoundingly long necks. I was fascinated by them. There were ten to twelve giraffes to a herd. We even got to see a couple of giraffes making out. It was then that I understood the term necking in a way I had never considered before. The neck of a full-sized giraffe is six to eight feet long.

The senior male member of the herd saw these two giraffes necking and approached. Using his head with his horns, he knocked the young male away as if to say, "She's mine!" He was very protective over her, like a father with a daughter. It was really touching.

Then there were the impalas, which traveled in huge herds of about a hundred. Every time I saw them, I would joke, "There's another herd of Chevrolets over there." Impalas are, for the most part, dinner for the larger animals. When they were grazing, there would always be one lookout impala with his back to the rest of the herd, keeping watch. Interestingly enough, they liked to stay close to their enemies so they could keep an eye on them. When one in the herd had eaten his fill, he would swap places with the lookout and let him graze for a while.

One morning, we ran into a herd of elephants fairly close by. The bull elephant was not happy with our proximity and flared out his ears—a sign that he was getting ready to charge. He charged the jeep until he got to within twenty or twenty-five feet of us and then stopped. He seemed to be saying to us, "You'd better back up right now or you'll have trouble from me!"

If I had been driving, I would have had a hard time keeping myself from fleeing, even if I knew intellectually that this would only cause the elephants to chase us.

In moments like that, I became very aware of just how close we were getting to wild animals. When you're riding around without incident, it's easy to put that reality out of your mind.

(I loved the elephants so much that, on a later trip to Thailand that Michele and I took together, I would end up buying three paintings that were painted *by* elephants! One painting was of an elephant, one was of flowers, and the third was of a landscape.)

One of the most exciting things I've ever seen happened one morning when we encountered a mother cheetah and three baby cubs under attack from a hyena. The cheetah was trying to protect her cubs from the hyena and managed to fight it off. She got lucky that day because there was only one hyena. Usually they travel in packs, sneaking up on their prey. A couple of the hyenas distract the prey while the rest attack.

It was hair-raising to hear the screaming and hollering by the hyena and the cheetahs. I was also stunned by the sheer meanness of the hyena. They are natural-born killers with the looks to match. The entire spectacle was like one of those T.V. segments I used to see on *Mutual of Omaha's Wild Kingdom.*

Another experience I will never forget involved a pride of nine or ten lions sitting on what appeared to be an enormous pile of sand. I expressed to my guide my amazement over our jeep stopping within five feet of those lions without provoking an attack.

He explained that over time, the indigenous animals realize that the jeeps, trucks and people that roamed their land were of no danger to them. So, they left us alone.

I asked our guide, "By the way, what is that...the sand hill they're sitting on?"

"Oh, that's a termites' nest!"

"A termites' nest that big? But that must be about five feet high and fifteen feet wide!" (I have a good eye for dimensions, thanks to my years in real estate development.)

"That's right. Termites are very important for keeping Africa green..."

Our guide explained that elephants and other animals eat the leaves and bark off the trees, causing them to die. Then they poop. Continuing the cycle, termites consume the animal waste, and *they* poop. And from their poop, new trees grow. Talk about the circle of life!

When I was in real estate in the States, I paid good money to avoid having termites in any of my properties. In Africa, termites were an asset and a necessity for the preservation of tree life.

We also visited Botswana, where we stayed in a safari camp that was entirely solar and environmentally green. It was fascinating to me that, from a comfort level, we had no awareness that we were without electricity.

The camp was on the headwaters of the river. We were surrounded by many varieties of gorgeous birds, including a bird named the Jesus bird because it appears to walk on water. We were also very close to the hippos and water buffalo that lived in the river. Both species are enormous and have temperamental dispositions. We learned that hippos kill more humans than any other animal in Africa. Interestingly, they are vegetarians so they won't eat their kill.

We were taken into the river on a huge motorized pontoon boat one night so that we could see the animals up close. There was no barrier between us and them. The experience was much like taking a walk in your neighborhood and walking past an off-leash dog—a dog the size of a house.

Much like the lion that flared its ears and began to charge us and then stopped, the hippos would rear out of the waters with their jaws open to signal us when we were getting too close for their comfort. The water buffalos were much more docile by comparison and wouldn't charge. They hung out in absolutely enormous herds of hundreds and roamed the grounds more than the hippos, enjoying spending time laying around in mud and water.

Among other highlights of our Africa trip was a visit to Victoria Falls in Zimbabwe (Africa's Niagara Falls) by helicopter, about midway through a trip. While in Zimbabwe, we also discovered an art gallery with some of the most astounding artwork either Michele or I had ever seen. The artist sculpted out of black and silver stone these pieces that were so incredible, we wanted to bring them all home with us.

Talking to the artist, I told him that I would help him find gallery space if he ever wanted to open a gallery in Atlanta. And for my time, he could pay me in a single stone sculpture. I have yet to find a proper gallery for his sculptures but I will never forget seeing them.

We also visited Capetown and stayed in a hotel. In the closet, we found our luggage that had been sent on ahead for us when we first left on safari and began our stays in the various camps.

Capetown was beautiful and quite modern. My most memorable moments while there occurred on Robbins Island where Nelson Mandela was imprisoned for twenty-seven years. The island had been turned into a national park where families lived and children went to school. Remarkably, our tour guide was an ex-prisoner himself.

We also took a day trip to the Cape of Good Hope where we were treated to the unexpected sight of penguins wandering around on the beach. That sight was definitely not something I would have associated with Africa. They were of the hot-weather penguin species, something of which I was unfamiliar until then. They looked like they had made a wrong turn somewhere and ended up near the equator.

The Wine Country area of South Africa, about an hour from Capetown, was one of the biggest surprises on the trip. The area surpasses even Northern California wine country in its splendor. It was quite mountainous and covered by vineyards. The scenery was just magnificent, as was our hotel, La Residence. We both wished we had set aside more time to explore.

We might have stayed one more night had we not been scheduled to leave the following day in late afternoon.

From there, we drove right to the airport in Capetown, flew through Johannesburg, switched planes, and then flew nonstop home to Atlanta. Arriving back in the States, it felt like we had reentered the earth's atmosphere after spending a month on another planet. Our African trip was for me the most exciting and wonderful trip of my entire life.

Returning home on May 11th, of 2015, we were both exhausted. After taking some time to recover from the time change and the rigors of travel, we headed to the Florida Gulf Coast. We had rented a house in Rosemary Beach for our annual pre-Memorial Day family gathering. (Janie had died on Halloween of 2012, I went by myself in May of 2013, and thereafter Michele went with me.)

There were a bunch of us at the beach house: Michele and I; my nephew, Alex; my sons, Scott and Drew, and their wives, Jaime and Nina, and kids, Max, Olivia and Devon. (Devon is my twenty-five-year-old step-granddaughter—Nina's daughter from a previous marriage.) Also with us were Michele's boys, Evan and Eric, along with her grandson, Robert ("Da").

The house where we stayed was on a cul-de-sac. From there, it was an easy walk down to the beach with its beautiful white sand. Being at the beach was very relaxing and we followed no particular schedule. Everyone did their own thing, going down to the beach and returning to the house as we wanted to. Of the seven nights we were there, we went out to dinner three or four nights and the other nights we cooked dinner at the house. We ate some great raw oysters at a local restaurant. Spending that week at the beach was a great way to decompress after our trip to Africa.

These trips to Africa and Rosemary Beach, as well as upcoming trips to Israel and Alaska, would end up being a sort of pre-honeymoon tour with my soon-to-be second wife.

Fifty-Two

As time went by and I sat with the idea of remarrying, it had started to grow on me. I wanted Michele to feel comfortable around her kids, and I knew that they preferred that she not be living with me without being married.

I also knew that Michele and I made a great match. And I was falling in love with her. So, I told her that I was going to start shopping for a ring and once I found one, I would surprise her with a proposal.

Knowing that her dad had been in the jewelry business and she owned a jeweler's loupe, I joked with her, saying, "Since you have that damned loupe, the perfect stone is going to be hard to find!"

Then, every few days as I was on my way out of the house in the morning, I would say, "I'm going to Israel today, babe. They have a stone they think I'll like and I'm going to fly there. I'll be home in time for dinner."

Other times, I would joke that I was headed to South Africa, Amsterdam or other sites where diamonds are historically mined and cut. (Belgium used to be the diamond-cutting capital of the world and then that distinction moved to Israel. Eventually, Israel lost that title and it moved elsewhere.)

Michele got a kick out of these jokes...for a while.

I did have contacts in Israel and they *were* actively keeping an eye out for a stone for me. Once I had the ideal stone, I would go looking for the setting.

I knew that Michele liked rectangular-cut and emerald-cut rings.

"You're not getting an emerald-cut ring from me!" I said. "It doesn't sparkle. It doesn't dance. It doesn't have enough facets. You're getting either a radiant-cut or a cushion-cut ring. Actually, round dances the most but I know you don't want a round one..."

"You realize that you know things you have no business knowing, right?" Michele teased.

"Some of that I picked up from your dad!" I reminded her. "And the rest of it, I probably picked up from *my* dad's salon customers over the years."

Early in life, I learned from my dad that there is no such thing as a stupid question. So, I have always asked a lot of questions of everyone, especially my dad. I knew that he knew more than most men about women, their hair, and their fashions. This has resulted in me carrying around a lot of knowledge about a lot of things related to the female population, some of which actually comes in handy from time to time.

Before long, my contact in Israel found a couple of stones he thought might be suitable and sent them to me. I selected the radiant-cut stone and bought it at a great price. Then I went to my jeweler here in Atlanta and designed the setting, which he cast in platinum. Knowing that Michele's favorite color is pink, I chose two pink sapphires for the side stones. I felt like diamond baguettes would be too predictable.

Over Labor Day weekend of 2015, Pookie and I were sitting in the living room with Michele.

"I've got something to say," I said, borrowing Annie's line. Then, while holding Pookie, I went down onto one knee.

I said, "If not for you, I'd probably be dead by now. So, since you're getting a package deal here, both Pookie and I would like your hand in marriage..." I then presented her with the ring in the ring box.

Michele began to cry.

"...And we would like you to wear this ring. I put a lot of time and effort into getting it just right for you. We hope you like it!"

"I love it!" she said. She was thrilled—and that was high praise from her, coming as she did from a family in the jewelry business.

(Sadly, in February of 2018, I would have to put Pookie down due to health issues. I agonized over the decision and finally consulted with Annie about it. "It's time to send him back to Janie," she agreed.

So, I had him cremated and then Annie and I went to the cemetery and spread his ashes over Janie's grave. I miss him terribly and still expect to hear his bark when I walk into the house. Sometimes, I swear I can hear him walking around the house.)

Michele and I would end up being engaged for almost a year. We began dating a year or so before Janie's passing and would marry in August of 2016, after dating for five years. I had been numb for a long time before meeting Michele, and was not remotely ready to jump into anything. I deeply appreciated Michele's patience with me, giving me the time that I needed to grieve Janie. I never forgot Janie, or lost my love for her, but the acuteness of the grief did ease a bit over time.

A month after we got engaged, Michele and I took a trip to Israel. After all my joking around that I was going to Israel to find the diamond for her engagement ring, we really were going to Israel—together.

Michele had never been to Israel. She had always wanted to go and was looking forward to seeing cousins who lived there. I had been there ten to twenty times, most of those times with Janie by my side. I hadn't been in about fifteen years, since before Janie got ill.

I loved Israel and welcomed the chance to spend time there again. I was especially looking forward to seeing the Unesco site, Petra, in Jordan.

While we were in Israel, memories came flooding back.

There was the time in 1980 when Janie and I had attended the bar mitzvah of an old friend's son. The event was being held at the Western Wall, previously known as the Wailing Wall. (Once Israel reclaimed Jerusalem, the wailing ceased and so the name of the wall was changed.) That was a special trip, with our kids being only seven and ten at the time. This was the era of the historic peace treaty that was struck between

President Carter, Menachem Begin and Anwar Sadat on behalf of Israel and Egypt.

Being so close to Egypt, Janie and I figured we might as well make a side trip. I will never forget the plane landing on the tarmac in Cairo—and stopping just shy of the airport. The flight was immediately surrounded by military vehicles and soldiers with guns drawn because it was Israel's first time flying an El Al flight into Egypt.

As we were exiting the airport, seven-year-old Scott had grabbed my hand and said, "Come here, Dad! I want to show you something."

He took me over to the gutter where a boy of eight or nine was sleeping with his head completely covered in flies. It was a horrendous sight, and it was hard to explain to Scott why that boy was in such terrible shape. I did my best to help my young son understand that he was seeing a sign of abject poverty.

It was also hard to explain to my two little boys why the Egyptians surrounded them and kept trying to touch them. (This was the time I mentioned earlier in the book, when the Egyptians kept calling my boys "Gingies!" and trying to touch them out of curiosity.) At the time, Scott was a towhead with white-blonde hair and Drew had curly red hair. To see children with that coloring in Egypt was a real anomaly and it took some doing to protect the boys from everyone who was grasping at them.

We also visited a tributary of the Nile where we saw women washing clothes along the edge of the water, and children and cows swimming in the same water that was used for sewage disposal. After seeing Egypt in 1980, I was cured of any desire to visit India.

We did see all the artifacts in Egypt, including the Great Pyramids and the Sphinx. I will never forget looking up at the pyramids and thinking to myself, *Those stones are huge and they look like they were cut with a laser! I wonder where they got them from, how they transported them here, and how they put them all together without cement.*

After visiting Israel, Michele and I stayed put for a while and truly settled into our new house. Then, in July, a month or so before our August 28th, 2016 wedding, we took an Alaska cruise.

Visiting Alaska had always been on my bucket list. My first cousin George (my mother's sister's son) was a doctor and had lived there from the time he started practicing medicine. He had wound up in Alaska, working for the public health service, as the medical doctor for villages in the Tundra. This was somehow arranged for him in lieu of his service in the Vietnam War.

George had only been required to serve in Alaska for twelve months but he fell in love with the area. So, after his residency, he and his family settled in Anchorage. He was now retired and often asked me when I was coming for a visit. The time had come.

We started the seven-day Alaskan cruise with a visit to Vancouver, during which I fell in love with the place. The skies were clear and the July weather was absolutely perfect—a balmy sixty-eight degrees. And the city was magnificent and clean.

Michele and I had often talked about renting a house in Florida for a month during the worst of the Atlanta winters. While we were in Vancouver, I realized I had it all wrong. Leaving Atlanta for a month in the sweltering southern summertime was the better way to go.

"Forget heading to Florida during the winter!" I said. "Let's make Vancouver our *summer* destination."

We took a boat taxi from the mainland to an island right off the coast, and visited a fabulous open-air market. We wandered around, did some shopping and then happened upon something that stopped us dead in our tracks. Michele and I looked at each other in disbelief. There was an art gallery featuring the sculptures of the very artist—Pinias Sibanda—whose work we had fallen in love with during our African safari trip!

After our visit to Vancouver, we were off to Alaska on our cruise. There were a surprising number of stops, including Juno, which was only accessible by boat or float plane.

"Juno is the capital and yet you can't drive there?" I said to Michele. "Why don't they plow through the mountain and put in a tunnel?" That might have been a good idea if not for the fact that on the other side of the mountain was another mountain.

The ship was small in the scheme of things—only three hundred passengers or so, as opposed to those enormous ocean liners that carry two or three thousand. A smaller ship can navigate through shallower waters, and get into smaller ports.

While we were in our room on the ship, we looked out to see an enormous ice chunk that had broken away from the glacier. It was such a sight that the captain (a woman!) did a 360-degree turn, spinning the ship around so that everyone on both sides of the ship could see it.

Despite the fact that Alaska is two and a half times the size of Texas, population in the entire state of Alaska was only about seven-hundred-fifty thousand at the time. Anchorage is the largest city and Fairbanks is the second largest. I tend to think of frigid weather when I think of Alaska, but being there in the summer was terrific.

There were several little coastal cities that relied mostly on salmon fishing and tourism for their economy. While we were there, the salmon were running, and that was quite a sight.

We took several float-plane trips, including one where we landed on a glacier. Float planes are wonderful little aircraft. (The last time I had been on one, I was seven or eight years old. Dad had taken me to a regional airport in the northern part of Westchester County and taken me up in a float plane. He wanted me to see the New York skyline from the air. The plane flew under the George Washington Bridge, and the flight was very exciting to me at that age.

Mom was not happy with Dad when she found out where he had taken me. As far as I was concerned, if Dad wanted to take me somewhere, I was raring to go. Dad was my best friend and I trusted him completely.)

On one of our excursions off the ship, we approached a stream by bus. We were let off the bus about two hundred yards from the top of the stream and then walked downstream to where the salmon were running.

As we looked into the water, we saw thousands of salmon running upstream and jumping out of the water. It was more dramatic than I had ever imagined it would be and a sight I will never forget. As the salmon reached the top of the stream, they laid their eggs—and then they died. The dead salmon are consumed by bears. Then the salmon eggs later become new baby salmon which enter the sea, and the cycle begins all over again. It was another circle of life moment.

Another indelible memory on this trip was made on a day when we went out in a small boat on an excursion to view sea animals. It was magnificent to see the stark and magnificent Alaskan landscape from the water. I mentioned to the guide that the boat seemed like poor protection in the event we encountered any large sea creatures, like whales. He downplayed the likelihood of such a thing happening.

We saw seals and sea lions swimming on their backs. Suddenly, we were surrounded by gigantic whales jumping out of the water. As they landed, they slapped their tails on the ocean's surface. To be in such a small boat while huge whales leapt from the sea around us was mind-boggling. Our guide told us that he was surprised to see whales so close to the boat.

As we neared the end of our Alaska trip, there was one day when my cousin George couldn't go exploring with us. So, Michele and I rented a car and drove around. We reached a mountain with a waterfall at the top, and stopped so we could hike up and see the waterfall.

Along the way we passed an older couple and their thirty-something daughter. "Excuse me," I said, "but do you mind if I ask why you are packing a gun?"

"Have you ever been in Alaska before?"

"No," I said.

"Well, that's why you don't know why I've got a gun! There are wild animals around here."

Needless to say, we stuck close to that armed man the rest of the way up the mountain. The climb took us straight up, about three quarters of a mile. When we reached the top, we were treated to the beautiful sight of the small waterfall rushing down the mountain.

As the time came to wrap up our trip and return home, George took us to a restaurant situated on a covered bridge. It was located in a ski area, and overlooked a small river. It was amazing and somewhat surreal to be able to watch the people below, catching salmon from the river while we ate dinner.

Fifty-Three

On August 10th of 2016, we returned from our trip. We had plans to marry at the end of August but no arrangements had yet been made.

About ten days after we got home, around dinnertime, I said to Michele, "Why don't we get married this weekend? You already have the ring. And we're only going to have family at the wedding, so it's not like we have to coordinate with a bunch of people."

We talked it over and both liked the idea, so we each called our children and told them, "Be here Sunday afternoon by 5:30. Michele and I are getting married at the house." I even kiddingly told the kids that I would understand if they had other things to do.

Then we called Maurice and Peggy, friends of ours, and asked them to come and be the non-family witnesses to our wedding.

Now, we needed a rabbi to perform the ceremony. Naturally, I thought first of my longtime friend, Rabbi Phil Kranz. I knew that he often went to Maine for the summer and might be out of town. Sure enough, when I called, I discovered that he was in Maine and had not yet returned.

We then thought of the rabbi whose classes I take—Rabbi Yossi New, the Orthodox Chabad rabbi.

He agreed but wanted Michele to go through a mikvah bath as well as to abide by some other Orthodox requirements that pertain to the bride. And given that we were planning a wedding for Sunday night, a few days away, that wasn't going to work for us.

Then Michele had an idea. "What about Rabbi Glusman?" Rabbi Brian Glusman is someone I had met at various functions for Michele's grandkids.

I liked the idea and got the phone number from Michele. When I called Rabbi Glusman, I said, "This is going to be a very casual wedding. Michele and I have been together for five years, are already living together, and feel like we are married. The wedding is merely a formality. We have been planning to get married for a while, but this ceremony is a last-minute deal. We are having only family here, except for our two witnesses. We would like everyone to be in jeans. It will be fun!"

Neither Michele nor I wanted to make a big deal out of our wedding. In fact, we waited until afterwards to tell our friends that we had gotten married. Janie had been gone not quite four years by that time, and we felt that it would be unseemly for us to have a big splashy wedding. Having a quiet, discreet wedding with mostly family felt much more appropriate.

I also wanted Jeff, my best friend since childhood, and his wife Judy, to come if they were able to make the trip. Jeff and Judy are the couple whose anniversary party I attended in San Diego while Janie was sick.

I often asked him, "Jeff, when are you two coming to Atlanta to visit?"

"When you get married, I'll come."

So, now I called him and said, "You'd better call the airline, Jeff! We're getting married. I know how you hate to fly, so don't feel obligated."

Being the wonderful chef that she is, Michele wanted to be the one to cook for everyone, even though she was also the bride.

We agreed that the ceremony would be held under the portico I had built outside the front door of our house. It was covered in vines and flowers and would be the perfect chuppah for the occasion.

The morning of our wedding, Sunday 28th, 2016, I played golf and returned home mid-afternoon. As I walked in the door, I was shocked to see Jeff from California. I was so happy to have him there.

"Judy's not with me," he explained. "I'm going to have to do a quick turnaround. I have a ten o'clock flight back to San Diego later tonight."

All the kids and grandkids showed up. Michele's son Eric (who is single) was there, as was Evan, who was there with his second wife, Catherine, and Robert, his son by his first wife. A year ago, Catherine gave birth to little Ruth McGuire whose nickname is Maggie. (Ruth is Catherine's mother's first name, and McGuire is a name associated with Evan's paternal grandmother.) When little Maggie was born, I changed Da's nickname to Bro, as I mentioned earlier in the book.

Scott came with his wife, Jaime, and my granddaughter, Olivia. Drew brought his wife, Nina, her daughter Devon, and my grandson, Max.

When it was time for the ceremony, we kept it very short and sweet, which was exactly the way we wanted it. Before the ceremony, we sat down to sign the ketubah, the Jewish marriage contract.

"You don't read Hebrew, do you?" asked the rabbi. "Are you sure you know what you're signing? Do you understand what you're committing to do with Michele?"

I laughed. "Well, I am not sure, but I assume I am committing to house and clothe her," I said.

"Yes," said the rabbi, "those two, and provide food. But you're forgetting one...You have to agree to provide sex for her."

"Oh, that's not a problem," I said.

After the signing of the ketubah, we all ate and drank and had a good time.

I knew that I had to go on with my life. I had my kids and grandkids to look after. And I remembered the promise I had made to Janie—that I would keep the family together. I felt that I was carrying out her wishes. Now, we had our newest member of the family, Michele.

I love my second wife, Michele. In some ways, she is nothing like Janie and in other ways, there are similarities. I always say that Michele is the mother of the world. She is an absolutely fabulous grandmother to my grandchildren and treats them like her own.

When I first convinced myself that I could try to start dating, I couldn't help but compare other women to Janie. I would be sitting over dinner with a new woman and comparing everything about them to my ailing wife.

I would catch myself doing that and think, "Do you *really* believe that about this woman? Or are you just comparing her to Janie? And if, so, is it fair or right of you to do that?"

I really contemplated that and ultimately decided that it wasn't fair to anyone—not to them, not to Janie and certainly not to me. I also realized that I was never going to be happy if I insisted on finding a carbon copy of Janie. So, I readjusted my thinking in that regard.

If you say to yourself, *Well, I need someone exactly like my spouse!* or you start comparing the two people, remember that no two people are the same. You will never find someone who is exactly like your late spouse. The person you loved is gone. You will be in for a world of disappointment if you insist upon finding a duplicate.

Life goes on—and you owe it to yourself to go on with your life. You may have kids and grandkids and you owe it to them too. And if you do remarry, remember that you will never forget the person you have loved and lost but the grief does get easier to bear over time.

Nobody gets out of this life without bumps in the road. Some of us have bigger bumps and more of them than others—but in the end, they are all just bumps in the road. As long as we are still breathing, we must go on.

Afterword

I never believed in the hereafter. Now, I believe that there is something after this life. My desire to believe is bolstered by these incidents where my father and Janie reached out to me at different points in time after they had passed:

The man who came and sat next to me during the Las Vegas show. He appeared right after I'd been talking at dinner about how upset I was that no one had come to my honorary dinner for the gymnasium, and how I was sure that my father would have come if he'd still been alive.

It still astounds me that I was able to look into the eyes of this strange man and see my father looking back at me. Not only that, but the man appeared in the seat next to me in the last locale my parents visited on their cross-country trip before heading back home to New York. (I happen to have a photo of my dad in the Las Vegas desert, wearing a cowboy hat.)

Then there was the incident with Janie and the flashing phone light. That was something I couldn't discount either. At the time, I wasn't even sure why I was asking Janie for a sign that it was okay to move forward with Michele, considering that I didn't even believe in such things.

The incidents of the flashing phone and the stranger with my dad's blue eyes cemented my belief in the hereafter. Then there were those smaller incidents of Janie landing as a butterfly on my golf bag and staying there for eighteen holes, and her landing as a butterfly on my finger.

I now believe in the hereafter—but G-d and I are still not quite on speaking terms. I just don't understand why He would make someone suffer through such a long, protracted illness. I have so many questions and no satisfactory answers. Questions like these:

If G-d wants to take someone, why not just take them?

If G-d is omnipotent, He should be able to prevent such protracted suffering. So, what is the benefit of all the suffering that is endured, not only by the patient but also by their family?

At some point in a case like Janie's, it reaches a point where the patient doesn't even realize where they are, so why leave them here on earth to suffer?

Any time I have asked these questions of a rabbi, I have gotten more or less the same answers, regardless of whether the rabbi is Reform or Orthodox. They all say something along the lines of, "It is G-d's will."

"Well," I always say, "I'd like to know *why* it is G-d's will! *Why* is it done this way? Is He punishing Janie? Or, punishing me? Did I do something heinous?"

I have so many questions and it's miserable to have no satisfying answers. All I know is that when it's my time to go, I hope to go to sleep one night and never wake up the next day. And if it does not go that way, and I see that I am headed toward an agonizingly long period of suffering for me and my loved ones, I plan to exercise my free will.

There is no way I am putting myself and my family through the kind of hell I went through with Janie. (Don't tell anyone but I have a stash set aside just in case I need to take matters into my own hands.)

To Families and Loved Ones of Those Diagnosed with FTD or Another Type of Dementia

As you know by now, my wife Janie had frontotemporal dementia, also known as FTD. This is a somewhat rare form of dementia. There are many forms of dementia, the most well-known being Alzheimer's Disease.

I am always fielding questions related to how and why I took care of my wife with FTD instead of putting her in a facility to be cared for there.

People are always asking me, "Why did you do it? And how did you do it?"

My answer is always the same: "I never even gave it a thought. I just did it. It was unbelievably taxing, draining, and wearing on me—emotionally, physically and mentally. But I would do it again if, G-d forbid, the situation ever arose again."

I have never been a beat-around-the-bush kind of person. I go after things and face them, head on. So, true to my nature, I walked right through the middle of the FTD nightmare with Janie. I put blinders on and kept my focus on what I knew I had to do.

At times, I found carrying such a heavy load to be unbearable. Despite the unbearable nature of caring for Janie at home, I want to emphasize that I have no regrets. When I sat down after Janie was gone, and reflected back on my promise to my wife that I would never put her in a facility, I felt good about having kept that promise.

I had no "What if?" questions plaguing me. I knew I had done everything humanly possible for her. I researched FTD extensively. I took her to multiple doctors to confirm her diagnosis. I made sure she had the best care possible. I kept my promise to care for her at home.

I even slept in bed beside her nightly, long after she left me mentally. When Michele and I started dating, I would kiss her goodnight and go home and get in bed with my wife. And I stayed in that bed beside her until the very end. I never even brought in a hospital bed.

There was nothing I regretted doing—and nothing I felt I had failed to do on her behalf. If I could have written a check to restore Janie to the way she was before her illness, believe me, I would have done it in a New York minute.

***

It was for you readers that I wrote this book—for those of you who are entering, or already suffering through, a similar journey.

You may be asking yourself, *How do I decide between home care and facility care for my loved one with dementia?*

There is no simple answer—and no right or wrong answer—to that question. It's a very personal choice. And it should be made in the privacy of your own home and heart. Listen to your heart. Do whatever you feel is best for you and your loved ones—all of your loved ones, not just the one with dementia.

Weigh your decision on every level—emotional, psychological, physical, practical and financial. The subject can become very complex so be sure to do your research thoroughly before committing to anything.

Whatever you choose, just remember that you won't—and can't possibly!—please everyone. There may be friends and family who fail to understand your choice, and judge it. But stay steadfast in what you've decided in your heart and mind, and press forward. The only way forward is to go through it.

Don't let outside forces pressure or shame you into deciding one way or another. No one is entitled to find fault with your decision, whatever it may be. Even if loved ones, friends and onlookers think they understand your situation, only you really know what it's like to walk that terrible journey, day in and day out. Until someone walks in your shoes, they have no right to comment on your choice.

Whatever you do, face the music, head-on. Make the choice—whatever choice you feel is best. Ultimately, all that matters is that *you* can live with your choices. And remember, if you do end up taking care of your loved one with dementia at home, it will likely become foremost on your mind and foremost in your daily routine and calendar. Still, your other responsibilities will continue on, unabated.

Depending upon your particular situation, you may still have the obligation to continue to show up for work, and continue to be there for your significant other, your children, your parents, and your home—not to mention all the other responsibilities we each may face in the course of a day.

These obligations, responsibilities, duties and commitments don't suddenly vanish so you can preserve your energy for the new priority in your life—being a caregiver to your loved one with dementia; they just get piled on top of your already heavy load.

If you choose to keep your loved one at home and look after them there, it's important to recognize that you can't close yourself off from the rest of your life. It will still require your attention. And the fact that you can't simply put the rest of your life on hold will make being a caregiver all that much more difficult.

The reality is that FTD and other forms of dementia leave you facing only bad options. There is no doorway to walk through that will make the illness suddenly go away. So, do your best with the cards you're dealt and hope and pray that when the end finally comes for your loved one, you can live with your choices.

Acknowledgments

So many people influenced my life that to mention them all might take another book. To the most important few who brought me to this place in my life, I want to express my appreciation.

To my mom (Lizzie, as I affectionately called her), thank you...For your love, devotion to family above all else, and your patience with me when I got out of hand. By example, you showed me what it was to care for loved ones, most importantly my grandparents and Dad.

To my dad (Stubby, as I affectionately referred to him), thank you...For giving me your personality, and for all you taught me about work ethic, toughness, and how to love. You were the guiding light in my life and my best friend for the twenty-seven years we had together.

To Janie, for whom I wrote this book...You were my friend, confidant, lover and devoted wife of almost fifty years. And you were the best, most devoted mother two children could ever have. You were also a devoted daughter, mother-in-law and aunt. You guided me through my career, criticizing me when necessary as well as encouraging me to reach for the stars. I will never forget you kiddingly saying to me, "I knew you would be successful; I just didn't know it would take so long." Thank you, too, for not listening to your mom when she told you, "Because you like nice things, you need to marry someone older and established." I would sign up for our ride through life again.

To Drew and Scott, my sons, thank you ...For your love, devotion and help in caring for your mother and me. And for the love it took to encourage me to "think outside the box." Your wives, Nina and Jaime, and the grandchildren you've given me—Max, Olivia and Devon—have all brought love, understanding and devotion to me at a level I didn't know existed.

To Janie's caregivers, Thelma, Deanna, Rose and Peaches, without whom I could not have completed this journey, thank you... You started out as strangers who came to care for my loved one, Janie, and ended up being truly "gifts from G-d" (to use the words of one of Thelma's references when describing you to me). You all cared for me as well as for Janie, especially at the end.

To Annie, our housekeeper for over forty-three years, thank you...Your love for the "first lady" was never wavering. You watched our children grow up and become adults and parents. Now our grandchildren have the benefit and gift of your love. Your dedication to Janie's care during those eight-and-a-half years was truly love. I am so thankful that you agreed to stay on after Janie's passing to "take care of me."

To my Michele—whom I never would have met if not for my kids having that think-outside-the-box lunch with me—thank you...First, for your persistence.

If you had not tried multiple times to contact me, we wouldn't be married today. You kept me going through the worst of times and agreed to marry me, and I truly believe that these are the reasons I am alive today! You have allowed me to live, thrive and love again.

And lastly, to Vivien Cooper, without whom this book would not have gotten written, thank you...It is often said that everyone has one book inside them. Mine was to be a catharsis for me and hopefully a help to those suffering, as I did, through the life-altering illness of a loved one. You led me through the most difficult and emotional period of my life, taking my words and thoughts and beautifully blending them into this book. Your talent, knowledge and patience are above reproach. Thank you for your guidance and your patience with me.